"Engelhard not only heeds the call of the wild, but also provides eloquent descriptions of its ever-diminishing decibel level."
 —LAWRENCE MILLMAN, author of *The Last Speaker of Bear*

"A compelling account of life on the frozen edge, serving as a literary conduit between North and South."
 —GLORIA DICKIE, author of *Eight Bears*

"Engelhard's self-deprecating northern odyssey takes him from the slopes of Denali, to the pages of a magazine peddling lonely Alaskan men. He guides snobby bear hunters on Kodiak Island, negotiates class IV rapids, goes head to head with thieving squirrels—and loses. Along the way he pokes holes in the myth of the stoic Alaska Man with humor and authenticity."
 —ANDY HALL, author of *Denali's Howl*

"Bound to become a new classic of the outdoors. Sure to be cherished by all who love Alaska and who long for wilderness."
 —BILL STREEVER, bestselling author of *Cold*

"Engelhard runs rapids and ascends Arctic peaks not in pursuit of accomplishment, but, rather, perspective—on human folly, amid nature's majesty in the Great North."
 —BEN MCGRATH, author of *Riverman*

"The verve, humor, sympathy, and passion of Engelhard's writing help us annihilate the distance separating us from the Alaskan wild."
 —CHRISTOPHER NORMENT, author of *Return to Warden's Grove*

"Evocative, erudite, and immersive."
 —NANCY CAMPBELL, author of *The Library of Ice*

"Takes the reader through adventures in the wild and of the heart with an engaging combination of wit and expertise."
 —LARA MESSERSMITH-GLAVIN, author of *Spirit Things*

"Engelhard manages something rarely even attempted in outdoor literature: stories focused not on the death-defying prowess of the adventurer, but on the wild glory of place."
 —ERIN MCKITTRICK, author of *A Long Trek Home*

WHAT THE RIVER KNOWS

WHAT THE RIVER KNOWS

Essays from the
Heart of Alaska

MICHAEL ENGELHARD

Cataloguing data available from Library and Archives Canada
978-0-88839-778-2 [paperback]

978-0-88839-800-0 [hardback]

978-0-88839-779-9 [epub]

Printed in Korea

Cover Photos: Michael Engelhard (Mathews River in the fall)
Frontispiece Photo: Lisa Hupp, US Fish and Wildlife Service
                     (Brooks Range river valley)
Author Photos: Back Cover – Barry Nelson (The author on the Canning River)
                     Inside – Rich Wilkins
Editor: D. Martens
Design & Layout: E. Morton

*We acknowledge the support of the Government of Canada through the
Canada Book Fund and the Canada Council for the Arts, and of the
Province of British Columbia through the British Columbia Arts Council
and the Book Publishing Tax Credit.*

Published simultaneously in Canada and the United States by

HANCOCK HOUSE PUBLISHERS LTD.
19313 Zero Avenue, Surrey, B.C. Canada V3Z 9R9
#104-4550 Birch Bay-Lynden Rd, Blaine, WA, U.S.A. 98230-9436
(800) 938-1114   Fax (800) 983-2262
www.hancockhouse.com l info@hancockhouse.com

*Hancock House gratefully acknowledges the Halkomelem Speaking Peoples
whose unceded, shared and asserted traditional territories our offices reside upon.*

To the essayist, the act of walking and thinking
gives way almost reflexively to the desire to write
about the terrain that has been traversed and
the reflections that the terrain has sparked.
–KENT C. RYDEN, *Mapping the Invisible Landscape*

I used to think water was first, but if you listen carefully
you will hear that the words are underneath the water.
–NORMAN MACLEAN, *A River Runs Through It*

And you really live by the river? What a jolly life!
By it and with it and on it and in it, said the Rat...
It's my world, and I don't want any other.
What it hasn't got is not worth having, and
what it doesn't know is not worth knowing.
–KENNETH GRAHAME, *The Wind in the Willows*

AUTHOR'S NOTE

While the word *Eskimo* ("netter of snowshoes" in a neighboring ethnic group's language) is now considered offensive in Greenland and Canada because of its colonial tones, Alaska's Yup'ik and Inupiaq speakers, especially of the older generation, still widely embrace the term. Most do not self-identify as *Inuit* (singular: *Inuk*), and it remains part of names of organizations and events like the Alaska Eskimo Whaling Commission and World Eskimo-Indian Olympics as well as of US federal statutes and offices. The same holds true for *Aleuts* (Unangax̂) and *Indians*, the latter pertaining to Athabaskans of the Interior and Cook Inlet (and related to the Lower 48 states' Apache and Navajo speakers), and to Southeast Alaska's Tlingits (Lingít), Tsimshians (Tsim-she-yan), and Haidas (Kaigini). *Athabaskan*, too, is a term linguists fashioned, lumping together Dene (their self-designation), groups as distinct from each other as the English and Germans. The umbrella term for all these ethnic groups is *Alaska Natives*.

Less than three miles from the cabin we rent, the campus of University of Alaska Fairbanks sits on a height that after 1917 was commonly known as College Hill and when I studied there, West Ridge. From a pullout above a sledding slope on its south side, on clear days now exceedingly rare because of wildfires and ice fog, you can see the Tanana Flats and the Alaska Range with Denali, North America's tallest peak. Bones, charcoal, and stone tools from the Campus Site have been dated to at least 3000 BCE. That's 20 times the age of these United States. The region's Kokht'ana (Lower Tanana Athabaskans in the anthropologists' tongue) call the hill Troth Yeddah', "Wild Potato Ridge," for the edible tuber growing there. In 2013, the USGS Board of Geographic Names approved a proposal to restore the landmark's original name. I humbly and gratefully acknowledge that the woods that became my home were home first to the Kokht'ana and their predecessors.

Those include two ice-age girl infants who died about 11,500 years ago in a camp on another ridge, 50 miles to the south, above the Tth'itu' ("Straight Water," the Anglos' Tanana River). Their skeletons, covered in red ochre like the adjacent gifts of stone spear points and incised antler foreshafts, are the oldest human remains so far found on the American side of Beringia, the 600-mile-wide land bridge that again lies inundated. Despite this and much more physical and oral proof for the depth and breadth of Indigenous occupancy, the state of Alaska took 63 years, until 2022, to formally recognize Alaska's 229 tribes.

I hereby also grant that the resource extraction I condemn enables my lifestyle and standard of living. "If one were trying to live sustainably, one couldn't live in Alaska," I often say. Or in few places at all, it seems. "The only level of technology that is sustainable," in the civilization critic Derrick Jensen's view, "is the Stone Age."

The following essays owe much to the fact that nature, culture, and history have shaped each other ever since humans stepped into the scene. Ethnicity and economies merely provide the varied conduits through which such energies flow.

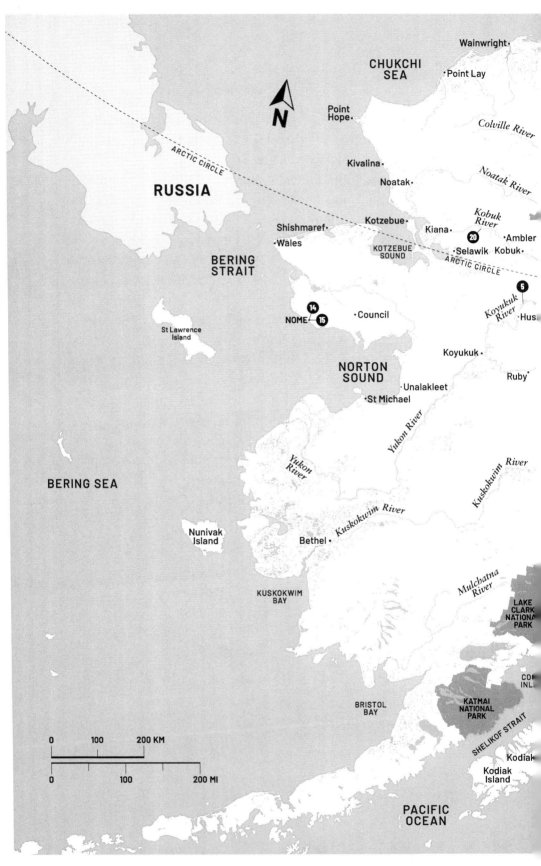

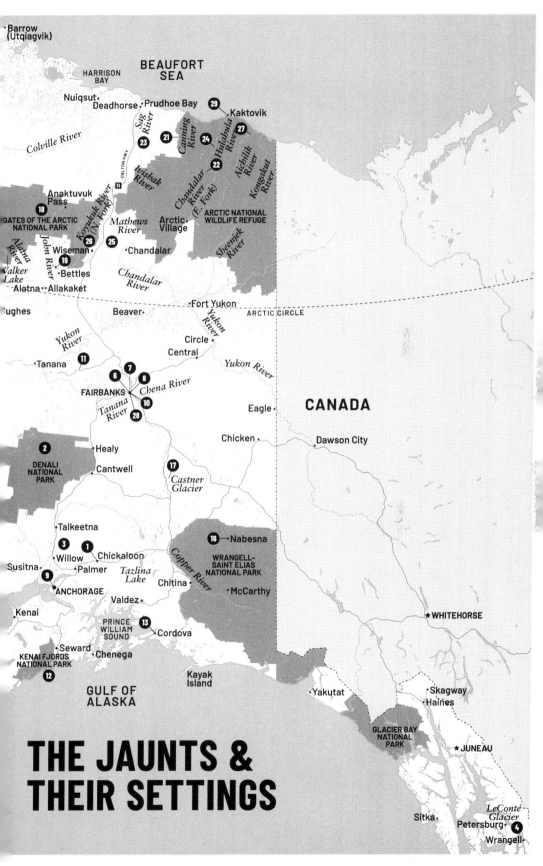

THE JAUNTS & THEIR SETTINGS

CONTENTS

CHAPTER 1

SOLD ON RIVERS AND MOUNTAINS
(A PROLOGUE)

A bad day of guiding beats a good day at the office, we say— except that out there, in the best of beyond, even on an otherwise good day, you can die. That sentiment rings true especially in Alaska, where guiding passes for a worthy career, a description, however, that mostly pertains to the profession's male-dominated and rather conservative trophy-hunting branch. The spring I assisted as packer with brown bear hunts on Kodiak Island, I got an unpleasant whiff of its clientele. Sitting at the campfire one morning, I saw a whiskered white head peeping from the woodpile. "An ermine," I shouted, as I've never grown jaded about wildlife and especially the snow-white weasels, rarely seen, whose tailed furs cloaked Europe's monarchs. Without missing a beat, a coarse Southerner in our group opened up. "I didn't fly over 3,000 miles to look at a fuckin' rat."

He was not just taxonomically challenged, but a jerk all around. Customarily, hunters, after claiming their trophy, let their assigned guide and assistant scout for those who have not yet been successful, thereby increasing those hunters' chances. This one refused, as he was paying for our services, he reminded us, and retained us at his beck and call.

The day of goodbyes came, with the floatplane moored off-shore because the pilot would not bring her closer to the rocky shore. The clients already had changed into traveling clothes, hip waders buried in their duffels. A certain prole piggybacking Georgia Man to the plane felt tempted to trip and submerse both of them. That day, professionalism won. Still, you don't want to mess with cooks, nurses, wait staff, barbers, car mechanics, or guides. The next one might be impulsive or in a really foul mood.

Another hunter, at the stroke of midnight, when his permit

expired, stood up on the ridge, fired his rifle, and yelled, "I'll be back," addressing the record male brownies that had evaded him. He'd gotten within shooting range of one that had rubbed itself bare inside his den, hibernating, and looked as if he'd slipped off his coat. The guy begged the guide to let him take the shot, if just for a claw necklace and head mount, but the guide, worried about his reputation, would not let him. That guide—a Hungarian, soft-spoken, with a hussar's gray moustache—who'd skipped across the Iron Curtain, told me afterward that stalking a wounded bear for the coup-de-grâce while it hid in the bushes gave him flashbacks of Vietnam. Hunters also sometimes asked their guide to cut out a bear's *baculum*, his penis bone, as a swizzle stick for stirring their cocktails or as a joke gift. I returned for a second season only because the work got me into some incredible places for free.

There were decent clients, too. An elfin Italian whom I shadowed on a black bear hunt in British Columbia's Chilcotin did not speak any English. My Italian pretty much was exhausted with the basics for romance, should an opportunity ever have arisen (though not with the hunter): *ciao, grazie, Chianti, amore, doppio espresso* (I don't smoke before or after) and *arrivederci*. Somehow, we communed through gestures and gibberish—I used to have some French and Latin—and I grasped that he simply liked being outside for the tracks and birds and all sorts of animals. He left me a handsome gratuity, but neither got a bear nor even saw one.

But enough about blood sport, about seeing the world through crosshairs in what the naturalist Charles Hood calls "gun-barrel tourism," on which I soon turned my weary back.

Proving the point that traipsing around cold and wet tundra or messing about in small, inflatable boats does not constitute a career, many youngsters pursue wilderness guiding at best for a couple of years between high school or college and the Skinner's maze of adult duties and cheeses.

Our supposedly more emancipated liberal set, like the odd black-sheep big game-guide poacher, commits its share of foul-ups. Some of those spawn negative headlines. One of my bosses, a former National Park Service ranger, was fined and blacklisted after she lifted a mammoth tusk from public lands to please an acquisitive client—a guy in one of her rafts had proved to be an undercover game warden. Operating from a Fairbanks storage unit, she'd also send you into the wild with a brick of baking chocolate in lieu of candy bars or rush into the airport lobby 15 minutes before your departure to reclaim her satellite phone or to hand you a map set, saying, "You're going to the Hula, not the Kongakut." And wilderness clients sometimes mimicked the trophy crowd. A corporate lawyer I had on multiple trips would not shave for days after his return to San Diego, to parade his he-man alter ego at the office, but eventually always did because his lady friend otherwise would not kiss him or be seen in public with him.

Some clients pledged they would take a dip in the Beaufort Sea at the end of our journey just so they could brag that they've swum in the Arctic Ocean. I never said anything; I had heard this before. They always reneged on their promise whether we arrived on a bluebird or an overcast day after testing the water temperature with a hand. One guy strapped a thirty-pound moose rack to his backpack, as a "souvenir," only to drop the tined shovels half a mile later. I hadn't said anything that time either.

Despite all that, forever young, I somehow got stuck on guiding, and with it. Alaska's landscapes and wildlife and lifestyle had certainly something to do with my choice. For a transplant from Europe, it was several dreams come true. The lure proved to be irresistible. Too much Jack London and Jack Daniels, perhaps, at a susceptible age. Like the Tanana River homesteader-poet John Haines, "I was not really born until I came here." My birth certificate was the syllabus for ANTH 242, my first college class here: "Native Cultures of Alaska." I'd been elated for days after my acceptance letter from UAF, the University of Alaska Fairbanks. Sure, the moniker "Golden Heart City" was a hollow chamber of commerce hype touting the town's mining origins and centrality in the Interior; but the university had one of the world's best Northern anthropology programs.

The decision to attend UAF had been made on a whim. I'd already secured a scholarship for a year in Edmonton, Alberta. I knew that Canadian city from a previous visit. It was big, and far from the mountains. Then, one day, I gasped at a photo of the Fairbanks campus in a brochure—that Denali view from the sledding-hill pullout vantage. My mind was made up. I swapped one U of A for another. Friends thought me nuts for declining the free ride in Alberta, but oil derricks pecking the ground like dumb monster birds marred that "Gateway to the North." It was also "Deadmonton" and "Canada's Richest Mixed Farming District," and, laying claim to Earth's largest Western boot, it was steeped in the cowboy culture I then still despised, which oozed out from Calgary.

I've based many life choices on scenery and concomitant open space, which did not always pan out. (It got me indentured for three years as a potter's apprentice in the Bavarian Alps.) Settling upon UAF was the most momentous of all crossroads.

My wilderness-guiding career started auspiciously, if spiked with challenges, with a rafting company in Chickaloon, South-central Alaska. To this day, I cannot pass by fluid turmoil, be it a gully a brook or a river, without assessing the flow and pegging my run, and more often than not launching a leaf or a twig. (We pitched driftwood limbs into big rapids now and then to study the water's will, where it wanted to take passive objects: a raft with a fainted guide, or one frozen in terror, or whose helmsman had been ejected.) I trained on the glacier-fed Matanuska, where the water rises when it gets hot, instead of dropping as it does in the desert Southwest. And yes, it was still "whitewater," tan sediment notwithstanding. Initially, we trainees chauffeured boulders in our boats to simulate the weight of up to six passengers. Then we graduated to taking fellow guides before we did any paying peeps likely to sue an outfitter if things went literally *kerplunk*. Proudly, if cheesily, I'd welcome boarding thrill-seekers to my office, its view. "Fortunately, they don't chain us to the benches anymore," I might quip, beginning to row.

A tour group of Japanese in particular sticks in my mind. Pouring from their bus carrying catered sushi lunches in plastic shopping bags, they all wanted the yellow Helly Hansen raingear, the XL-size, not the smaller drab olive tops and bottoms we'd recommended. Perhaps they thought they would be easier to spot if they fell in, or it could have been a cultural thing. They ended up waddling down to the boats a bit like penguins. We learned to please whims if they did not compromise safety.

And we learned the requisite dirtbag jokes: What's the difference between a guide and a savings bond? A savings bond matures and makes money. What's the difference between a guide and a large pizza? A large pizza feeds a family of four. (We would not settle into beer-bellied respectability, ever, we swore.) And, at low water: We scrape to make a living. These lines, it goes without saying, riffed on our workplace, Edward Abbey's "River of No Financial Return." They were thinly veiled ruses, attempts to solicit gratuities ("tips" or "beer money"), which we couldn't, not officially, but which made up a substantial part of our income. Even the frugal ancient Greeks had placed coins for the Stygian oarsman under the tongues of their departed. Most Europeans, to our dismay, believed that the price of a ride included the baksheesh. But at least our EU day-trippers' weren't heavyset as a rule. Their financial slip-up inspired yet another wisecrack: What's the difference between a [insert nationality here] and a canoe? A canoe tips.

Our outfit, among other options, offered trips past Lions Head, a cliffy 2,000-foot outcrop on a stretch of Class III-IV whitewater that took your breath away, depending on runoff levels. It was the scenery that was breathtaking, and also the water temperature. The flow was so charged with silt that wet clothes and filled hip waders would quickly pull you under, despite your lifejacket. Unfazed, we'd zip through Greg's Hole, Sandwich Rock, and Double Trouble. *Sandwich*, in this case, did not allude to a lunch food but to the action of rafts pinned against that rock. What had Greg done to gain river rat immortality? You never wanted to have a hydraulic feature named after you.

The third half-day shift was the Midnight Sun Run, which ran even when the sky was overcast. When a passenger went overboard, after pulling him or her into the boat by the life vest's shoulder straps, you'd land as fast as you could, to build a fire. Easier said than done, as readers of the London short story know. Your hands would be shaking, and the client too, and the wood could be wet and the current so fast that beaching without someone on shore grabbing on to the bowline was like stepping off one of those airport conveyor-belts that push humans toward processing—one that had gone haywire. Once, missing the pullout completely, I landed below it, clinging to branches inside an alder thicket to prevent getting sluiced farther downstream, and then towed the boat back up on its bowline, ignominiously, against a waist-deep current of melted glacier, cussing, with the seated passengers watching. On a different occasion, a "swimmer," unaware that he had been dumped and Maytagged only because of a ship-pilot's error, handed me that season's biggest tip. I'd gone where I was not supposed to go: into a monstrous, churning hole. And that maw gaped deeper and wider with every rehash of the story around a yard fire or on the van shuttle to and from the river.

There are no atheists in foxholes, allegedly, and the same goes for big water. A priest at the Pearly Gates got upset when Saint Peter high-fived a long-haired, disheveled river guide whose breath reeked of booze and then waved him through, while the priest had to queue at the end of the line. "During your sermons, people were napping in the pews," the saint told the complaining cleric, "but when this guy was running rapids, everyone in his boat was praying."

Some of the world's peoples hold rapids to be sacred sites, the abode of gods and ancestors, destination for souls after death, or, where salmon leapt, a source of sustenance. To the dismay of the Park Service, Grand Canyon boaters place token offerings—sometimes wildflowers or cans of beer—on Vulcan's Anvil, a pitch-black plug mid-river above the gorge's most formidable maelstrom, Lava Falls, asking for smooth runs. Rapids are liminal, portals between traveling right-side up and upside-down. (Ancient rock art often depicts the dead upside-down, their priorities sorely upended.) Guides and tourists of no faith and all faiths joined in the Church of Flowing Water to show reverence at these thresholds. I knew of a real church with that name that a doryman founded. He wanted to officiate at weddings on his trips. We all connect in different ways with whitewater's froth-and-cord energy.

We tempered the sacred with the profane. For us guides, "No shit, there I was" became the opening phrase of heroic yarns, just as "Once upon a time…" and "Sing to me of the man, Muse, the man of twists and turns" had become that of older, no less fantastic genres. "Inevitably, events morph as they are turned into stories," as the author of a book about climbers' pranks puts it, because "Distortions arise from shifting memories, altitude-addled brains, and subjective viewpoints," and because "Longings create their own realities." Heartily if unknowingly, we also drew upon the likes of Melville, Stevenson, Conrad, and Dana. And yet, like the sailor, cowpoke, bullfighter, huntress, fly fisherperson, or trapper of fur-rendezvous days, our breed developed its own repertoire of oral nonfiction that prepped me well for putting pen to paper—or rather, index fingers to keyboard.

You were lucky to be back at the warehouse around 2 a.m. and to catch a few zees in a camper trailer that extruded foam insulation and that squirrels besieged, before rigging for the morning round that left at seven. I glimpsed a darker side of this business when an Anchorage cardiologist died, likely from a heart attack, after a raft flipped on the most intense tour this outfit advertised, a gauntlet of class IV and V rapids in three tight canyons on the Kenai Peninsula. This remains the only water of that magnitude run commercially in Alaska. By comparison, sane boaters think of Class VI as un-runnable. Our office phone promptly rang off the hook—in those days, they still had hooks. Callers inquired about "the trip on which that guy died." Other commercial outdoor ventures report this pattern too. There's no such thing as bad publicity in this line of work, I guess. That raft's guide, blameless, had been thoroughly traumatized.

Halfway through the twelve-week season, management (the owner's friend) informed me that they had to let me go for lack of bookings, on the Matanuska, though not on Sixmile Creek, where the doctor had drowned and which then exceeded my skills.

Still, a longing to belong had become deeply entrenched. The next two and a half decades I bounced from guiding gig to guiding gig, from outdoor program to outdoor program, with stints in Alaska's Arctic, Kenai Fjords, the Big Bend, Moab, the Sonoran Desert, and the Grand Canyon, veering from riparian rodeo into horseback guidin' but always yo-yoing north. When I tired of wealthy, demanding clients and the service industry, I switched to educational outdoor programs for youths—at-risk as well as fairly law-abiding ones—trying to shape the future by shaping young bodies, young characters. I vividly recall an Outward Bound (OB) rafting course exclusively filled with village teenagers. We had to make a shopping run into town, because none had brought their long underwear. It was a summer trip, wasn't it? Never mind that the water could be 45 degrees or less and that cold water kills 20 to 30 Alaskans each year, more than half of them in recreational small-craft accidents. Fifteen minutes of immersion will sap your warmth and strength enough to make self-rescue problematic. Meaning: you'll be too numb to swim. We instructors had paddled across Tazlina Lake in a headwind, trying to reach its outlet, while the students snacked and lounged on what they referred to as the "party boat," the rafts we had strapped together. In camp, after we'd introduced Leave No Trace practices at our portable stainless-steel toilet, two girls, ignoring the thunder jug, promptly vanished behind a boulder to do their business there. Instead of conducting stretch circles before breakfast, we lured sleepyheads from their bags with mugs of hot chocolate. De-rigging at the takeout, some of the kids asked if they could blow the safety whistles they'd worn for the previous week. The following five-minute concerto fortissimo for 22 instruments should have split eardrums.

We at Outward Bound had a schematic for judging rapids and possible courses through them, which I'll share here at no extra charge. The acronym with which we taught this was WORMS— it's also what you feel in your belly perched on a boulder while scouting Lava Falls. One day I realized that WORMS can aid in the plotting of a life's trajectory: W stands for water; what are the major currents, and where would they carry an inanimate object (you, paralyzed)? O is for obstacles, not always obvious. R for run; what is your ideal track after mulling W and O, "the line" in the boater's lingo? (Stray and you'll pay.) M denotes markers; these can be onshore or river features, rocks, pour-overs, standing waves or constant ripples that tell you where you are in relation to where you really want to be. (They are important, since your perspective shifts once you get into the boat.) In life, these interme- diate goals can be marriage, a first child or home or publication, a promotion, or your first Himalayan peak. Lastly, there is S for scenarios, the big what-ifs. It's always good to have a backup or rescue plan in place. I never told students that I was much better at WORMSing rapids than doing it for my own life. The reason, I believe, is the Os that pop up unexpectedly, or Os that lurk unseen but still can upset you. Or you might be the biggest O to yourself. I also may have misread social currents on occasion.

This, I promise, concludes this book's self-help section and anxious soul-searching.

When instructing hoods in the woods or spoiled teenagers began to irk me and I was missing the tips, I relapsed into guiding. And when "the daily"—seven trips a week—became "the deadly," I swung back to being OB Wan Kenobi. Some summers, I moon- lighted as a rent-a-guide, an even lower life form, subbing at multiple companies in a bid to stitch gigs and the wages of fear into steady employment. Wags spoke of "poverty with a view." Working for two dozen different outfits spurred me to explore alone or with friends, as on guided weeklong or three-week trips there was simply not enough time for that. This pained me, especially in locations as new to the guide as they were to the clients.

I had quit anthropology in part because, like the cultural critic and English professor Marie Louise Pratt, I couldn't stomach that such interesting people doing such interesting things too often wrote such boring books. The fact that they didn't tell jokes about their profession may have signified something. Nor could I handle the postmodern constructs then in vogue, which diluted the rich flavors of reality beyond texts, even nature's importance, in a flood of vertiginous words. (Jacques Derrida will give you a taste: "To pretend, I actually do the thing: I have therefore only pretended to pretend." He also always dreamed of "a pen that would be a syringe," a statement open to unkind interpretations.) "What *is* both necessary and sufficient—for honest literary work," Edward Abbey emphasized in "A Writer's Credo,"—"is to have faith in the evidence of your senses and in your common sense." Amen.

My academic training and interests, however, informed my guiding. The unfinished PhD had been meant to reveal symbolic dimensions of a landscape through the views and behaviors of a hunter-gatherer society, Gwich'in Athabaskans in Arctic Village. In plain English: I wanted to learn how those who lived lives of nomadic subsistence until recently construe place—how maps form in their minds, how locations forge personalities.

I was a lousy grant writer, and the money for this had not come through. I probably could have received funds to study how many beavers those Gwich'in were trapping and where. Much of the research the Park Service and similar agencies financed had to be "applicable," that is, it had to translate into management guidelines. "In some cases, we manage people more than we do wildlife," one official told me. That was certainly true for footloose caribou and the hunters trying to fill their freezers with them.

During fieldwork in northwest Alaska, first in Kiana, on the Kobuk River, I discovered a storied landscape that predated colonization, which for me backfired, making me question the parks bureaucracy. Accompanying Alaska Native elders on their hunting and fishing, I shared in the rootedness of foragers who had maintained fluency in nature's idiom to an unequaled degree. They still lived, to quote a historian of nomadism, through the abundance of land "rich in memories, spirit and meaning." Each slough, each mountain pass, bear's den, boat portage, tent-ring stone circle, or lookout hill spoke of a past still sharply present. The landmarks and affiliated tales condensed a perspective as much as they did practical knowledge. They focused the traditions of people whose history and identity largely reside outside of walls. They defined home turf, not glamorous wilderness. They endure as part of a moral universe, pithy reminders that keep groups and individuals centered.

While I embraced my subarctic life in a Fairbanks cabin without running water, ironic for someone destined to become a river guide, I was shocked to find that paradise has its shadows, too. A straight line connects the Klondike gold rush and sea otter and fur seal trade with Cold War nuclear bomb tests in the Aleutians and plans to nuke out a deep-water port on Alaska's Chukchi Sea coast or to dam the Yukon River for hydroelectric power—flooding 10,000 square miles of waterfowl nesting and feeding grounds and human hunting territories, thereby changing the weather—with current projects: a second road to the Brooks Range, violating Gates of the Arctic National Park; one through Izembek National Wildlife Refuge; and the Pebble Mine (a pit two miles wide and half a mile deep—nothing pebbly about it) in one of the state's prime salmon-spawning watersheds. In a stroke of quasi-karmic retribution, a wildfire this summer erased most of the mine's supply camp. For Abbey, who went on two river trips here, Alaska was "the last pork chop," "the final big bite on the American table"—drool, baby, drool! "A man feels free to destroy an entire valley by placer mining," he had noted, having seen Fairbanks from the air, "in order to extract one peanut-butter jar full of gold dust." That was in 1983. Today, even in unproductive years, hydraulic shovels at the Fort Knox Mine north of town scrape the equivalent of an elephant's weight from a hole that puts Arizona's Meteor Crater to shame.

Regardless of what I set out to write nowadays, the climate intrudes. Drill pads and rigs and pump stations with ATCO trailers linked by roads atop gravel dikes still loom over the cradle of polar bears and of caribou, as they do over the North Slope village Nuiqsut. In pursuit of a heinous habit, ConocoPhillips now wants to chill rapidly thawing permafrost to shore up its Prudhoe Bay structures. Drill, baby, drill!

Since the first Beringians set a skin-clad foot here, craving mammoth steaks, people have always desired things from Alaska. Trailblazing aimed at boom-and-bust riches—be they otter pelts, nuggets, land, salmon, whales, timber, tourists, or oil—always has been a mark of (and a stain on) the settler psyche. I, no exception, mined the North for experiences, memories that, barring brain injury or dementia, would cast their warm glow into future rheumatic years.

I once did not get a guide position for which I'd applied because I was "too outspoken" about my environmental convictions. Folks on vacation didn't care about overgrazing or dams or alfalfa, golf courses, or Vegas, and tamarisks sucking the river dry, the manager told me. Venting my spleen, I would be a bad influence on junior guides, he said. A corporation specializing in glamping—"glamorous camping," a fad here to stay, I'm afraid—bought that mom-and-pop business later. They'd send one gaggle of guides downriver to set up solar showers, a buffet, and tents with folding cots before a second clutch transporting clients beached their boats at this mobile Club Med. You bet these sun-struck dudes in sarongs sipping martinis in camp chairs in the shallows or under umbrellas didn't want to hear about uranium tailings eroding upstream. "The water is so dirty," clients sometimes remarked. We always filtered it for drinking and cooking, and I worried more about stuff too small to be caught: invisible radioactive particles and heavy metals.

I always had to stick my oar in in Alaska, too. On one Kongakut raft trip, I ranted and raved about Big Oil's plans to defile the Arctic National Wildlife Refuge, which, together with the Grand

Canyon, is my favorite place on this Earth. Halfway through our journey, I learned that the two guys in my boat were retired petroleum engineers. No tips that time, either—a guide's raft, more than other job site, feels like Forrest Gump's box of chocolates. Or a *Titanic* lifeboat, post-iceberg.

For the longest time, I quelled my unease about working in tourism with the belief that an educated public and especially people touched in person by wild things and places would stand up for them, instead of ruining them or standing by, which amounts to the same. But while there will always be some hearts and brains receptive to "the message," I'm not so sure anymore about the majority. As a reviewer once wrote about a different author, I "belong to the more misanthropic end of the green spectrum."

In the spirit of full disclosure, I should also mention that I won a Rasmuson Individual Artist Award once. Finally, grant money! They were fossil fuel funds, though, like so much of the dough circulating here. Each Alaska resident gets an annual dividend check from the state, which invests money from the taxes oil corporations pay. Some see this as a payoff and donate their crude windfall to good causes. Wish I had had that luxury. Eventually, I could not even use the grant money when my poorly planned trip to Mongolia went belly-up.

In hindsight, it has all been worthwhile, despite the fact that my resume looks like a condemned apartment block, with the latest gig always the likely charge to bring the whole edifice of my economy down. Guides pride themselves not so much on whom they have slaved for but rather, where. Late-season burnout occurred, and a sense of humor certainly helped. Escorting strangers on longer adventures, informing them, keeping them fed, warm, safe, and engaged or at least entertained never grayed into routine. I stayed keenly aware that my day on the job could and should be theirs in heaven. In the stern of a paddle raft and under rain-battered tarps, singing "Michael, Row Your Boat Ashore," I've rubbed shoulders with the mildly famous and immoderately rich and with people of different backgrounds whom otherwise I would not have met.

On a Conservation Lands Foundation fundraiser on the Colville, which wends through the National Petroleum Reserve–Alaska, I cooked for *Fight Club* actor Edward Norton's dad and for a Moab rancher who had bought up property and torn down its ranch house so the land could revert to its natural state. Another musical mob, on a ski trip in Denali, belted out "Michael got run over by a dog team" to the tune of the grandma-and-reindeer original. I had come under the runners during a scout for the National Outdoor Leadership School (NOLS), when an instructor lost control on the downhill and his mutts knocked me on my face. Unlike the trophy hunting set, our subculture thrived on ribbing and one-upmanship, especially between the competitors NOLS and OB. Still, I don't think that wreck had been intentional.

I felt blessed, overall, considered myself chosen, though I was missing out on promotions or similar forms of advancement, and my earnings were seasonal and more than other professions affected by economic swings. There were health benefits instead, fresh air, and plenty of exercise. River work did not come with insurance but did with creaky joints, a bum lower back (from heavy lifting, not from rowing), and a charmed if erratic love life. The first romantic encounter with my wife took place in the privacy of *Orca Bay*, a trailered dory parked inside my roommate's garage. We did not rock his boat; dories are tippy nutshells, modern incarnations of Major John Wesley Powell's. The son of another river legend, the man who pioneered dories in the Grand Canyon, later sank *Orca Bay* at the mouth of Havasu Creek. R.I.P.

My feats as a professional boatman ran the gamut from blisters to close calls, from antics to inducing annoyance, soberness, tears of the good kind, and rapturous bliss. I once retrieved the wedding ring a rapid had sucked off a client's finger when I cleaned the raft at the warehouse. I got to show a moose to an Inupiaq boy who'd never seen one; it had been his biggest wish for that OB-week on the Little Nelchina and Tazlina. Elsewhere, a parent told me that her kids, who had expected their float trip to be boring, confessed afterward that it had been their favorite part of the family's sojourn in *Amerika*. The country needed image-boosting just then, during Bush Junior' reign. I've stayed in touch with a few clients over the years, and several booked repeat adventures. They were "clients," not "customers," because we did not sell products from a store but engendered delight that, sustained on longer trips, could affect lives or at least shine for years. And, unlike customers, the clients were not always right. In these woods, many were babes whose faltering steps could get them into trouble but which also could be their own reward. "At the gates of the forest," Ralph Waldo Emerson wrote, "the surprised man of the world is forced to leave his city estimates of great and small, wise and foolish." Being one such myself, I saw how "The knapsack of custom falls off his back with the first step he takes into these precincts." And off the backs of boys, girls, and women. That change at its best was transformative.

You really couldn't put a price on those memories. Students of mine, to their parents' dismay, became river guides or Outward Bound instructors. Sailors in the wake of the solo circumnavigator Robin Knox-Johnson, they had "painted their lives with bright colours, not pastel shades, and that brightness is like a drug and they want[ed] more of it." So, I know some of our journeys touched some adventurers in a positive way—positive, as far as their nascent biocentrism was concerned. Our joint re-wilding, doing without, and headlong dives into beauty bonded us.

As a writer and wilderness guide, I unearth stories that I then carry forward. I sink roots deep into landscapes to create new stories that drive and sustain me. Life, like memory, is episodic by its very nature; hence this autobiographical volume of essays covering three decades. Literary trends and reputations come and go. But truths endure. Chaucer, still the pre-modern lodestar for stories written in the English language, immortalized seekers and raconteurs, spinners of tall tales and jugglers like myself, entertainers on the move and on the make. In his poem "The House of Fame," he nails the dynamic in my guiding and writing: one of action and stillness, of socializing and solitude.

> For when thy labor done all is
> And hast made all thy reckonings
> Instead of rest and novel things
> Thou go'st home to thy house anon
> And also dumb as any stone
> Thou sittest at another book
> Till full bewildered is thy look
> And liv'st thus as an eremite
> Although thy abstinence is light.

My "reckonings" before and during each backcountry trip comprised calculations of distances; fuel and food requirements; backpack and airfreight weights; the whims of weather and wildlife; the goals, abilities, and personalities of my clients; and the largesse of gratuities. My "abstinence," economic and otherwise, is a project in progress, though off the job, I do enjoy time alone. And I have a longing for pilgrimage, having gone on a 58-day one in the Arctic and a 40-day one in the Grand Canyon.

Guiding is but the latest calling in a long tradition of bards, pilgrims, pathfinders, organ grinders and carnival strongmen, voyageurs, Pony Express riders, riverboat pilots, and showboating mountain men. Bunkum artists, dubious narrators like Marco Polo, John Wesley Powell, or Frederick Cook—the latter stole ethnographic data and falsely claimed firsts for the North Pole and Denali's summit—remain all the rage in postmodern prose. But I have a standing to maintain. While the following, loosely linked chapters could be labeled "creative nonfiction" of the memoir type, and there's no guarantee that time has not put a shine on events that in the moment weren't so shiny, I have journaled diligently and done my homework of added research.

You may have heard this old saw:

How can you tell when a guide is lying?

His or her lips are moving.

Thanks to the printed word, I reach an audience without mine doing that.

CHAPTER 2

TOUGH TIMES ON DENALI

Why would you climb Everest? Because it's there, British mountaineer George Leigh Mallory allegedly told a reporter before his 1921 attempt to attain the highest point on Earth. He post-holed into the twilight of history on his third try, in 1924, joining the pantheon of alpinist gods. His remains were discovered only in 1999, and there is still doubt whether or not he was the first to summit Mount Everest. Why indeed climb any mountain? Why breathe? Why love? Why speculate about the meaning of life? The answer: We cannot help it. It is part of our nature.

Why did I want to climb Denali? Because it teased me each clear-enough day, as I biked to the campus library above Fairbanks and the Chena River floodplain. Because it just hovered there on the horizon, divinely remote, a cool and ethereal presence boasting immaculate symmetry, its pearlescent north face spanning the highest base-to-summit relief of Earth's mountains. Because it seemed unreachable and, in its aloofness, perfectly captured the Great Land's spirit. I did not want to take this peak's measure because of its height or to break any records but to escape gravity, to cast off into the oceanic blue that engulfs its bold crest.

A chance to climb Denali came sooner than expected. Laurent Dick, a friend who lived outside of town, was planning his first ascent. Laurent had grown up with mountains, but his birthplace, Switzerland, had become stifling, and he craved purer air and landscapes less tainted. When we first met, he was a student of photojournalism with a yen for nature photography, striving, like myself, to wring a living from his passions.

Everybody whom Laurent asked to join him had prior commitments; but soloing Denali is considered unsafe. And so, I was on. Even with two people, the safety margin was slim. As the official trip leader, Laurent had submitted his mountaineering resume with the permit application for the Park Service to review. If they had thought it insufficient, a ranger would have tried to talk us out of the climb. Except for Mont Blanc in the French Alps and an attempt on Mexico's Popocatépetl that nosebleeds and vise-like headaches cut short, my scoreboard was less than dazzling. I had never topped 16,000 feet nor endured the rigors of Arctic cold fronts. I did not know how well I would handle the lack of oxygen or maladies of mountain sickness at 20,300 feet. The globe's atmosphere thins near the poles and bulges at the midriff, so the barometric pressure on Denali is lower than that of a peak of the same height near the equator. Physiologically, climbing Denali therefore feels as it would a Himalayan mountain 3,000 feet higher. Put differently, if Everest lay in the Alaska Range, you couldn't summit it without bottled oxygen.

With the invitation (and permit) issued, duly impressed by the destination, I started to borrow gear. My neighbor loaned me skis, a pair of crampons, and his *pulk*, a Scandinavian-style plastic sled with harness to which I would hitch myself to pull part of our load. My outfit represented a strange mix of Aspen and bush Alaska: plastic ski boots, Polartec fleece, and Gore-Tex pants combined with a fur-ruffed down parka and beaver skin hat. There are certain things modern technology cannot improve.

We fretted over gear and food lists, adding or subtracting items following advice from Denali veterans or our current readings. I was preparing mentally with an account of the pioneering *winter* ascent cozily titled *Minus 148 Degrees*. Riven by doubt, group tensions, and a crevasse tragedy, eight climbers became trapped in three separate camps above 14,000 feet during a six-day blizzard. "No one had lived on North America's highest ridges in the winter twilight," the author, Art Davidson, writes. "No one knew how low the temperatures would drop, or how penetrating the cold would be when the wind blew. For thousands of years McKinley's storms had raged by themselves."

Tempests hone the cold's edge into a scalpel. Denali's summit routinely registers minus 40°F, while lows straddling the Arctic

Circle suck air from slopes, not just around heinous Windy Corner. On this peak, said to brew its own vat of nastiness, a weather station once recorded minus 75.5°F, which with the wind chill factored in translates to minus 118.1°F. Exposed skin freezes within 30 seconds under such conditions. Worse, humid Bering Sea and Gulf of Alaska westerlies and southerlies dump truckloads of snow. "All of a sudden, the air turns opaque," one survivor said about the onset of such a blow. "You can't see anything, and the wind starts immediately." For park rangers, storms might be Denali's biggest danger, thrashing campsites and trashing gear, knocking climbers off their feet and forcing them to crawl between tents. Backpacks get whisked away and mittens ripped off vulnerable hands.

"The masses of mountains, which form the shoals of the aerial ocean, have a sensible influence on the ambient air," the father of ecology, Alexander von Humboldt, observed in the staid diction of early 19th-century natural scientists. This Prussian polymath, the "Last Man Who Knew It All" before knowledge became compartmentalized, laid the groundwork for the concept of altitudinal life zones—and no-life zones—by mapping vegetation belts in the Andes. On his belly on Ecuador's Guagua Pichincha, he'd peered over the crater's lip, watching blue flames while gagging on sulfur fumes. He fingered humans as drivers of climate change. Rarefied air he had known firsthand. Clambering up a knife ridge steeped in fog on Chimborazo's snow cone, injured, bleeding, and with bloodshot eyes, he felt a nauseous urge to vomit. (Flashbacks to "El Popo" here for me.) With a botanist companion, he reached almost 20,000 feet, a record that stood for three decades. Humboldt endured oxygen deprivation in the service of science. But a mere 15 years earlier, in 1786, a Chamonix doctor had surmounted Mont Blanc with his peasant porter, becoming the first guided modern on record to bag a peak as "sport," simply for fun.

Nearly 6,000 miles from Chimborazo as the condor sails, at the same elevation Humboldt had achieved, a weeklong super-blizzard on Denali in 1967 killed seven climbers in a group of twelve—America's deadliest mountaineering disaster. The rope teams had summited from the north, the Wonder Lake side, via Karstens Ridge and Harper Glacier. A search party looking for survivors found one corpse bracing the pole inside a collapsed tent. Wind speeds up high had approached 300 mph, the National Weather Service estimated, and conditions on those bitter July days may have been the worst Denali had seen in a century and the worst mountaineers had ever encountered.

In June, I was hoping, we would face a mountain less cruel. Like Thoreau setting out for Wachusett Mountain, we were "resolved to scale the blue wall which bounded the western horizon, though not without misgivings."

When we finally loaded the truck, the amount of gear and provisions we'd be carrying more than two miles up vertical wasteland struck me as fit for a mule. I thought I was in decent shape, having schlepped food, tents, rifles, and bears' skins and their skulls for trophy hunters through Kodiak Island all April.

Bad luck swooped down on us right away. Cracking walnuts on the ride south, I broke a filling in one of my canines. A short stop at the Healy gas station, where I bought Super Glue, took care of the problem.

In Talkeetna, we checked in with the National Park Service for our mandatory briefing and to hand over our fee for recreating on public lands. A few last-minute purchases at the local sporting goods store, and we were on our way.

Our pilot was Jay Hudson, owner of a family business that had been shuttling the curious and ambitious to and from the mountain for half a century. His wheel-and-ski-equipped Cessna quickly gained altitude, leaving behind the tourist town that resembled a block set a toddler had scattered. The Susitna River glinted between gray gravel bars; cloud shadows flowed across the land, lending it texture and contrast. Soon, green foothills yielded to the monkish habit of the Alaska Range. Jay aimed straight for the V notch in a rampart of minor peaks; this was One Shot Pass, the shortest and most direct route to Base Camp, at 7,200 feet on the southeast fork of Kahiltna Glacier. Battered by tailwinds or downdrafts, and often trapped under a low cloud ceiling, pilots have to get their line right the first time. "There are bold pilots and old pilots, but no bold old pilots," an Alaska saying warns.

When Jay aligned our Cessna with Kahiltna's crevasse field, the pass framed the plane like a gun sight—its wingtips appeared to be grazing precipitous couloirs and avalanche chutes on both sides. Ahead of us, as the glacier's backdrop, Mount Foraker and Mount Hunter flanked "Deenaalee," the "Tall One" of Koyukon Athabaskans living to the north. Perceiving the world as a maze of relationships, the region's Dena'ina inhabitants referred to the two subaltern peaks as Denali's wife and child. Though the Interior's peoples had named many mountains, many remained unclimbed before Alaska became a US territory. Icy heights were the home of spirits and giants that should be respected, and what thing of value could be found up there, anyway? Some Athabaskans meeting an early expedition noted that "mountain sheep fall off that mountain," doubting the climbers would fare any better. They wondered if the White Men were looking for gold at the top.

Hunters and gatherers went out in nature to find food. "Country folk go out into nature to shoot things," as the Norwegian standup comedian Are Kalvø more bluntly puts it. We urbanites go to find ourselves, or transcendence, or challenges.

It is all the more remarkable, therefore, that the first person to summit Denali because it was there was Athabaskan, the Koyukon-Irish guide, trapper, and dog musher Walter Harper. Harper had been raised the traditional way, with his mother's people, after his father left. At his family's Yukon River fishcamp, he caught the eye of the dogsledding Episcopalian missionary Hudson Stuck, Archdeacon of the Yukon and of the Arctic. The proponent of "muscular Christianity" was impressed with the strapping lad, whom he placed at the boarding school in Nenana and later employed as a trail assistant, translator, and riverboat pilot-mechanic on the Fort Yukon mission launch *Pelican*. In the summer of 1913, Stuck, Harper, then 21, the guide and prospector

Harry Karstens, and another youth on a journey of three months and four days tackled the mountain from the north side. They sledged gear across the cracked Muldrow Glacier, along a route they had marked with willow branches, when one of the dogs broke through a snow bridge and slipped from his harness. Walter was lowered into the crevasse to rescue it. He was not immune to the alpine grandeur. "We saw the finest avalanches this morning," he wrote in his journal, "coming down from the north ridge of Mt. Denali one after another shaking the whole Muldrow Glacier…" A match one of the men smoking pipes carelessly tossed ignited their cache there, which they had covered with the silk fabric of a tent. They lost provisions, wool gloves and socks, film, and, fittingly, most of their tobacco. After extensive repairs, having sent the dogs back to their basecamp near Kantishna, they continued up the northeast ridge, which an earthquake the year prior had shattered. Karstens and Harper had to cut a three-mile staircase through the dangerously poised jumble of ice blocks and slabs. Gulping air, with less than half the oxygen available at sea level in each lungful, the men suffered "high altitude stupidity," insomnia and breathing difficulties, "fits of smothering" and "blind staggers", for which their medicine chest held no remedy. Felt insoles and six pairs of wool and felt socks left no room in Stuck's size-16 footwear. Harper, six feet tall, a born prankster with a shy and ready smile, was the only one feeling entirely himself, and so, for the summit bid on "climbing-irons" or "creepers" strapped to moose hide moccasins, was put in the lead, where he remained all day. The first human to set foot upon the top of Alaska's great mountain "had well earned the lifelong distinction." Stuck, in his own opinion "somewhat overpassing his narrow wind margin, had almost to be hauled up the last few feet, and fell unconscious for a moment" in the little snow basin that occupies the top of South Peak.

The mountain had been elusive. During what was billed as its first ascent, in 1910, two Fairbanks Sourdoughs of a party of four planted a 14-foot spruce flagpole slightly below the false-summit

North Peak, proof they hoped Fairbanksians could spot by tele-scope. A two-cent saloon wager and a sentiment that the honor should go to Alaskans had launched these miners' bid for glory—no soft-handed Easterners were to best them. The pole traveled strapped to the back of one climber, which the others in turn relieved. They'd brought only basic clothing and gear, long johns, bib overalls, unlined parkas, no ropes, iron-tipped "alpenstock" staffs, and homemade sheet-metal crampons like a knight's foot armor, and on summit day, three thermoses with hot chocolate and a bag of donuts. Their journey by horse, mule, and dog team took almost four months. From Fairbanks, North Peak is not visible, but Stuck and company sighted the Sourdoughs' flagpole, confirming a feat that had been decried as a hoax.

As soon as the propeller sputtered to a standstill, Jay unlatched the door and we started to pile gear into the Kahiltna Glacier's snow. In less than 15 minutes, we had the plane unloaded. It tax-ied back to the improvised airstrip of compacted snow, dusting us in a wake of spindrift. As the Cessna lumbered off again, its drone boomeranged between cirques and arêtes. Laurent is trilingual and had breathed in Alpine traditions since childhood, so I picked up some fancy French mountaineering terms.

He had warned me not to expect solitude on this venture. But I was still unprepared for the bustle at "Kahiltna International"—up to one hundred women and men at a time peopled this outpost. Denali's gateway was a makeshift encampment, a tent city forti-fied against the weather's moods. It replicated frontier society: Jabbertown, Bachelor City, Braggartsville, Testosteroneton, not-withstanding the presence of women climbers. Babel transposed into the North. Flags of different nations snapped in the breeze, gear sprawled everywhere, and people hobnobbed or reclined in lawn chairs in front of their compounds. Austrians joked with Canadians. Italians drank wine with Kiwis and Japanese. Koreans talked routes with Argentines, Poles, and even a few Chinese. Unfamiliar accents and languages mingled with cooking scents.

Some residents had built elaborate snow kitchens, complete with benches and shelves. Climbers waited in line at the entrance to the outhouse, a euphemism, really, for a portable toilet half-sunk into a snow pit. Tax dollars had paid for it, and the National Park Service choppered it to Talkeetna regularly to be cleaned. I figured it was the most scenic "bathroom" in North America. In fact, this seat lacked walls, rather qualifying as a "throne." Plywood on three sides, up to your shoulders, barely guaranteed privacy. You felt like a king surveying his domain, but wind or no wind, you certainly would not linger over the view. Everywhere, people coiled ropes, adjusted crampons, or sorted provisions. Bamboo wands tipped with orange flags marked food caches in the snow.

The runway hummed with activity as more planes landed and departed. Despite the chaos, a sense of purpose and urgency galvanized the crowd, like an army preparing to storm a hill fort.

The characters you bump into on the mountain are a big part of the experience. Some couples climbed Denali for their honeymoon. One of the rangers at the 14,200-foot camp had been a rodeo clown in a previous life. He was still saving people's skins, but now in a much bigger and colder arena. On a whim, he had once circumnavigated the Great One on skis, in the middle of winter. Vern Tejas was rumored to be around, a mountain-guide rock star who shaves his head and sometimes played his fiddle on the summit, who had been the first to solo Denali in winter, and who once rode a mountain bike down Aconcagua, and scaled the highest peak on each continent at a record age of 57. Over the decades, he'd amassed over 50 Denali ascents. For his winter solo he'd adopted a smart crevasse self-rescue device: a 16-foot aluminum extension ladder. He stood between the middle rungs with the ladder strapped to his climbing harness like a 1930s cartoon figure wearing a "bankruptcy barrel." If he stepped into a crevasse, the ladder should catch him and he'd shimmy onto it and across—that at least was the idea. The Talkeetna flyboys, too, were chips from a different block. Doug Geeting, who used to tow advertising banners high above oiled flesh roasting on California's beaches, was not only one of the most daring pilots around but also a writer and award-winning folk musician.

After we'd dug out a level foundation and set up our tent, Laurent checked in with the base camp manager. Annie Duquette lived on site for the entire season, in a Weatherport, a Quonset-style shelter scarcely more comfortable than a tent. She acted as air traffic controller, Park Service liaison, shrink, nurse and mother figure, and source of information about weather and climbing conditions. The woman the climbing rangers called an icon did pull-ups from a bar installed in her hut when things were slow. On call 24 hours a day, "Base Camp Annie" made sure things ran smoothly in this off-kilter microcosm representative of what is commonly, though erroneously, called "the real world," a built world of shallow time and deep confusions.

I only found leisure to fully take in my environs after we had settled in. Mount Hunter rose more than a mile above the Kahiltna, at an angle close to 40 degrees. Since we arrived, already two avalanches had scoured its face: billowing, thunderous slides, choking crystal-breath death that raced halfway across the glacier. It had taken the snow clouds minutes to settle. Each time the mountain let go, camp business ceased and all attention centered on the spectacle.

During pauses of calm, I was comfortable enough to lounge about in our flat wearing only a T-shirt. Laurent visited neighbors, gathering news about conditions higher up; but I did not want to meet people just yet, preferring to absorb the warmth and time alone. The camp stove roared along merrily as I kept feeding the cooking pot snow. This was the only source of water around, and we'd fired up as soon as our tent was pitched. With the devotion of monks, we would melt snow for several hours every day, avoiding the yellow kind, because dry air and exertion sapped our body fluids.

A late sun pinked Mount Foraker's spine, while silver-lined clouds hooded Denali's crown. The scale of things made it hard to judge distances. I knew it was eight miles from our camp to the summit, but straight lines were impossibilities in this terrain. The enormity of our endeavor was corroding my confidence. "Double-ferrying," we would in effect climb the mountain twice. We'd carry or sledge one load up and cache it and descend for another night at camp, which would help us acclimatize. "Climb high, sleep low" was the motto. The next morning, we'd break down the tent and haul it and the rest of the gear to that cache, which would become the new camp. "It is this going down and doing it all over again that is the heartbreaking part of climbing," Stuck had complained about the procedure.

Perhaps we did not belong there. Indigenous people, who always had shunned the mountain, understood this; human bodies and minds were not designed for such hostile environments. Overwhelmed by splendid isolation, I curled up in my down sleeping bag early, deciding to take one step at a time.

The next two weeks passed in a blur of snow, insomnia, and oxygen deprivation. The aura that powers this Goldilocks speck in our universe seemed too weak to sustain this unique panting speck on the mountainside. Eventually, the monotony of movement numbed all thought; our bodies shrank into nothing but focused breathing, our minds into clenched fists. Eventually, even the pain evaporated. We lived like ticks in dog fur, lodged in the mountain's skin not for nourishment but for protection. At 16,200 feet, Laurent had developed symptoms of altitude sickness—a hammer headache, shortness of breath—and we had to descend again. Next, we sat two days stormbound in our tent, which whopped like a helicopter, so loud that we couldn't talk. It reminded me of the famous film scene set in the Klondike in which a starving miner wielding an axe chases Charlie Chaplin's Little Tramp, the roommate transformed into a five-foot-five chicken, around a cabin teetering on the brink of a snowy abyss.

Running out of reading material, we studied the prescription drug pamphlets in our first-aid kit. I suffered from an abscessed tooth (not the canine), flushed to the gills with painkillers and antibiotics from the rangers' med tent. (The doc on duty had served as a dentist on Himalayan expeditions.) Many climbers afterward turned around, descending, as they ran low on fuel and provisions. We had plenty left and also already had cached one load on top of the Headwall, an infamous bottleneck and the only technical stretch on the West Buttress route, where you climb a nearly vertical 800-foot icy slab aided by fixed ropes. Back at the 16,200-foot saddle, a Japanese man sat outside his snow cave, sucking on a cigarette, sunbathing *in flip-flops*.

We finally summited, owing our success to stubbornness and extra fuel and food rather than good sense. The view from the top, though, scrolled out with more detail than a map, made each minute worthwhile. Beyond the calm of the occasional basin, lesser peaks of the Alaska Range broke on Denali's escarpment like surf frozen in mid-motion. Glaciers scaly and wrinkled with age scraped their way through the massif's heart. Did the mountain's roots reach as deep as its heights soared, to balance it? There had to be some counterweight. Clouds like blinding white airships hung above a horizon that from our vantage appeared to be visibly curving. If the crampons' bite had not grounded me, I would have floated off into deep, blue-black outer space.

On our descent, the Football Field, Archdeacons Tower (named after Stuck), Denali Pass, the Autobahn (climbers' black humor; through slips and 1,000-foot falls, this slope precipitates more deaths than any other place on the mountain), High Camp (the base for our 18-hour summit day), the Buttress, the Headwall, Basin Camp, Windy Corner, and Motorcycle Hill passed by, dreamlike and without incident. Early on, we noticed choppers windmilling toward the summit and knew something was up—a medevac or retrieval mission, most likely. Our thoughts were with those climbers, whoever they might be. We later learned they were 13 Taiwanese training for Everest. A storm had caught them on their descent near the Football Field. They carried no maps, ropes, altimeters, compasses, and no sleeping bags in which to bivouac.

With the visibility at 15 feet they nevertheless had to overnight. Exposure killed one of them in the rocks by the Archdeacons Tower.

Misfortune and bad judgment trail some people like their own shadow. The following year, after summiting Everest, having ignored his turnaround time and been surprised by another blizzard, the Taiwanese team leader weathered one night in the death zone at 27,000 feet. Near comatose, he was evacuated in the highest helicopter rescue in the history of Mount Everest. He survived but lost all his fingers, toes, and his nose. Eight climbers died on the high slopes that day, in the harrowing events Jon Krakauer retold in *Into Thin Air*. "Denali should not be a preparation for anything," I had heard somewhere, "It's a serious mountain itself." Clearly, it had not prepared the Taiwanese climber for Everest.

A pair of charcoal and iron-powder hand warmers costing one dollar had saved my own toes, which remained numb an hour after leaving High Camp on summit day. With sunrise bronzing the slope, lending it the illusion of warmth, I'd hoped that circulation from movement would soon perfuse them. When it did not, my feet wedged like wood blocks inside the ski boots, we'd stopped and I'd slipped two oxidizing pouches into my vapor barrier socks. Regaining sensation, I had been able to continue.

Back at 11,000 feet, we switched from crampons back to the skis and *pulks* we had cached there, faced downhill and let fly. After days of hauling loads and moving like zombies, the burst of speed brought on head rushes. We kicked up white rooster tails, flashing past strings of climbers who still trudged up the mountain. With the recklessness of people in need of beer and a cleanup, we zipped across narrow snow bridges softening under the June sun. In tricky places, I flipped my *pulk* over, which slowed me like a dragging anchor.

Before we reached the base camp on the Kahiltna, we slogged up a hump whose name had amused us on the day we set out. Returning, it made sudden sense: Heartbreak Hill. It could have been called "Just when you thought you made it..."

Foul weather was upon us once again. Steeped in fog thick enough to spoon, the camp brought to mind an underworld that shadows populated. Half-buried tents clustered together as if seeking company, and the maze of trails and embankments looked unfamiliar in the flat light. Fluff fell from the ripped bellies of clouds. Rope teams were abandoning the mountain, eager to head out for the solstice bash at Talkeetna's historic Fairview Inn. But in this Hadean stew, not even Alaska bush pilots dared to fly. Glued to Annie's radio, we waited for updates. We visited, we bragged, we compared gear, exchanged addresses, and dug up and shared supplies the marauding ravens had overlooked.

Halfway through the morning, a pale sun elbowed its way in, and baby-blue gaps showed in the scrim. Almost immediately, overdue planes started buzzing in; the ensuing commotion resembled the rush to the last choppers leaving Saigon. Climbers scurried about, shuttling gear to the runway, except that three feet of fresh snow cushioned the ground where the runway used to be. More levelheaded or seasoned mountaineers assisted the pilots by stomping out a landing strip with snowshoes and skis in a klutzy square dance. Some planes briefly touched down in mock landings to compress the snow. One unfortunate soul plowed into drifts, where his Cessna bogged down. Another flipped but was lucky enough to crawl from the wreck unharmed. (With the help of a steel cable, a chopper later airlifted the mess to Talkeetna.) A few of us pushed stuck planes by their wing struts, blasted with whiteout from the engines, needled by snow the propellers whipped up.

After repeated sorties to the glacier's deck and shuttles to town, our bird dropped from the sky once more. We boarded in a hurry. A last peek through the Cessna's scratched Plexiglas panes showed the locus of our desire falling away. From up high, base camp looked abstract and lifeless, a porcelain diorama already fading into a memory.

At the Talkeetna airfield, Laurent and I gulped down balmy air, staring in disbelief at a world that wallowed in tender greens around the parked Cessna.

Having stuffed our faces with real food—pizza and salad at the McKinley Deli—we ambled to the bunkhouse for a shower. In the crowded dorm, I stepped over an ancient, groggy guy with sparse wild hair in a sleeping bag on the floor, to be told afterward by Laurent, in a voice hushed with awe, that that was Fred Beckey, a German-born, womanizing climbing-bum legend and guidebook author with close to one thousand first ascents in the Pacific Northwest and elsewhere—"a larger-than-life figure," in the words of *Alpinist* editor Katie Ives, "on an endless road trip, speeding down highways and dirt roads" in a pink Thunderbird with skis on a trunk rack. To Laurent, it was as if the Dalai Lama had graced a 7-Eleven with his unannounced presence. (Beckey, kindred spirit to the Sourdoughs, kept climbing until four years before his death at the age of 94. But he never figured out what it was that had finally slowed him down.)

A glance at the half-blind bunkhouse bathroom mirror convinced me that I'd lost ten years and about 20 pounds on the mountain, though looking only slightly less worn than the celebrity in the dorm. I was glad to have done this and glad I would never again have to do it. We relished water hot enough to raise welts before charging the historic Fairview Inn like polar explorers would have chased a mirage. But, wonder of wonders, this Shangri-La did not dissolve. I opened its hefty door to find the place packed, though it was only four in the afternoon. For a minute, I just stood immersed in cigarette smoke and warm humanity, flabbergasted by the den atmosphere. The current of voices, the clinking of bottles and glasses overlaid with women's laughter, the bellows of climbers happy to be alive, belied the mountain's composure. Climbers outnumbered the locals, both working hard on hydration. You could easily recognize who was outbound and who'd just returned. The latter looked burnt, raw, reduced, somehow, to an essence. I tried to read failure or success in the lined faces. Regardless of outcome, Denali had honed edges in everyone, edges that cut into new and lasting truths.

The rounds kept coming, and I didn't know who was buying. By the time dusk, or what passes for it on summer solstice in these latitudes, dimmed the windows, our waitresses had kicked off their shoes and no longer ran tabs. As the home planet wobbled precariously on its axis, spinning, and racing back toward winter, I became nauseous. Before I left, I caught sight of Laurent atop the bar. Swaying like a bamboo wand in a gale, he was planting a miniature Swiss flag on the summit of an oil painting of Denali, and having a tough time with it. But, till dawn at least, for him and for others in there, wild abandon would cloak the sight, lodged firmly as ice screws, of a body laid out in a black rubber cocoon at 14,200 feet.

CHAPTER 3

TIBET IN THE TALKEETNAS

To Fura Kancha Sherpa, a chip off Nepal's Khumbu Valley, Southcentral Alaska's Talkeetna Mountains must be mere foothills. He looks young, despite a lifetime of high-altitude sun and nine successful Everest bids, but somehow, underneath, also older. His co-guide, Dylan, calls Fura, who grew up around the animals, "a true yak whisperer." In reality, the shy, rail-thin drover, under a ball cap concealing baldness, whistles or hollers to keep them doggies rollin'.

A guest worker for the short summer, Fura greets two float-plane loads at Sheep Back, a lake headed by shark-tooth peaks in whose shadows he's guarded seven yaks since the previous backpacking bunch flew back to Talkeetna two days ago. Crosswinds at our destination detained us in town that long, and I'd crashed at the staff house. Tomorrow, Fura will retrace his steps to Moon Shadow Lake, providing logistics for Alpine Ascents' weeklong trekking trip—us—on the way. I'm tickled to be a client, a guide being guided for a change, here on a story assignment.

We fire-chain food and gear from shore up a grassy bank. Camp has been left standing—a blue-and-white kitchen tent, a carport-style dining tent, and the yellow dome in which clients will sleep. Besides Dylan, a Washington-based, ski-patrolling seismic engineer-mountaineer with a blond beard and fledgling ponytail, there is Piper—his well-behaved avalanche-rescue border collie—and Maren, the Talkeetna assistant. She skijors with huskies and is getting her pilot's license. At times when clients hike bundled up, she goes T-shirted, her Scandinavian face always flushed, hair in golden plaits for convenience. A father-son pair completes our group. Alaska virgins, both will sprout stubble here. Rick's white, closely cropped crown and good-old-boy manner befit an erstwhile Vietnam recon pilot and retired Pacific

Island missile-range commander. His son Eric, equally barbered, tall and buff as a quarterback, recently launched an Austin craft brewery. A frilly bicep tattoo flaunts this first-time backpacker's love for Texas, hops, and his Brazilian wife.

I'm eager to meet the creatures of legendary reputation. Smart, sociable, selected for tractability, and boasting personalities—Einsteins, compared to run-of-the-mill cows—the beefy brutes were first bred millennia ago in Tibet, from spunkier wild stock that still roam the Himalayas at 16,000 feet. They are wealth on the hoof, the currency of survival. "Yaks' bodies are full of treasures," a Sino-Tibetan proverb says. To this day, yaks supply nomads' and villagers' needs: meat, milk, and cheese; butter fueling votive lamps and potent, smoky tea; spinning fiber; leather "bull" boats shaped like troughs, for stream crossings; dried-dung briquettes, cud's blessing in treeless country. Yaks plow fields and thresh grain and compete in races. Their "ox treasure" testes, allegedly tasting like venison, boost Chinese libidos. On the exotic meat market, they fetch 50 bucks a pair. Yaks deliver oxygen tanks and espresso to Everest's basecamp and in Alaska yield farm-raised steaks and wool softer and warmer than that of merino sheep. They caravanned salt, and one carried the exiled Dalai Lama to India. Divine messengers, they romp in dances and myths. Some go so many months unattended they turn semi-feral. Still, unlike bison, yaks do not constantly want to gore you.

Before the Depression, Canada-born yaks in Fairbanks had been crossed with Scottish Galloway cattle to enhance the Interior's meat production. The resulting infertile "galloyaks" endured cold but not farm drudgery, especially being milked. According to the former director of the university's Agricultural and Forestry Experiment Station, you could do it, but it wasn't easy. Their era allegedly ended when one savaged the college president's garden. The following winter, galloyak-heavy school-cafeteria menus revealed a third drawback: the meat was tough, almost inedible. In Alaska and elsewhere, today yaks are farmed for meat 30 percent leaner than beef and a sideline of fiber or yarn. They're content on subarctic hay, sedges, and willows. More docile than their closest *bos* cousins, bison—some yaks carry three-year-old kids—they'll still herd up at the scent of a bear or a wolf and charge and fight to the death to protect their young. Free-range ranching is not feasible here, but in a bit of regional ingenuity, one Delta Junction yakker separates calves from his cows by scooping them from the corral with a salmon dip net instead of roping them with a lariat.

While our piebald energy bundle sniffs ahead, nosing the burrows of ground squirrels that pop up like whack-a-moles, we explore a ridgeline, easing into amazingly bug-free surroundings. We weave uphill between star gentians and harebells, between outcrops that frost fractured and lichen scabbed, and from which alarmed marmots shrill. A hidden mist machine allows only glimpses of jade lakes, snow shrouds, and crumbling gray pyramids. Clouds erase those during our return and then spatter drizzle.

On our return, near camp, where fireweed slashing the landscape is its sole vivid aspect, we run into our party's bulk, the magnificent seven. The "boys"—Jack, Joseph, Levi, and Pemba ("Saturday")—graze haunch-to-haunch with Nima ("Sunday"), Dawa ("Monday"), and Pratima ("Trim, with a Nice Smile"). Sherpas are known for their prowess as porters, guides, and summiteers in their own right, and the term refers to both a vocation (in lowercase) and member of the "celebrity ethnicity" that put the first man on top of Mt. Everest and brought forth the male and female record holder for most ascents of that peak. The Sherpa people name some yaks and children after the newborn's birthday. Our handler's first name, Fura, means "Thursday." "Kancha" designates a family's youngest boy. Appending the birthplace or clan can resolve any remaining confusion. But Kathmandu phonebooks are pretty much useless, globetrotters say. The Alpine Ascents yaks bearing Nepali names were reared in Alaska, the rest shipped from Asia to Talkeetna. A calf dropped there this spring came as a surprise; the cow's knee-long hem cloaked her pregnancy. Native and foreign muskies in the off-season mix in the company owner's pasture, and a few are herded to the uplands for these trips.

Proud, doting pastoralists worldwide adorn their cattle. Bronze bells on bright, hand-woven neckbands broadcast our yaks' whereabouts. Swastikas on Dawa's collar symbolize Buddha's auspicious footprints, the karmic wheel—cosmic recycling. Young Pemba, a bull, sports red woolen ear tassels, markers that we soon learn to heed. Joseph punk rocks a mane strand dyed orange. Hair loss has exposed his neck folds, skin thicker than expected.

Piper has fully morphed into "Griper" over the black, wandering boulders steeped in musk. It's the shepherd instinct. Her barking bothers Pemba. Pemba charges and Dylan barely deflects the yak by snapping open his hiker's umbrella. (When did *those* become a thing?) Piper is no match for this four-legged battering ram. Tibetan wolves and winters, however, kill bigger, wild yaks.

I'd pay to see such forces clash.

I linger entranced by the hillside foragers. Straining to reach without stepping, they go bug-eyed. One, relieving a scalp itch, pulverizes a tussock. Rubbery lips and tongues uproot greenery audibly. Horns of a shortbow's bend and span scratch pronounced humps. The grumblings immortalized in this species' Latin name—*Bos gruniens*, "grunting ox"—set counterpoints to the buzzing of bees at flowers and the lapping of wavelets at the shore. I recline on cushiony tundra crinkly from drought, where munching white muzzles, belly-hair skirts swaying, and the temple-bell clanging of clappers lull my monkey mind.

By the time notes of barbecued salmon rouse me, the yaks, though not hot or mosquito-ridden, have ambled into the lake. At a later camp, one will claim a cottongrass island for itself. Distant relatives of the bison and water buffalo, yaks simply love to dally chest-deep in water—Tibetan toughs on a ruminative break when we put on layers of clothes so our lips won't turn blue.

The next morning, we watch the ancient routine of beasts being burdened. Maren yee-haws them in from a bowl in the hills. Fura tethers them to climbing rope strung between a picket and rock. The odd shirker has to be dragged into position. Each hand-carved packsaddle fits a particular yak. The two feisty ones, Pemba and Jack, require Dylan or Maren to grip a horn. With horses, mostly the back end spells trouble; with yaks, upward thrusts of the armed anvil head. Singing to calm them, Fura fastens chest bands and cruppers to keep things from sliding. Having cinched girths and trucker-hitched balanced coolers and bulging bags in his job's sweatiest moments, he finishes, pulling taut nylon webbing, bracing a knee against the load. "A knot not neat is a knot not needed," we told students at Outward Bound; for want of a taut knot, a load—or life—can be lost. Knots, to the former Alaskan fisherwoman Lara Messersmith-Glavin, are "rituals of the hands that have been passed down for countless generations, binding with texture and shape." The eternal or endless knot of Tibetan Buddhism, a good-luck Möbius-style representation of birth, death, rebirth, and the interlacing of all things, may well have sprung from the mind of a herder who took monastic vows.

The yaks, lugging tents and heavier personal items, leave after the hikers, passing them later so camp will be ready when we arrive. Traversing alpine terrain under lightened backpacks, we like this arrangement. Eric broke his neck playing football. Rick has had both knees replaced and survived bone cancer; arthritis gnarled his hands into roots—yet he walked 600 miles on Spain's Camino de Santiago last summer. I have lower back problems and a crook shoulder, unhinged repeatedly.

For several hours every day, when I'm not with the hikers, I escort the lumbering column of bovines fanning out, stopping and grabbing mouthfuls, stoking boulder physiques. Even green-horns recognize individuals by their bodies' cast, by fetlocks and forelocks, by demeanor, by the head-butting instruments' bold, unique flare. Dawa, the runt, always sans baggage, always lags. Hiking-pole prods won't rev her behind into second gear. Pemba enjoys mushrooms. He also hassles Nima, who retaliates fiercely or, bursting forth, gains distance. After one bout, Pemba's cargo needs retightening. The hormonal youngster never challenges

Jack. That one just sitting on you would feel like burial under 200 bricks.

In creek beds, the mob vanishes into thickets, except for horn tips or the occasional hump. Mistaking one for a grizzly's, I flinch. Galloping quickens the gamelan orchestra's beat, but caught mid-line or up front, I manage to dodge these mini-stampedes. Cairns form exclamation marks at the route's cruxes, bad-weather beacons reminiscent of stacks in Tibetan passes, where travelers adding stones ask for blessings or appease inscrutable, glowering gods.

By day three, our fair-skinned maid, wearing headphones and acting as sweep, sounds like a hoarse carnival barker. She's a softie with animals, though, which ours perceive as weakness. Fura, leading and smiling at rookie efforts, speeds up slackers by lilting their names. The marathoners in fat suits huff toward Yak Pass, tongues lolling under a withering sun. Like the Sherpas, who breathe faster at rest and circulate blood faster through vessels wider than those of lowlanders, yaks evolved at high elevations. They break ice crusts to feed, chew snow when water is absent—having fewer sweat cells than a cow conserves fluids in arid environments. A lung capacity three times that of cattle pushes more and smaller, oxygen-rich red blood cells through tissues, withstanding minus-40-degree temperatures. Yaks shed the dense, dark-brown winter coat underneath guard hairs to prevent overheating. Both fibers have been crafted into rugs, ropes, tents, bags, slings, wigs, and lately, designer long johns and soundproof insulation for a Dutch museum. You can whisk away flies with the tail hair, or have an attendant do so, singling you out as royalty. The donors' surefoot-edness, outclassing horses and mules, shines on the far side of Yak Pass. Dainty as Boston debutantes, they trail Fura 800 vertical feet through ball-bearings scree. Yaks can jump six-foot fences, and their gallop, as one rider (not in our group) put it, is smoother than a horse's, "like a Lincoln Continental."

For years, I worked with mustangs and quarter horses—which I believe to be the most fickle of domesticated animals—guiding trail rides, charging in Civil War reenactments (on the Union side), and teaching at-risk youths in a "Buffalo Soldiers" program. I've brush-popped strays and, riding drag, punched livestock in Wyoming, West Texas, and British Columbia's Chilcotin country. Not really the cowboy type, I've always loathed cattle, those crusty-assed locusts leaking methane as they denude public lands. But yaks may yet cause me to revise my opinion.

On day four, we pitch tents among choice blueberry patches after squelching in sandals through marshland and a dammed creek to aptly named Beaver Camp, six springy tundra miles downhill from Lake Camp and Flattop Mountain, above whose brow a golden eagle spiraled on thermals. Throughout our descent, Denali domed on the horizon—blindingly white, weightless, holy, attended by Hunter, and by Foraker, humped like a yak—kin to Mount Kailash and Machapuchare. It seemed unreal, not at all like the peak I had climbed. Ruth Glacier visibly wended from its flank, with black curves of moraine rubble from cliffs that would make El Capitan blanch. Darkness briefly intruded when Eric, getting a cell signal, over lunch told us of another mass shooting. I've long opposed communication devices on wilderness trips, except signal mirrors, and only recently, grudgingly following outfitters' mandates, have accepted guide satellite phones for emergencies. Charter bush pilots nowadays expect weather updates from parties in the field on the morning of a scheduled pickup; time and fuel are precious. In the sweet bygones, you'd sit on an airstrip in the best kind of nowhere on the agreed-upon date, and you'd get a lift, eventually. I recall a time on the Sadlerochit River when we heard our pilot buzzing to and fro above the fog. But he could not locate a hole and left to return two days later. My client, afraid he would starve, had started to stockpile Butterfingers. It's a delicate balance, I admit. Where rescue in ideal conditions is but a phone call away, the zest of self-reliance goes stale. Decisions become less deliberate, less consequential. Perversely, the promise of backup security may deceive people into taking greater risks. As for client phones: noise from the maddening outside world dissolves here-ness. It deflects the adventurers' attention away from nature and ruins the sense of remoteness. No news can be good news indeed. "Such was my seclusion," Buddha supposedly said, "that I would plunge into some forest and live there" in pursuit of enlightenment.

Music from the kitchen tent—thankfully some bluegrass-y number, not Fura's beloved Bollywood soundtracks—announces dinner is being prepared. Dylan, Maren, and the packer have bathed and rinsed clothes in the creek. The yaks, bedded down on our ridge near dusk, wear bug nimbuses. In the slant light, the insects resemble crazed, gilded dust motes. Fura anoints the quietly suffering martyrs with repellent daubed onto latex gloves, out of compassion but also so they'll stay put. They've fled infested sites in the past, bolting for miles to drier or windier camps. Brushing her teeth, Maren jogs orbits around her bedroom before diving in as if piranhas were chasing her. The yaks' peaceful chiming joins sibilants from a brook tumbling off the plateau. A waxing, Cheshire-grin moon mocks the weakening sun.

Never hobbled, the yaks normally don't wander far. Now they crop halfway up a mountainside, now ten yards from our tents, homing in, as a rule clustered, on the richest green. The term "herd mentality" is unflattering, really; safety can be found in numbers, together with warmth, comfort, and room for distinctiveness.

Willows, dwarf birches, cow parsnip, and alders choke the stretch between Beaver Camp and our pick-up location. Over the years, the yaks have dozed trails through the lush under-growth, wider, more entrenched than caribou paths. Still, we get bunched up behind them, because they're flagging in untimely heat. Scattered spruces appear, rust-brown, upright, beetle-killed corpses forecasting the apocalypse. It's a visual version of Eric's amok news. Each adult tree within miles has expired. Each one remains upright, a potential torch. At peak wildfire pitch these days, Alaska's forests aflame spew the same amount of carbon dioxide as all of Florida's carbon-fueled bingeing.

A feast for parched minds and the eyes, Moon Shadow Lake blues a basin ringed by knolls. Bearberry leaves have begun their blushing and fireweed the loosing of silky seed fluff. I take a bracing swim, pinpointing Flattop Mountain, hazy with distance. Tomorrow, the wranglers will hike the yaks out, an overnight trip. Fura lifts his last can of "fish beer" in celebration, his cherished Sockeye Red, which Eric praises, too. The taciturn Nepalese then cleaves a skewer from a birch log with the crooked blade of his *khukuri*, a Gurkha melee weapon and sickle, a Swiss Army knife many times older than Switzerland.

Crrrck. It is steak night. Should Dawa worry?

As the first floatplane, shattering stillness, alights the next morning, I bid farewell. My silent *namaste* salutes fellow incarnations: dreadlocked sadhus, shaggy saints, patient, beautiful souls.

CHAPTER 4

MAROONED

The students recline in a half-circle in camp chairs facing the scalloped bay, afraid to miss out on the scenery. By week three of this month-long ed-venture, companionship, paddling skills, and new landscapes have begun to fill any void TV or video games may have left. The spectacular setting helps translate the course curriculum—politics and ecology of the Tongass National Forest—into realities that will take root as memories. Luckily, no clear-cuts dissect today's view. In this part of Southeast Alaska's archipelago, hills dark with yellow cedar, hemlock, and Sitka spruce wrap around the bases of sudden massifs, part of the nation's largest public forest. Peaks throng above the tree line, as do, higher still, barbed vanes of cirrus. Along the shore's scrawl, a dozen sea kayaks lie where we landed, like beached gaudy pilot whales. Gulls shriek in a winged blizzard near the high-water mark, pecking at dead things between the rocks. The tide carries notes of kelp, brine, mudflats, and decay—creation's inimitable perfume—while less than ten miles from us the hemisphere's southernmost tidal glacier dips its crystal tongue into the ord. Mediterranean after-noons too rarely bless Alaska's Inside Passage; before we even pitch tents we take advantage of this one, teaching a lesson on glacial morphology. The warmth and my co-instructor's voice lull me, and my concentration keeps slipping. A different, animal, form of attentiveness takes over as I scan the beach for bears on the prowl.

Some bright, sheep-size creature *does* register in my field of vision, on an island afloat in the bay. Pacing from one end to the other, it appears to be testing the perimeter of its confinement. Could it be a wolf? I reach for my field glasses, tense enough to alert the group.

A head too small, angular as slab marble, offsets a body shaped like a boulder. Shag fluffs fore- and hindquarters into ridiculous bloomers. A mountain goat. At sea level. The incoming tide has barred its retreat, stranding it like an ice chest washed off some tour boat or a bergy bit gone astray. At first glance it could be a billy or nanny. Both sexes sport jet-black spikes the local Tlingits carve into potlatch spoons—curved, functional keratin art. Our guidebooks say that adult male goats are the ones most likely to go gallivanting, from alpine reaches down crenellated ridges and into the shelter of conifers, lured by any ungulate tough guy's Eldorado: salt licks, or deep meadows to browse and populate. Elusive as well as exclusive, the white ghost of the Coast Range was not described scientifically until 1900 and claims a genus all to itself. Earlier encounters with parts of its body had resulted in misunderstandings; on his journey along this rugged shore that ice gouged, Captain Cook traded for mountain goat hides, which he thought came from "spirit bears," black bear mutants, off-white like cream, that pace British Columbia's coast. (These bears are sacred, and Indigenous people would never have killed them.)

The students are standing now, firn lines and medial moraines temporarily consigned to their minds' garrets. Our intern, Neil, sprints to his kayak, slides into the cockpit, and, pushing with his knuckles, seal-launches from the beach.

"What are you going to do?" someone shouts. "Drape it across your bow?"

"Don't know," he replies. "Just taking a closer look, I guess."

Why not leave it be? I wonder. What feeds this need for proximity, this urge to interfere? "To cherish," the forester and ecologist Aldo Leopold mourned in A Sand County Almanac, "we must see and fondle, and when enough have seen and fondled, there is no wilderness left to cherish."

This fondling is not just a pat on the head. We nurse oil-slicked otters and eagles back to health. We radio-collar caribou to understand their timeless but timed rounds. We keep bears in cages, to edify, engage, enchant, entertain. We make room for wolves where we used to poison them and, just as absurdly, installed mountain goats in Nevada and Colorado, where trophy hunters can chase them. Others flock, in Sweden, to cull hundreds of lynxes. Our relationship with the wildlings has been monetized and depersonalized. In Japan, there's a bear-meat vending machine now. And in a kind of moral mathematics, the Canadian government calculated the dollar value of a polar bear—$400,000. That tally includes the bears' worth as tourist magnets as well as "cultural, artistic, and spiritual values for Aboriginals."

The sociobiologist E.O. Wilson claimed that an attraction to other life forms got inscribed in our genes when animals shaped hominid nature on Africa's steppes; hunter-gatherers acknowledge this debt with respect. Evolutionary psychologists also warn us that we neglect or corrupt this relationship at the cost of societal dysfunction. To further complicate matters, this innate drive ("biophilia") can manifest as the opposite: a dark urge, born of greed or fear, to abuse and eradicate our brethren-on-Earth. Be they dachshunds or Komodo dragons, head lice or monarchs, cobras or Siamese cats, these others leave few people unmoved.

Regardless of its motivation, the reaching-out of a species that exiled itself behind barriers of artifice can be a bleak and beautiful thing. I only hope nobody will suffer injury or indignity on this occasion. While Neil disembarks on the low-slung island, the goat gallops up and over a rise. Neil walks to the top, neoprene skirted, paddle in hand, to see what we have already seen from shore: the goat cut a wake to an outcrop close by, muzzle pointed skyward, like a chunky retriever.

By the time Neil has inserted himself in the kayak again, the billy has climbed this miniature Ararat doomed to submerge. Against the sea's backdrop, the goat seems out of its element but still more of this place than we Gore-Tex-ans from afar. Possessed of a mineral quality, a poise and resilience older than flesh, it stands bolted to rock—an extension of sweeping summits, hewn from Le Conte Glacier's trunk, solid and blunt as winter itself. Its stubborn form embodies the land's pluck and fiber. Like snowfields crisp in the distance or the void on explorers' charts, the goat not only invites speculation but even more so the projection of desires. I would trade with this bearded recluse in an instant. I'd travel unburdened by gear. I'd grow hairy and hunchbacked and rank, sniffing out mates and competitors. I'd become agile enough to dodge grizzlies and wolves, fearless enough to bed down on vertiginous ledges, and smart enough to avoid our kind.

With a lapse into pastoral metaphor excusable in a Scotsman, wilderness sage John Muir compared this breed to others, considering them "nature's cattle," better fed and protected from the cold. He detested filth and might have been a germaphobe: domestic sheep were unkempt and dirty compared to the "clean" wild animals like the mountain goats he observed in his wanderings. But he also acknowledged the grit in their existence. During a sledding trip above Glacier Bay, on the ice flow that still bears his name, he found bones cast about in an ancient blood rite. Their configuration spelled out the death of a frail or sick or unlucky one. Presumably, wolves had caught up with a wild goat two miles from safer ground, where breakneck terrain matched with breakdancing athleticism would have given it the advantage. Despite their famed surefootedness, missteps occur, and the abyss claims its share of mountain goats every year. Loose rocks and avalanches strike down others. Inexperienced kid goats may fall to the talons of golden eagles, which hunt alone or pair up to corner them. Current logging practices in the Tongass, stripping slopes of cover and feed, further skew the odds against survival.

Pulling away from those sobering thoughts, I watch Neil bump the outcrop with the bow of his kayak. He waves a paddle blade in the animal's face. What is he doing? Trying to save a goat by making it dive? It's unlikely to drown, even if it gets flooded out. But Neil might yet discover the flip side of hands-on approaches to learning. If the goat chooses to answer intrusion with uncivil resistance, our rookie instructor will have a hard time explaining hoof scratches on his kayak deck back at the warehouse.

Clearly vexed with being crowded, Billy indeed takes him on, defending its quickly shrinking domain. He jerks horn daggers into Neil's direction, hooking the air, unwilling to yield as much as an inch.

On shore, the students holler and cheer—for whom, I cannot tell.

Eventually, the goat's aversion to humans overcomes any fear of the unfamiliar. (It knows nothing about tiderips or orcas or reefs.) With shoulders tucked in like a boxer's, it pivots and leaps high and wide, charging its twin in the burnished sea. Before long we lose sight of it as it pedals across the bay, into Muir's "endless combinations of water and land," to be culled from the gene pool or to sire a feisty clan somewhere in the high country.

CHAPTER 5

MATING DANCE UNDER THE MIDNIGHT SUN

With each paddle stroke, muscles play in her tanned, well-rounded shoulders. Straight chestnut hair falls to the nape of her neck, barely concealing the swan-like curve.

"Such a beautiful day, *non?*"

It is indeed. I cannot believe my luck. Here I am, with an exotic woman, on a remote northern river, a forget-me-not sky smiling above everything.

What more could a man want?

It all began with an ad. Or rather, with the idea that, after so many years of romantic shipwrecks, of forever stumbling into the pits of physical attraction and carnal confusion, a soul mate could perhaps better be found by comparing souls.

I therefore decided to have my profile printed in *Alaska Men* magazine, the path-breaking periodical that has been "bringing you Alaska bachelors since 1987." *You* meaning the female half of the Lower 48 states and a few overseas. *Bachelors*, meaning, "husband material," according to the magazine editor herself. This illustrious and illustrated gem also gave the world a T-shirt with the slogan *Alaska Men—The odds are good, but the goods are odd* and the Firefighter Calendar, a male equivalent of the swimsuit calendar and Playboy centerfold long overdue. In fact, the odds in places like Fairbanks or Los Anchorage are about even, and as for oddity—you be the judge. I heard from a woman on a winter flight into Fairbanks that her seat neighbor showed her a series of photos of his woodstove and cozy cabin, only to lose interest when she answered his question about whether somebody special was waiting for her "at the other end" in the affirmative. At the annual bachelor auction in Talkeetna, which allegedly draws women from as far away as Mainland USA, one lot in black-frame glasses and a hipster hat, outgunned by bare-chested beefcakes with fur codpieces and roses in their teeth, modestly flashed a *Respect Is Hot* sign. You have to be on your best game. Nights are long here in December, and beds can be cold.

I certainly qualified for the honorific "Alaska Man." Although German-born, I had been a resident of the Big Dipper State for almost four years. I lived in a cabin, a plywood cracker box on the outskirts of Fairbanks. It had an archery range—a hay bale—out back, where I trained to become the Great White Moose Hunter. But I soon quit practicing, losing too many arrows to the swamp, and those were expensive.

Undaunted by the objectification of my body, I filled out and sent in a questionnaire, together with a picture of my expressive, clean-cut features against the backdrop of a bush plane. (Not my own—the plane, that is.) Asked to describe my ideal first date to the readers, I did not hesitate for a second: *My ideal first date would be a weeklong wilderness trip together, because I believe that's where your compatibility and true colors show quickly.* They ran a full page in the magazine, and I was happy with the way I looked and sounded on glossy paper.

I was hoping for the mother lode this time around.

As a safety precaution against infatuated stalkers, crank calls or bomb threats from jealous exes or current boyfriends, I had my phone number unlisted and rented a mailbox at the post office in town. (*Paranoid* was not one of the character traits I had cared to mention in my sales pitch.) As it turned out, the readership was rather diverse and not at all limited to the continental United States. I got fan mail from England. One letter arrived from Quebec, in broken English, another from a black nurse in Kotzebue. A fisherwoman, sounding lonely, trawling off the coast of South Africa, cast her net wide and wrote to me on yellow legal-pad paper. One of my female pen pals grew up in a lighthouse. She admitted she talked a lot with dead people. I received notes from prison inmates that made me blush, although I pride myself on not being prudish. Some epistles contained locks of hair. Others were smudged with lipstick kisses, or steeped in mysterious perfumes.

Quite a few women were suspicious. They wanted to know why I'd chosen a portrait shot as my photo. Was I obese, or missing a limb? Foolishly, I had believed in the old saw that eyes are the windows to the soul. I quickly became an expert graphologist, a reader-between-lines. Occasionally, the exotic stamps intrigued more than the enclosed words. But every time I peered into the dark innards of my mailbox and spotted the white or pink wink of envelopes, I trembled with the prospect of having hit the jackpot. Letters and pictures of women in various poses and stages of life lay scattered all over my 14-by-14-foot plywood palace without running water. (Hence the self-described *rustic minimalist* in the magazine.) I bought a cardboard folder and organized my correspondence alphabetically, a little boy locked into the candy store overnight.

A flurry of letter writing ensued with a few fortunate candidates. And bit-by-bit, as I got to meet their souls, and they mine, the choice became clear.

Monique was a French woman living in Albuquerque, a lover of literature and a painter. I personally prefer Edward Abbey's rants to Simone de Beauvoir, and much of photographic realism strikes me as uninspired. But I felt I had to make some concessions. Monique had divorced her husband, a former salvage diver, when he turned into a couch potato. My kind of woman exactly. As I could not peep through her soul's apertures in the diminutive photo she'd sent, I asked for an enlargement. The watercolor sketch that promptly arrived in the mail showed nothing but a pair of hazel cat's eyes afloat on lush paper. Long lashes and brows arched like calligraphy brush strokes sent harpoons straight into my chest. Perhaps too soon, we swapped phone numbers; but the first time her sweet, melodious lilt bridged the distance between us I could have gobbled up the receiver.

When she finally walked through the gate at the airport, my heart danced a little jig. I was going once, going twice…she looked like a French version of Audrey Hepburn. Except, with her delicate five-foot-four figure, she was shorter than I expected—about half as tall as the grizzly encased in glass at the Alaska Airlines counter. Monique had told me her height, but it had never quite registered, and I am bad with numbers anyway. (In my profile, that translated into *concerned with quality rather than quantity.*)

She knew, however, that the way into the heart of a Taurus is through his belly. In my modest kitchen nook, she went straight to work, preparing a dish of braised scallops, green asparagus, potatoes au gratin, smothered in a killer sauce of heavy cream and Cognac (no cheap brandy for her), something with a nasal-sounding name I can't quite remember. That first night, we slept chastely apart, myself in the stuffy loft reached via ladder and hatch and Monique on the floor of my domicile, which tilts slightly, because I live on permafrost in the taiga that wraps around town.

On our first full day together, we did touristy things. Aboard the sternwheeler *Discovery* we plowed the silty Chena River, while a bush pilot demonstrated taking off and landing in a floatplane, the romance of glorified cab driving, and the theme music of *Love Boat* played in my head. We stopped at Susan Butcher's place, where the acclaimed musher welcomed us from her backyard. Leaning on the rails of the big white riverboat, we watched Susan's handler race her Iditarod-winning team. The huskies looked a little hot on this subarctic summer day, as they pulled a sled around the yard, their driver barely visible behind dust clouds.

"But there is no snow," observed my lovely companion. "We Alaskans do things differently," I reassured her.

We spent a pleasant-enough evening at the Malemute Saloon of the old Ester Gold Camp. Monique got further glimpses of Alaskan manhood and mores from the upright-piano player, a token Sourdough dressed in 19th-century garb, who kept spitting with great relish into the sawdust that covered the floor. The original "Sourdoughs," I explained to her, were Klondike miners who carried fermenting pancake starter and after a few winters probably smelled like it.

During my weekly soccer game, Monique sat at the sidelines. Our team was Buns on the Run, and our sponsor, a fast-food breakfast place, had donated shorts too tight, with the business name emblazoned on their backsides. Instead of watching the odd goods milling about on the ball field, Monique chatted with the wives and fiancées of my teammates. While I appreciated having a trained nurse in attendance—we were losing, and things were getting a tad rough—a shadow of domesticity fell onto my soul. I imagined that scene as a replay of my mom watching my dad kick a pig's bladder around some Hessian cow pasture, 32 years ago. It had happened that way. I had happened that way.

The day after, a small plane delivered us to the banks of the Koyukuk River, north of the Arctic Circle, where its turbid flow skirts the village of Allakaket. Our great adventure was about to begin.

Between piles of gear, I wrestled with the Klepper, the collapsible double kayak made-in-the-old-country that was to be our craft. I remembered that the brand name is a Teutonic term for a nag ready to be sent to the knacker. Out of their packsack, the canvas deck and rubberized bottom, the keel, ribs, thwarts, gunwales and rudder parts, more closely resembled the remains of a seal butchered on shore. I could not make sense of the gibberish German instructions, even though I was still fluent in that language. (*Manually challenged* was another trait that never made it into print, because it clashed with *self-reliant* and *down-to-earth*.) With the help of my fine-boned visitor from the high desert and advice from a number of Native Alaskan spectators, I eventually figured out where all the *Flügelmuttern* and *Kreuzschlitzschrauben* needed to go. We assembled the thing and shoved off.

"Should we look for a camp, Mai-kel?" Monique now warbles from the bow of the boat.

I just love the way she pronounces my name.

"*Biensure*," I flaunt my command of the Gallic tongue and contemplate adding a "*cherie*" for good measure.

We make camp in a clearing overlooking the river. After humping the contents of our boat up the steep bank, I prove my resourcefulness and worth as a paramour by whipping up a dinner of pasta and tomato sauce, robust bush fare, not some kind of frou-frou city cuisine. (It was all there, out in the open, black on white in *Alaska Men*: *...not obsessing about the mundane details of life...*). On a previous trip, on the Noatak, I lost a minor piece of equipment when the kayak flipped—the cooking pot. I emptied the can of Coleman fuel for the stove into my water bottles. With a Leatherman, I then sawed the one-gallon tin can in half. The upper part, hammered at with a rock, made a nice lid, the bottom a beautiful, if sharp-lipped, pot. For the rest of that journey, a gas aftertaste tainted my meals, and I had to dip drinking water straight from the river with my cup. So what? A little sediment and spare fuel in their diet never hurt anybody.

"Voila!" I beam, handing Monique her plate.

I see admiration in her eyes, and her radiant smile reveals a chipped front tooth cute enough to die for. My knees feel like the green Jell-O I keep hidden as a surprise dessert.

After we've cleaned dishes with gravel and sand, low-impact style, we set up our shelter. I left the roomy three-person dome tent at home and brought the doghouse instead. We are comfy inside, lying on top of an unzipped sleeping bag—a *shared* sleeping bag.

"Tell me about your life in Alaska," she demands.

Great, I think, time for some pillow talk, and proceed to recount the adventures of the spring I was working for big-game hunting outfits on Kodiak Island and near Katmai's volcanoes.

"I hauled supplies from sea level up into the mountains, and 40-pound bearskins and skulls back to the boats. It was the perfect preparation for an ascent of Denali the following summer." I can tell she is impressed when she snuggles closer. I go on to recount an episode in Glacier Bay National Park, failing to mention that I flew there to meet another blind date. (She turned out to be— but that's a different story.)

"I was out sea-kayaking, trying to get close to a griz' on a spit of land, to get a better picture of him. Next thing you know, he jumps into the drink and starts dogpaddling after me."

The instant these words come out of my mouth, I realize they are a mistake.

"There are bears out here too, *n'est que pas*?" Her voice almost falters.

"Sure—I don't know, actually." What else is there to say?

"Ssssh! What was that?"

"What?"

"That sound. Like a splash."

"Probably just a piece of cutbank slumping into the river."

"No, lis-ten!"

And we both do, and her body is rigid, and I can sense tension coming off her like heat. The economy-size can of bear repellent lying handily at the foot of our love nest probably does not help much to alleviate her fear. I stay quiet, but all I can hear before drifting into sleep is an ominous rumbling in the distance.

Before long, the sun tilts upward on its low arc and light caresses the tops of black spruce trees on a bluff, which resemble big bottle-brushes. I walk to the morning-still river, urged by my bladder. Water like mocha roils at the tip of my boots. Something about this strikes me as odd. Scanning the beach, I cannot locate our paddles.

"Monique."

"Yes?" comes her voice from the tent, still heavy with sleep.

"Did you put the kayak paddles away last night?"

"No. *Pourquoi?*"

"They must be here, somewhere."

I look inside the boat, behind the tent, behind bushes. Nothing. Suddenly the truth hits me in hot and cold flashes. The river has risen. It must have been raining hard last night and only upstream. Unloading the boat, I had simply dropped the damned wooden paddles and, like a tenderfoot, left them lying on the beach. The deluge snatched them.

"*Merde alors!*" Monique's words, not mine. She is wrapped in her sleeping bag, her sculpted collarbones exposed to the new day, which suddenly promises to be bleak.

I just stand there, *six feet tall, blue-eyed, confident and comfortable in the outdoors*, God's gift to womanhood, a James Blond of the boreal woods.

After a quick and tense breakfast, we are back on the water. I guess we could line the kayak downstream, following the brush fringe of the Koyukuk, but I decide to forgo a bushwhacking ordeal. Not easily browbeaten by the weather's antics, we pole downriver instead with unwieldy lengths of driftwood. This is very awkward from a sitting position, and the poles only help with propulsion where the river is shallow enough. When I try it kneeling, the kayak threatens to capsize. The current is sluggish; at this pace it could take us weeks to get to Hughes.

The next few days are best forgotten. They stretch before us endlessly, an impression that can only in part be credited to the untiring Arctic sun.

The poles break frequently and need to be replaced. When they do, the Klepper truly behaves like a horse carcass. It turns sideways, grinds into gravel bars, or helplessly drifts toward dangerous strainers—fallen trees skimming the surface. They vibrate in the stream's passing, potential deathtraps with the power to pin and rip or flip boats, to keep swimmers' heads underwater. When Monique deigns to look at me, deep lines furrow her once-comely brow. At some point I try to cheer her up.

"This could be Venice, and I could be your *gondoliere*." (Did I mention *great sense of humor?*) More ice-queen frowns are my only reward. Could it be a cultural thing? Perhaps the French don't like the Italians.

What's the difference between a Frenchwoman and a kayak?

A kayak buoys you.

In the evenings, I lie in my sleeping bag by myself, with sore shoulders and blistered hands, too tired and raw to even think about touching this attractive woman next to me. Instead, I calculate food rations and distances in my head.

Six days out, we pitch the tent on a half-moon of gravel on the inside curve of a river bend. By now, I wear boxing gloves made of bandages from the first-aid kit. Nevertheless, tonight is the night. Tonight, I will make my move. Tonight, I will check my soul mate's compatibility. During dinner, Monique had talked to me again, even laughed at some half-hearted jokes. (I had served her pea soup "au cretin," with a flourish: a filthy bandana draped over my arm.) I start by removing the wraps around my fists, bending stiff joints. This will be bare-knuckles. Last man standing.

Just as I roll over, crunching footfalls draw close to the tent. They stop abruptly. Silence. In one fluid move I reach for the bear spray, roll out of the sleeping bag and poke my head through the tent flap (...*athletic*...). I am determined to protect this babe in the woods, if necessary, at the cost of my life.

"Hi, guys. This is tribal land. Part of the village of Hughes."

"Why? How close are we?" I ask the young man with slightly Asiatic features, who waits respectfully ten feet from the tent.

"'Bout half a mile."

"I had no idea we were that close," I apologize. Trusting that the river would get us where we needed to go, I had not brought maps either.

"There is a camping fee, if you guys spend the night here." I look for my wallet, which I *did* bring. Even the bush is getting expensive these days. I pay, our Koyukon host nods, and leaves. Back inside I realize the spark of desire has been snuffed out. It could have been the interruption, but more likely, forking out 15 bucks for a campsite without showers, picnic tables, or even a barbecue pit, has cooled my ardor.

Next morning, we land at the village. Skilled hunters who have steered small watercraft for thousands of years are gathered on the riverbank to observe our deft maneuvering. Word must have gone out, or else they saw us coming. On the improvised boat slip, I busy myself with the load, trying to avoid eye contact with the elders. With their broad, leathery faces, their quiet stance and demeanor, these are true Alaska men, the genuine article.

"You know, they make real nice kickers [outboard motors] now," one of them volunteers.

I nod. "Goddamn paddles, too," I curse under my breath.

Back in Fairbanks, we are saying our adieus at the airport. "Will you call me when you get to Albuquerque?"

"Perhaps."

A quick hug, a peck on both cheeks that elevates me like a European head of state, and Audrey Hepburn disappears through the gate, a figment of my inflammation.

One week later, Monique called from Albuquerque, admitting she had a six-year-old boy and never intended to move to Alaska.

As soon as I found out, I built a bonfire and torched my pile of letters in the yard, *given to histrionics*. From the bench on my rickety porch, I watched fat ash flakes dance above tangles of fireweed that was already beginning to turn. I considered the odds of another long winter holed up in my cabin. Baking twelve kinds of Christmas cookies for myself. Probably talking to the ravens again, by March at the latest. To hell with it! I sighed and fed my complimentary copy of *Alaska Men* to the flames.

CHAPTER 6

BIKING COOL

Each fall I compile a to-do list for winterizing my bike, hoping to get around to these things before first flurries of "termination dust" make tinkering outside undesirable. *Slightly deflate tires for better traction on snow.* (No money to buy studded ones.) *Put on low-temperature chain grease.* (Makes riding in low gears feel like riding in low gears.) *Dig "poagies"—mitten-like insulated shells—from piles in storage trailer and attach to handlebars.* (They help you keep fingers, which are useful for shifting gears.) *Add various reflectors and change batteries in headlamp.* (December nights in Fairbanks last 16 hours, and not even the gaudiest auroras give off enough light to navigate by.) The local high-end sporting goods store advertises a "Cold Weather Clinic" for bikers. But, except for its clanking ball bearings and wobbly pedals, my trusted steed is fine.

Needless to say, each fall I step outside my cabin some morning to find snow piled on the seat of my still unmodified ride. I *did* compromise my vision of a small-town home by forsaking Moab, where I'd guided for Tag-A-Long Expeditions and instructed for OB, once again returning to Fairbanks, because my girlfriend found work in Alaska's second-largest city and because I missed its wilds more than I thought possible. Luckily, living a few miles from town—without running water, at least until spring melts the snow on the cabin roof—feels decidedly rural. It keeps face-to-face interactions with people limited, meaningful. As for the biking, even a cursory survey of trials and tribulations shows that riding the wintry urban range equals the best Moab's slickrock can offer.

This is no place for tight spandex outfits that cost as much as a custom-tailored tux; heavy wool army pants, baggy enough for two pairs of long underwear, will keep vital parts functioning.

Footwear consists of knee-high, homemade nylon-shell mukluks with felt liners. A hooded down parka, beaver-skin hat (preferably with ear flaps), and fleece mittens complete the outfit. A full beard or balaclava comes in handy on breezy days and keeps the cold from peeling your face. (But I take off the mask when entering banks or convenience stores.) Because of the cushioning effect of these garments, wearing knee and elbow pads is unnecessary, unsightly, if not impossible. Helmets don't fit over Soviet-style fur hats, and the only chance for abrasions is doing a face plant on salted roads.

Allow ample time for dressing and undressing.

Much gear is field-tested for suitability and adapted accordingly. During my first winter of riding at 40 below, I wore a sweater with a metal zipper. Had I remembered that metal is an excellent conductor, I could easily have avoided the nickel-size frost blister on my Adam's apple. On a different day, my lip stuck to the bike's padlock, which I tried thawing out with my breath. When boiling water, tossed up, blossoms into a diamond-dust Mohawk, air pumps shatter; knobbed rubber expires spontaneously; wrenches fuse with your fingertips; cranks and pedals snap; and pedaling cranks snap at you. In such cold, minutes turn into days and tires into Fred Flintstone's wheels. It's a cold that stings, burns.

In short, while desert bikers worry about dehydration and heatstroke—or rattlers, like the six-foot diamondback, thick as a bodybuilder's bicep, we all missed by less than a yard on an Arizona excursion with troubled youths—their subarctic counterparts have to work hard to keep their noses from falling off.

Another hazard, surprisingly, is air quality. While Moab may taunt you with dust squalls or headwinds, "ice fog" is the boreal biker's bane. Suspended, freezing moisture mixed with soot from too many households burning green birch or spruce and from cars left idling because they likely will not restart gets trapped below an inversion layer. The atmospheric chokehold can make you hack like a consumptive. It's as much fun as having your respiratory system sandpapered. Even on clear days, cold and dry air, sucked in deeply, sears your windpipe and bronchial tubes. (Rumors that it will make your lungs adhere to your rib cage are just that—a tale to scare tenderfeet.)

Rather than landing jumps or doing wheelies, my great feat of balance is staying upright on two wheels on level ground. "Black ice" forms near traffic lights and intersections where car exhaust briefly melts snow that refreezes. I've learned to avoid rash braking and steering maneuvers, and have perfected the paratrooper shoulder roll. Although I am not skirting sheer drops like those along Moab's Portal trail, I have found opportunities to practice equilibrium. I once parked my bike outside the supermarket in town, only to find a thief had lifted my quick-release seat. With a backpack full of groceries, I pedaled five miles standing up. (Nobody has enough bottom padding to sit on *that*.) Steering with one hand between a wall of plowed snow and a bully truck, while flipping off its driver with the other, also demands deft motor skills.

My Moab friends mostly complain about flats from goat heads or cactus spines. Up here, glass from broken whiskey bottles poses a considerable risk. (Some stores have specials on six-packs of hard liquor, so business is brisk.) On Alaska's main highways, potholes from frost heaves open unexpectedly like big-game pitfall traps. Snowplows can suffocate or filet you, or mangle your ride. Moose and snowmachines—also called "Sno-Gos," "Ski-Doos," or "snowmobiles"—cross at unpredictable intervals. In the dark, bulls may mistake bikers for rivals or possible mates. No less ornery, one cow had chased me in our driveway, and I saved myself, barely, by putting a birch trunk between her and me. On the upside, nobody, not even the most desperate dirtbag, will steal a bike model named Mountain Tamer.

Though admittedly there is less topographic relief around Fairbanks compared to, say, Moab's Poison Spider Mesa trail, similar weight loss and aerobic workouts can be expected. This is mostly due to snowdrifts on the road and excessive sweating in bulky clothing. For extremists, there is the Iditabike, a 200-mile winter race tracing the historical dog-mushing route partway.

(Bring pepper spray, to defy village dogs and the odd winter-walking bear.) It's not quite as fancy as Moab's Primal Quest, during which bikers with eight-grand Revel Rangers rappel off Gemini Bridges' sandstone arches, but in a pinch, it will do.

Let's not forget moments of transcendence, either; those fractals of beauty that wait by the roadside. Snow dervishes spinning on blacktop. Gamboling ravens. Mock suns, from ice flakes quivering in the air. White bunnies or ermines killed in hit-and-runs, stiff, flattened like boards… On days when I'm too chicken to face traffic, I shortcut through the woods behind campus, rolling through moose tracks and picket fences of birch shadows alternating with sunlight. But it's really a tradeoff, because I risk spats with cross-country skiers over their manicured trails.

When gawking at migrating geese and cranes that chevron the sky or feed in the Creamer's Field wetlands, be sure to keep an eye on the road.

I am not that exceptional, overall. While not quite as busy as Moab, Fairbanks hums with ultra-cold biking activity. There's the French expatriate, an accomplished classical violinist, who hauls bags of dog food on a cart for the huskies that share his backwoods home. There's my friend Robert, who is wearing horned felt helmets he sews and who wraps birch bark around his bike frame, which appears cobbled together from saplings— the Biking Viking, the *Fairbanks Daily News-Miner* calls him. I know him as BBB: Birch Bark Bob. Had he not dropped out of UAF's glaciology courses, he would have penned his dissertation on paper-thin bark scrolls, with snow-goose quills and ink from stovepipe soot.

Another guy pulls an enclosed trailer with a clear plastic window when even vodka crystalizes. (Is he carrying babies in there?) My neighbor, a Zamboni driver at the ice arena in town, commutes on a bike with rearview mirrors and milk crates, wearing white, inflatable "bunny boots" and headphones. United in suffering, we do not gather in racing gangs, or feral packs. We are not recreationists but pragmatists on a tight budget.

Our minimalism emulates Klondiker "wheelmen" who reached their destinations not on shank's mare but on steel ponies, rolling, pushing, sliding, and sometimes sailing. In 1897, greenhorn mobs boarded steamers bound for the goldfields while bicycles, invented 80 years earlier to counter horse shortages after the Napoleonic Wars, had become a nationwide fad—Sears that year stocked models called The Scorcher, The Winner, and The Flyer. African-American "Buffalo-Soldiers" bicycle corps patrolled the Yellowstone country, scaring horses and cows. The cavalry officer and polar explorer Adolphus W. Greely thought this form of locomotion equal to the telegraph, perfect for quickening long-distance communication through messengers on two wheels. And Robert Service, the Bard of the Yukon, who missed the Canadian rush by seven years, biked from his cabin to his Dawson bank teller job and to court his stenographer lady friend.

As soon as news of the bonanza broke, a New York syndicate pledged to construct a bike path to it, "a roadway, lightly constructed of steel, clamped to the sides of the mountains where it is not possible to arrange for a roadbed on a flat surface," with a roadhouse every 50 miles, "a place of refuge whither the wheelmen, and especially the wheelwomen, can flee for safety when the elements behave badly." The schemers proclaimed they would have nothing to do with "common methods of transport, such as railroads, boats, pack horses, dog-sleds, and Indians." One reporter wrote that by 1900, scarcely a steamer left for the North that did not carry bikes.

Commercial, single-gear models were advertised as the miner's best choice, as were snowshoe attachments clamped to the frame and bicycles with a ski instead of a front wheel. The Rambler Road Wheel, which dealers touted for Alaska conditions, came with a detachable, heavy-tread tire easily repaired by "man, woman, or child." The Klondike Bicycle, probably never built, sported solid rubber tires, weighed circa 50 pounds, and in the words of one 1897 guidebook was designed "more for strength than appearance." Rawhide shrunk onto its tube frame would allow prospectors to touch it without their skin sticking to steel in low temperatures. It was really a shape-shifting cart; the rider, dismounted, would haul a quarter-ton of goods on four wheels before retracting one outrigger pair and shredding back down to pick up the next load. Bikes proved to be more efficient on hard snow than on boggy, boulder-strewn summer terrain. Dawson stores hawked them to tenderfeet, and a local newspaper speculated that canine freight teams were doomed. Best of all, even a ready-made snow bike cost only the fraction of a sled or the optional dogs.

Dozens who heeded gold's siren call surmounted the Chilkoot Pass between Skagway and Whitehorse. When that boom petered out, a few would cycle down the frozen river-highway from Dawson to Nome, having mastered the eye-straining trick of staying in the two-inch double-track firmed up by sled runners. Riders coming upon mushers at blind trail corners created snow angels or drilled headfirst into drifts. One rookie remarked that he had been bucked off horses many a time but never before seen a mount that could get out from under him as quickly as a wheel.

Freshly disembarked at Skagway, "swift-foot" velocipedists had grunted contraptions, some lacking pedals but burdened with 200 pounds, up the aptly named Dead Horse Trail to White Pass. With the required minimum of a thousand pounds of food and a thousand pounds of equipment, they faced ten round-trips from sea level to about 3,000 feet. The Reverend John Jameson Wright, catering to his flock's spiritual needs on an "evangelistic tour" of the mining camps, pumped his legs for warmth at 40 below. A peeling nose at the roadhouses signaled a salty trail dog; without one, people might think you had ridden in on the sleigh-coach.

If the "dog-punchers" eyed bicyclists guardedly, as they did East Coast dandies or cabin-fevered odd ducks, one can hardly blame them. Bizarre do-it-yourself arrangements flourished. Two Argonauts anticipating the Yukon River, which debouches from Lindeman Lake, had left New York with conjoined bikes from whose iron crossbars hung a rowboat that held their possessions.

Winter caught up with them outside of Skagway, perhaps at a tent cluster dubbed Rag Town. In March, with onions selling for a dollar and 50 cents each, a luckier soul whizzed in the opposite direction from Dawson to Skagway on an eight-day grocery run without mishaps. As the Philippine-American War flared, a bike carrier rushed headlines with the *Klondike Nugget* to Grand Forks, 14 miles from Dawson, and to miners on creeks close by.

A Palo Alto bike dealer, hearing the news of the strike, promptly sold his inventory to drag a 90-pound sled loaded with photographic equipment across White Pass. In rough spots, he put the bicycle on the sled, but he made up time downhill and on ice-lidded lakes. One single-speed demon had so many flats that he stuffed his tires with rope. Another, fueled by roadhouse mush, griddlecakes, coffee, and muskrat mulligan, skirted open water, dodged ice jams—or face-planted into them after crashing—and zipped full-tilt over glare ice. At times, kiting before the wind, he backpedaled to slow down. Somebody had planted a ghoulish trail marker, a red, shorthaired dog, on its nose, stiff tail straight up and paws at a trot, "a circus clown doing his trick." On his thousand-mile journey, this man carved wooden replacement pedals that lasted only a day. While he circled a camp, showing off, a Native Alaskan spectator was said to have remarked, "White man, he sit down, walk like hell." The strange sight of the last of 1900's spring stampeders, biking sea captain John Sutherland, frightened some Athabaskans, who shot at him, because their shaman said all the fish would die if he stayed alive. The next day, pacified, one of them punched this Scot to test if he was real and then offered to buy the magic hoops.

Then as now, congealed grease, frozen bearings, and knee, elbow, or collarbone fractures were common. Then as now, a boneshaker rigid with cold or gunked up with slush might feel like a white elephant fused to your hands. Dr. Arthur Conan Doyle, the creator of Sherlock Holmes and a one-time Arctic traveler, in 1896 had endorsed the conveyance: "I believe that its use is commonly beneficial and not at all detrimental to health, except in the matter of beginners who overdo it." Other physicians feared that, a combination of sunburn, exertion and the effort to maintain balance could cause "bicycle face," a possibly permanent condition characterized by a clenched jaw and bulging eyes.

Cold-weather bikers then, too, were clotheshorses by necessity. Docking in Skagway on a cruise to Siberia with John Muir, the nature writer John Burroughs noticed women in short-skirted bicycle suits meant to keep hemlines out of the spokes—two of Boston's best wheelwomen had headed north early on, exercising their shapely legs, hoping to enlist a thousand fans belittled as "bloomer girls" on their own mounts to join them. Men wore a flannel shirt or a onesie union suit inside a fleece-lined overall topped by a heavy mackinaw coat or drill parka, two pairs of thick wool socks inside felt boots not so snug as to cut off circulation, plus a beaver-fur ear-flap hat, fur nose guard, and fur mittens. No weight-weenies, they also might strap a fur robe or bearskin over the handlebars. The mukluks of one wore out, and his toes bruised badly on the ice. Fastened to the springs behind the seat, the canvas pannier of yet another contained a spare shirt and socks, more woolen underwear, a journal in waterproof covering, pencils, and several blocks of sulfur matches.

It's never been about looks for the Fairbanks set. With our snotsicles and waxy cheeks, our pluming breaths, and bent silhouettes, we sitting men (and even the women) may resemble those hoary Yukoners or the doomed of Scott's Terra Nova expedition. But some inner flame fuels us, a hard-won awareness and pride: what is sport for some is transport for others. Regardless of trends, we are biking cool.

CHAPTER 7

A BATTLE OF WITS

He's not the worst enemy I've ever made. But he's the one who has dinged my self-image as a smart guy consistently. Sheltering under our cabin on the Fairbanks outskirts, as an ermine does in the winter, he launches his forays, always scanning for owls, foxes, weasels, and the lynx that visits and imprints the snow with pugmarks, though far too seldom. That lynx deserves its own chapter, but our paths crossed just once in the flesh, very briefly. My wife, Melissa, saw it first, from the kitchen window, doing the breakfast dishes. When she shouted my name, I thought the woods were on fire. The ensuing minute-long staring match with the whiskered forest recluse so far remains my only encounter with it. Amber eyes in a face like a mask plumbed mine from ten paces away, while tense prying or bafflement propelled a black-tipped bobtail twirling in a lynx version of head scratching. Scientist-trappers entice lynxes by dangling grouse wings or shiny CDs from branches as wind-spun bait. The lynx at our cabin, floating across the morning's snow crust on saucer-size paws when it decided it had had enough of the strange creatures inside the box, did not even leave tracks. How easily we could have missed it, the last of Alaska's charismatic land mammals that I'd never met. And it wasn't a notch in my naturalist belt, no non-material trophy or checkmark on some wildlife bucket list. I just longed to see a lynx, like the kid in my boat on the Nelchina did a moose. The Devon nature writer Miriam Darlington, smitten with otters and owls, describes a "wild-animal effect" that "brings us into the present, into the perfect moment, time outside time when beings can just be." Some people care about stock portfolios, their careers, Facebook likes, or the latest cool thing; I cared about this. What did it matter, having an outhouse and bad internet, having to plug in your truck in the winter to warm its engine and battery and to pay for snowplowing, or having to fill gas tanks every month and a water tank every two, if life gave you a lynx, let alone peace or the aurora's jumpy sky rivulets. I was always open to the woods' gifts when I stepped outside or walked up our cul-de-sac dirt road. Neighbors announced sightings on a small blackboard by the battery of mailboxes, to alert others. Melting back into the spruces like a dream of frost and smoke, this lynx reminded me that, right at our threshold, the wilds start, a world mirroring ours in which the flighty, the fastest, the strongest, the camouflaged, the armored, the venomous, or, in this case, the stealthiest survive.

My animal fiend, by comparison, prospers through sheer bravado. He's a red squirrel, expert at dining and dashing. I'm certain about the sex, since there's much posturing, and because of the decibel level, of course.

Our vendetta goes back some time. The previous summer, he'd scolded from a ringside seat in a black spruce when I played badminton with Melissa. His laser-gun snickering threw me off my game. "Sentinel of the taiga" my butt. I lobbed spruce cones at him. He's also parked his haunches in my wife's hanging flower baskets, as if at a spa. And a few years ago, returned from vacationing, we had found his "drey" inside our outhouse, a grass-and-moss sphere, or "drey," in one ceiling corner, resembling the landscape artist Andy Goldsworthy's work, yet invasive, a grotesque smacking of *Alien*'s creature pods. He'd not claimed the insulated insides of the cabin's walls, at least, which happens to other Alaskan fringe dwellers.

This fall, when he's not haranguing, or battling the competi- tion, tailgating it like greased lightning, he has taken to raiding the house-shaped bird feeder outside our living room window. Fearing trouble, I'd hung it from a tree branch on a line a dumb- bell anchored. My safest bet would have been a post with a plate top for the feed—a design whose overhang stumps rodents—but the soil already had frozen, and I lacked the tools and materials anyway. Sure enough: at random hours, he'd perch on the bird feeder sill, stuffing his mug with expensive seeds after evicting all chickadees—the boreal and the black-capped, these nervous bursts of energy, Melissa's downy delights. Pecking away, vying with hoary redpolls that puff up their rosy chests and feint at each other, they're priceless, marking winter's winding down. Their tut-tutting warning of predators (us!) near the feeder gives way to the sweet, strangely mournful *fee-bee-ee* that male black-caps whistle more often and louder as the days lengthen, in response to rising hormone levels.

Bingeing or "hyperphagia," a behavioral change at the opposite end of winter in ground squirrels, and bears before denning, builds fat reserves. Although Red does not hibernate—he just slumbers wrapped in his stole tail—he is hyper, all right. "Squirrel" is also a verb, and the root of an adjective, for a good reason. Few other creatures are as energetic; few bodies this small can contain such an excess of life, zipping up and down trees like electric current. He uses tree stumps as hikers do a creek's stepping stones, yet instead of hopping from one to the next, he bounds, arcing sure-footedly, unerringly, fluidly, loaded with springs, always aimed at his next meal. Once in a while, a pinecone on the outhouse floor, the bloody horsehead under our bed sheets, reminds me that he returns at his leisure. He does so frequently, gnawing at posters of national monuments tacked to the walls for dreaming of summer. He favors Canyons of the Ancients. Perhaps, he lines his nest with these clippings, like Depression-era hobos tucking newspapers into their boots. (Or is he getting high on the ink? Denying us comfort?) His gluttony isn't wanton, not entirely, but an investment in a rich winter coat. At subzero temperatures he holes up in root crotches or under rotten logs, snug as a nut in its shell. A "scatter hoarder," he caches spruce cones and possibly also the sunflower goodies throughout our ten-acre lot, banking extra insurance. Mental kin to Clark's nutcrackers, he knows where to withdraw his safety deposits months later—while I can't even remember my account number or where my checkbook is. Near the path to our outhouse, I've passed by mounds of whole cones, and farther out, by "kitchen middens": tree stumps, smothered in scales and stripped cores, fallout from a chainsaw massacre. Red rotates cones and wild raspberries from our yard in his dainty hands, like nibbling corn on the cob. I'm surprised, and at the same time not, to learn that red squirrels are omnivorous, with nestlings, bird eggs, baby bunnies, and voles on the list of edibles. On a slow day, they pick mushrooms, which they dry in tree crotches for winter consumption, and pilfer each other's caches. A scientist in the Yukon discovered a coyote jawbone stashed away, though one must assume that it came from roadkill.

Whenever I caught Red in flagrante delicto, with his paws in the cookie jar, I flew out the front door, down the porch steps, roaring. He'd wait till the last moment, gorging himself, before jumping off and bounding across the snow to safety. Though I could have grabbed him by his plush tail, a decoy fooling aerial predators, I was afraid he would bite me. Over the course of two days, a thief of bird feed in England, a gray squirrel "from hell," attacked and bit 18 people before it was put down. Not to be bested, a "deranged" NYC nutso bloodied snow during its own reign of terror when it assaulted a woman at her front door. "It was angry, vicious and incredibly strong," she reported, and it chased another woman down the street. People on that Queens city block wouldn't leave home without a can of pepper spray or a shovel and heavy gloves. The Park Service must have scenarios like these in mind when it forbids tourists to feed squirrels. Perhaps this was all part of a trend, Nature's payback rung in by rodents, none of which were sick with rabies. A beaver already had savaged a septuagenarian Massachusettsan. Another, in Belarus, sliced a femoral artery, killing the fisherman who had grabbed it for a trophy shot. River otters (no rodents) in Anchorage, too, had been hounding people and pets. Lastly, Alaskapox—a small-mammal virus infecting humans—was making headlines.

Chigurrrh had menaced Melissa, mock-charging her, mistakenly pegging her as the weaker sex. But despite the risk of getting sick or mutilated by grabbing him, I did not really want to hurt the slinky wee skunk. On his hind legs, ogling the suspended diner and incoming birds, the beady-eyed orange gnome almost looked cute. His tail curved up over his back, which gave him a defiant, mohawk-punk air.

My repeated attempts at counter-terrorism through hazing failed miserably. He appeared promptly at his chowtimes. At that point we had not yet heard about suet laced with chili peppers, which thwarts squirrels but does not affect birds, most of which have a weak sense of taste and smell.

So I lay in wait, determined to study his wiles. Unable to climb the line from the ground without opposable thumbs, he'd hustle up the smooth birch vis-à-vis the bird feeder to the proper height. Then he'd lunge into space, grubbing paws spread and extended, trying to stick his landing. He mostly did—until I moved the feeder's line farther out on the branch. (Having no ladder, this required pitching the weighted end over it without knocking myself senseless.)

When Rusty missed three times in a row, I smelled victory.

I next spotted him snaking through twigs at the limb's drooping tip, gauging angles for reaching the roof. His balance was astounding, and even the thinnest growth still supported him.

His head-dive yielded another round at my trough of plenty.

He may have monkey agility, but I got the great apes' gray matter. Tightly winding and taping cellophane sheets, I bandaged the birch and two nearby—the bucktoothed trapeze artist excelled at stringing together canopy routes. He tackled the main tree a few times, sliding off while I pumped my fist behind the windowpane. Unfazed, he catapulted at the third Christo trunk, gaining toeholds in plastic not wound nearly tightly enough. The rest was his freefalling stunt reprised.

The score was Einstein 0, Despicable Squeaker 4.

That scoundrel. That red-handed son of a sow! (Male squirrels are "boars." All adult squirrels are swine.) This clearly called for diligence, not gut-response tit-for-tat.

Melissa suggested lubricating the feeder's roof after sheathing it with tin foil. I thought the cold might neutralize salad oil and that his claws would shred the aluminum into tinsel. So, instead,

I pierced the lid of a Styrofoam cooler, through which I pulled the bird feeder's line. This deflector above the roof, tilting on impact, would repel him as duck wings do water or a starship shield does attackers, should he repeat his leap of faith.

An hour later, he'd remounted the birch and was peering down through its branches. His tail twitched like a tense mountain lion's or a peeping Tom's eyelid. He streaked back under the bird feeder, where he stood all but scratching his head, and once more to his lofty lookout, as at ease on the shrink-wrapped wood as a hurdler on the track. Impressive. You try that, scurrying down a tree trunk headfirst.

Still, it dawned on me then. Up there, he could no longer spy nutty Nirvana. From that perspective, the lid blended in perfectly with the snowy yard. And he simply couldn't grasp how what he saw from below vanished again and again.

Homo sapiens 5, *Headache hudsonicus*: 4 (final score). His full Linnaean name is *Tamiasciurus hudsonicus*, "Shadow-tailed Nut Hoarder of Hudson Bay"—if only he would relocate there. And if ifs and buts were candy and nuts, oh what a Christmas we'd have! (He could get to Quebec without touching the ground, vaulting from treetop to treetop for 2,400 miles through North America's share of the world's largest land biome: boreal forest.) Appalachians, knowing his ilk as the "fairy diddle" or "mountain boomer" that mauls their log cabins, complain that the creature is "too fast to get a sight on it with a gun." During lean springs, Athabaskans consumed the scrawny bodies. Medieval Siberian peasants paid land taxes in non-elitist squirrel pelts, couture for the commoner, and one hundred could get you a cow. Nowadays, fly-fishing vendors offer twelve cents per "usable" tail to be tied into lures, while fur buyers shell out up to six bucks for skins made into caps, coats, or glove linings. Let's up this bounty to previous standards, I say.

I have a hunch this one is playing the long game and will best me in the Darwinian contest. I chose to stay childless for economic and "green" reasons, not merely from self-interest.

In his five-year lifespan, he will sire at least 20 babies looking like leftovers from appendectomies, litters of healthy, clever "kittens" or "pups"—young squirrels are spared the shame of porcine designations, never mind the impossibility of pigs begetting cats or dogs. How many of these fruit of his loins will ripen to adulthood among lynxes and owls, I do not know. He likely will murder some offspring of rivals and they some of his.

Perhaps he is plotting with a northern flying squirrel currently, brainstorming a lateral, James Bond approach to the calories he will need, or how to cripple our truck. He rarely pops in anymore; a cat burglar demoted to bum, mining leaf litter, hoping gray jays and chickadees dropped suet crumbs. I realize now that I miss him, miss our autumnal sparring, the thrill of a worthy opponent. In his poltergeist ways, he's as unique as that big, furtive cat with brush tips on its ears.

Sometimes, only cuteness or rarity separates the precious from the pest. Being a carrier of sickness certainly matters, as does perceived cleanliness. Roaches and rats fit the bill. Bats in a garret, for most folks, do not. Melissa finds their needle-fanged goblin faces adorable. The rustling leathery wings of one madly brushing the walls in my Fairbanks cabin one July morning, frankly, gave me belly flutters. The whole vampire thing, the name of that northern myotis—*lucifugus*, "fleeing the light"—the freakiness of a flying shrew, or perhaps simply the home invasion had me rattled.

The word "pest" has lost specificity, spreading from "deadly contagious disease" into "any noxious, destructive, or troublesome person or thing." Its expanded meaning adds judgment, the anthropocentric perspective. From a geocentric point of view, *we* are the pests. Globe-spanning *Homo sapiens* should emphasize with, if not outright applaud, fellow opportunists. But "All of these are animals that aren't staying in what we've decided is their place," Bethany Brookshire writes in *Pests: How Humans Create Animal Villains*, her probe into zoological beliefs and perceptions. And "You mess with our food,"—or *our* birds' food—"you mess with us." Like Alaska's black, brown, and white "problem bears," hooked on dog food, garbage, and smokehouse salmon, squirrels are constant reminders that we're not in control, not even within our own four walls or yards. For that, we can never forgive them. When our interests do not clash with theirs, we prize squirrels as photogenic wildlife, park ornaments, bucktoothed cartoon characters, kids' cuddle toys, threatened national icons in Scotland and England, or like the lynx, grace notes of a lifetime.

The flame-furred brat robbing our "chickies" taught me one thing. A curious forest cat; voles; porcupines; grouse; ptarmigan; raucous ravens; red foxes fighting, screaming like banshees; and coyotes yodeling, recent arrivals; owls hullaballooing (two kinds, great horned and boreal); this midget marauder—Brookshire calls hers "F***ing Kevin," the tomato-destroying possible "godfather of a squirrel mafia"; spring and fall cranes ribboning overhead, announcing themselves with rubbery croaks; woodpeckers machine-gunning a chimney pipe, making you think it's an earthquake; snipes oscillating at dusk, winnowing high above a clearing; wasps and mosquitos turning porch meals into slapstick routines; snow bunting transients flurrying on my way to the mailbox; warblers stunning themselves on our windowpanes; a bat in the bedroom; and a moose trapping your spouse in the john, to which she'd escaped so fast she lost a slipper...they're a package deal.

Love it or leave it, I say. When you make your home on the margins of civilization, you knowingly join a trans-human community, one in which your goals might clash with those of winged or four-legged tenants, all having claims older than ours. In May, a horned grebe pair returns from the Aleutians to a roadside pond the size of a tennis court between our cabin and campus. By July, five or six grebelings bob in the parents' wake. Though I have no proof, I want to believe they're the same pair every year. But I don't have to leave my recliner to watch nature drama. On a window's bug screen, a jumping spider silhouetted against blue sky and black spruce is stalking mosquitoes. Our Fairbanks subdivision, in short, hums with more animal action than some European national parks. I am waiting for wolves to move in.

CHAPTER 8

RECOVERY

The scene on the highway's exit ramp caught me off guard. Something in the grass transfixed a stout woman, in her sixties perhaps, with glasses and frizzed brown hair, dressed in sneakers, jeans, and a sweatshirt, who stood away from her parked truck. Bicycling closer, I noticed she was Native American, and the object of her gaze was a bird plump as a chicken and glossy as obsidian. Fascinated with all wildlife and fond of aerobatic clowns in particular, I stopped on the gravel shoulder. The raven's left wing dragged; feather tips skimmed the grass. The chisel bill hung ajar, as if its owner were panting, displaying the mouth's soft pink lining. With each blink, white nictitating membranes closed on the bird's eyeballs like camera shutters freeze-framing the world.

"It's injured," the woman stated the obvious. "I'm trying to take it to a vet."

I asked if she needed a hand, and she went to the truck, returning with a sweatshirt. Noon sun, undeterred by clouds with gray guts that sagged toward the horizon, ironed my back. As cars sped past, curiosity flickered behind their windshields. Oblivious to the streaking of traffic and pain, the bird faced the more imminent threat we represented. Each time the woman approached, it hopped beyond reach, tucking the hurt wing close to its body, as a person would a dislocated arm. Circling around, I distracted it long enough for the woman to throw the shirt over it. She stooped, nimbly for somebody so compact, and scooped up the raven before it could wriggle free.

We walked to her truck, whose door I opened.

"Would you like to come to the vet?" she asked. "You could hold it while I drive."

I wedged my bike and backpack full of groceries into the truck and got in. En route to the opposite end of town, she rang a friend who had worked in bird rehabilitation. She already had phoned that friend for advice as soon as she spotted the bird.

"I got it and am driving to the vet now. A guy is helping me."

Through fabric my fingertips sensed the bird's heart. Unable to tell terror from resignation, I listened to its labored breathing, worried that it might suffocate or overheat. A scaly leather foot tipped with lacquered claws had escaped from the wrap and pushed against my belly. Occasionally, as frost heaves or cracks in the pavement shook the truck, wings brushed against my breastbone like spruce boughs or a book page turning. I had never been that close to a raven before.

My grandmotherly accomplice, Margaret, recalled how she had trapped a raven accidentally when she still lived in her village up north. She had been setting snares to catch rabbits; to her surprise a raven stepped into one of her loops. She released it and, getting stabbed in the process, came to respect the bird's moxie and imposing bill.

Research for a school paper she had to write turned up much scientific information, but Margaret had zeroed in on a wealth of raven lore, knowledge rooted deeply in time, accounts and beliefs that branched far beyond North America into Siberia and Europe.

Charcoal sketches in the caves near Lascaux depict "crows" that imply spirit messengers or human souls. Two ravens named Thought and Memory perched on Odin's shoulders, gleaning news of the world on daily excursions. And without stars to guide them through summer's nacreous midnights, Norse settlers released *hrafnar* from their single-mast ships as scouts looking for land, pagan answers to Noah's doves.

Throughout the northern hemisphere, this bird attended shamanistic flights of trance. It was teacher and totemic ancestor. It stared bug-eyed from the trunks of family trees—totem poles along the Pacific Northwest coast, genealogies hewn into cedar trunks. Kwakiutl dancers acknowledged the bond by wearing masks with four-foot bills closing with whip-crack claps. Crow-hopping under the spell of gourd rattles, they *became* birds. Other raven masks split like seedpods, revealing a second mask and thus the deception of first impressions, the hidden nature of things. In the mythology of Margaret's own people, the Gwich'in of Canada's Yukon and northeast Alaska, Raven acted as trickster and transformer. In the course of his exploits, he endured violence or deformity, comparable to the bird I was cradling. Vulgar and petty, scheming and greedy and often not very shrewd, he was the sacred and the profane, the light and the shadow inside each of us. At the beginning of "Distant Time," he created not only humans, but also animals, some of which watched over people as guardian spirits. As part of a bargain between species, people honored obligations, obeyed unwritten rules, and offered gestures of care, feeding dried fish to a wolf they had killed, or not disturbing a raven on its nest, lest the weather would turn cold. In an age that for believers is present to the same degree that it is past, Raven stole daylight for his creations, which until then scrambled around in the dark. Inspired perhaps by the bird's love for shiny objects, or by a solar eclipse, one tale passed on over midwinter fires recounts Raven's theft of the sun. A chief in the sky had given the orb to his child as a toy. When the toddler dropped it and it rolled into the room's corner, Raven covered its glow with his wing. Then he flew back to earth with it, illuminating the world of people.

In Tlingit versions of the myth, Raven is white or translucent, a marker of supernatural status, as in Melville's whale tale or those about unicorns or British Columbia's "spirit bears"—even the white rabbit pulled from a hat shares this magic. The robbed owner, angry at the deceit, held Raven in the smoke of the home's fireplace, forever besmirching the bird though not its reputation: the trickster got his hide scorched for humanity.

His benevolence still can assume the form of ravens that guide hunters to fresh wolf kills, moose or caribou, whose bounty feeds entire families. Villagers in Alaska constantly scrutinize the living environment, and a raven rolling onto its back in midair is "dropping a package of meat," announcing good fortune for the attentive.

I told a few anecdotes of my own. On a snowy Fairbanks side-walk, I once found leftovers of a raven meal: a scuffle of rune prints, banded feathers, and at the display's center a grouse foot. My wife told me about a raven who killed a pigeon in town and dragged it under a car to take it apart unobserved. Guilt? I think not. More likely, he wanted to keep his mates from claiming a share. During a Grand Canyon trip, fat twin marauders in search of food violated my backpack and pulled out smelly socks. (I had been mad enough to fling rocks in their direction.) Another time, one nabbed a Ziploc full of snacks a kid on an OB course had hoarded and flew across the river to hack into the bag on a rock shelf, tantalizingly within the kid's view. Similarly, a mile above timberline, on Denali's buttressed heights, ravens had made the connection between bamboo wand markers and the food caches climbers left in a snowdrift, excavating peanuts, cheese, and beef jerky with great gusto. The climbers considered them flying rats, but I'm not the only one with a soft spot for them. In downtown Sitka, I observed motorists patiently waiting for ravens to grab a meal on rain-slicked Harbor Drive, instead of honking their horns or trying to squeeze by or run over them. Mobs of bachelor ravens engaged in pretend fights sound more like chimps than birds to me, always bringing a smile to my face. I've also heard ravens chuckle and mutter when they're alone, like writers spending too much time in their head, which made me rethink the whole concept of animal communication. A professor on sabbatical, pointing a parabolic mike at ravens raiding a Fairbanks landfill, is adding snippets to dozens of vocalizations already recorded. He hopes AI will be able to crack the croakers' code.

There's still much about raven behavior we don't understand. The Juneau naturalist Bob Armstrong spied on a bunch in the alpine zone that passed rocks to one another. Whenever a bird did not like a rock it received, it would attack the giver of that flawed gift.

Margaret and I realized we had common acquaintances in this city of 70,000 that can be as tight as a ground-squirrel warren, among them my former Gwich'in-language teacher. Our conversation, which had begun as a trickle, meandered around the invalid bird and its kin before the current, deepening, roiled raw stuff to the surface.

Between raven stories nestled Margaret's confession that she was a recovering alcoholic. She hinted at divorce, at a step- or adoptive parent. Her children and grandchildren lived as far away as Tucson, and she rarely saw them. Beading had given her strength to pull through. "It keeps my hands and mind busy all the time," she told me. She talked about her style, how she kept finding motifs and patterns in nature, which she then translated into art. Craft and expertise ran strong in Margaret's family. Her mother had passed on the gift; at age 14, she had fashioned a fringed hide shirt encrusted with beads and shells for Margaret's great-grandfather, a chief. It now hung in a display case at the university museum on the hill above town—a flash from the well of history, a snippet of culture enshrined.

When we finally reached the clinic, the raven felt heavy and warm, like a swaddled, if flawed, foundling. The weight on my belly tapped a fount of nurturing that, for a person sworn to childlessness and not having pets, welled up unexpectedly. I imagined how easily a bystander could have mistaken our trio for a family rushing its infant to an emergency room.

There was an entrance for dogs and another for cats, but none for birds. We stood in the air-conditioned office's neon glare, with sterile surfaces and posters that advertised pet health care pressing in on us. I sweated where the cotton bundle touched my body. Margaret tugged on her T-shirt, admitting coolness to her skin. While a receptionist had her fill out some paperwork, my arms tired, and I braced them on the Formica counter. The bird squirmed again and let out a rusty squawk; I tried to keep a good grip, mindful not to break feathers or injure it more.

Before long, a veterinarian's assistant took it into another room. She returned to hand Margaret her soiled sweatshirt.

"I'll have to wash this," Margaret said calmly.

"What will become of the bird?" I asked the receptionist before we left.

"The vet will see what she can do. We'll check with a rehabilitation place here in town, and when the bird is ready it will be released where you found it."

Back at the truck, Margaret volunteered to drive me home. On the way there, we talked some more. I wondered aloud if it was even legal to pick up or keep wildlife. "Let 'em come find me, if they want," was all she said. Before I stepped from the truck, Margaret showed me photos of her traditional, yet innovative beadwork, which she sold at church bazaars: garlands offsetting inspirational poems, necklaces culminating in bear pendants, discs of tanned hide erupting with floral designs, and wall hangings with the sign of her people's adopted faith. I asked for her phone number in case I ever needed a customized gift.

As much as I intended to inform Margaret about the outcome of our rescue mission, I needed to trail this story to its end for personal reasons, too. My writing, if not my curiosity, had almost ground to a halt. The world did not provide any new plots. Words did not come easily anymore, and when they did, matched flowers pressed in a book more than they did the green fertile chaos that threatened to swallow my yard. But the minute I closed the cabin door, I grabbed pen and paper, and sentences began to form.

Next day, I rang the clinic to inquire about the patient's condition. The diagnosis was bleak and the outlook even more so. As the result of heavy trauma, typically from collisions with cars or windowpanes, the raven had broken a wing bone and dislocated a shoulder and would never fly again. It shared the fate of many residents who'd turned into trespassers, an opportunistic lot that includes ants, magpies, rats, coyotes, deer, and here in Alaska, gray jays, bald eagles, bears, porcupines craving salt not stopping at plywood but gnawing on rubber mats, and, in my swell neck of the swale, a certain squirrel. Lacking foresight to dodge development as well as familiarity with technology's traps, these camp followers glean from our tables, our henhouses, our backyards, our interstates. Who hasn't seen sly raven moves outside of supermarkets? Who hasn't seen them dive into greasy Dumpsters, haggle over scraps, or, heads cocked sideways, gauge the speed of traffic before dashing onto asphalt to peel off rabbit flesh? We've built havens free of predators but filled with tidbits and trash, and they flock to them. Such scavenging devalues them in the eyes of some people, who regard them as vermin. But is the ravens' defiance of human plans and conventions not wildness of a particular kind?

We are bound to them for better or worse. In their close affiliation with us, ravens can flag environmental health risks. Mosquito-borne West Nile virus, which kills thousands of birds and expands in tandem with global heating, has not yet reached Alaska. Corvids in the Lower 48—crows, ravens, magpies, nutcrackers, and jays—among the species most susceptible to the disease, suffer worse than infected humans, who may never show symptoms, with death rates approaching one hundred percent.

Some creatures have become so familiar that we no longer perceive them. They blend into the landscape as if plumage or fur were a camouflage coat. When we *do* take notice, we sometimes call them "common," but there is nothing common about this rogue bird, except for its manners. Of all our wild neighbors, it is the one that most reminds us of ourselves. It walks on two legs. It's garrulous, social, and smart. It plays creatively, even into adulthood. In the Gwich'in village of Old Crow, the mycologist Lawrence Millman watched the birds, which some people mistake for crows, hanging off a power line and somersaulting.

At Prudhoe Bay's oilfields, ravens begin to nest in late March, at minus 30 degrees. With no twigs free of snow, they requisition unusual nesting material: welding rods, plastic cable ties, copper wires, survey stakes. Some assemble to meet incoming cargo, waiting at the airstrip for the plane's arrival. They know that we know that they know. During the unloading, they probe food crates, rip open the packaging, and sometimes hide loot in industrial structures, away from prying foxes. As soon as the snow melts, they waddle after lemmings; they pilfer eggs and chicks from migratory birds. They mostly ignore oilfield workers but avoided a researcher who previously trapped them, with paper lunch bags as bait, recognizing the enemy even when she wore borrowed coveralls and a hard hat in disguise.

Ravens handle cold snaps of minus 50 degrees or below far better than they do cars. On days of extremes, adding air insulation, they swell into fluffy footballs. Their physiology lets them prosper anywhere between the Sonoran Desert and the Arctic Ocean. Reminiscent of Raven's mythic coup, they capture minute amounts of sunlight with their heat-absorbent plumage and retain precious body warmth. Sheer size, combined with stockiness, helps these largest of passerines to preserve life under winter's coarse cloak. Aided by their adaptability, they've conquered half of the planet's land surface.

Anchorage birders this year sighted a blue-eyed, ghostly-white raven, a leucistic rarity lacking melanin pigment like the Tlingit's light thief. In flight, facing off with an anthracite pal, it seemed to be dancing with its shadow. Its fantail on photos looked ratty, an old feather duster. Perhaps the "dancing" had been bullying, the fate of those who stick out. Defying expectations, a white raven makes us heed the world and its workings again.

On clear winter days, you can watch mundane ravens spreading their wings, sunbathing on the ground, or rolling exuberantly in heavenly down. If you sit still enough, long enough, in a Fairbanks parking lot, vignettes of urban raven life will accumulate: Seven birds aligned on the back of a truck, eyeing its bed strewn with garbage and clucking at the sudden booty. A pair locked together in midair tumbling, tails-over-heads, scattering feathers as if in a pillow fight. A scruffy loner extracting ketchup packets from a plastic bag, stashing them in snow piled around the foot of a parking meter for future consumption. They live like street bums or heroes fallen from grace; some people take this as a sign that the ancient spirits no longer inhabit their animal manifestations. Fledged under Alaska's raw skies, the birds still belong more in this place than I, a transplant from afar.

In Distant Time stories, the trickster and culture hero often tripped over his own appetites. Left alone, its descendant, the specimen we had brought in, also was likely to meet a bad end. It would starve or fall to the next predator crossing its path. The vet was still trying to contact the only licensed bird rehabilitator in town. If that person could not give it refuge, the raven would be euthanized. Appalled by the news, I wanted to take it home but discovered I needed a permit and appropriate setup for keeping a wild animal. The vet refused to release the bird and, detecting my frustration with clinic protocol, reminded me that I had interfered with nature's laws when I helped retrieve it. But I'd stepped in only because our kind caused the accident in the first place.

I called again the next day, a Sunday. The receptionist kept me in a limbo of Muzak laced with commercials. When she came back on the line, she informed me that the bird had been put down. I pictured the vet thrusting a syringe through the iridescent mantle into the warm flesh I had held. As jet-black button eyes lost their luster, I wished for one less story to tell.

When I phoned Margaret at work the following morning, she had already heard about the mercy killing. "Too bad," she said while I held on to the receiver. Regret and compassion colored her voice, and an entire life's weight rested upon those two words.

CHAPTER 9

NOTES FROM THE ROAD TO BESTSELLERDOM

I had planned the promo tour for a collection of northern wild-life stories I'd edited the way a field marshal plans a campaign. A four-day Book Blitz South would target eight locations in the Anchorage and Mat-Su area: independent and chain bookstores, a café, a museum, a luncheon for professional communicators, and a nature center up in the mountains. In preparation, flyers had been printed and hung, emails and press kits sent, and the events listed in several papers as well as online. Reservations had been made at a cozy but pricey downtown B&B, at my, not the publisher's, expense. The publicist had worked overtime, constructing a collapsible poster stand from struts, spars, screws, and an old lamp foot; the book's cover printed on cloth, in San Francisco no less, could be hoisted on this contraption like a sail on a mast.

I realize that words alone rarely draw crowds any more, unless you're a politician. Authors on book tours are therefore encouraged to play Indian flutes, tap-dance, wear clown suits, juggle their books blindfolded, or at least to behave inappropriately. I enlisted support troops, inviting writers who had contributed pieces to the anthology. Owls and falcons were to be the crowning glory. The presence of live raptors and their handlers from two rehabilitation facilities was no mere publicity stunt. My failed raven rescue in Fairbanks had inspired the story collection, and one contributor's essay described the visit of an education bird—Gandalf, a great gray owl crippled in an accident—to her eco-literature class. I admired these volunteers and their wards, and piggybacking their act with mine was supposed to benefit everybody involved. My girlfriend, now wife, who also was the book's designer, acted as liaison, trip photographer, finance officer, motivational coach, quartermaster, and driver—I haven't driven since 1980, when the army made me—wrapped into one.

(In fact, people who see me walking around town have asked her if I was training for something.)

As we rolled into town, thousands of animal lovers thronged the streets. Alas, they had come to see—dogs.

In my ignorance of Alaska pastimes, I had overlooked that the Book Blitz weekend coincided with the Iditarod, the world's most prestigious sled dog race. At the B&B, all the other guests turned out to be volunteer dog handlers, one a British police officer visiting from Hong Kong. Another husky groupie, a Connecticut retiree, had attended the race start eight years in a row. None quite struck me as "the literary type." Still, the outdoor theme and commercial vibe were encouraging, and we promptly spotted some potential readers in the crowd: a bearded guy wearing a wolf-pelt hood complete with the animal's head, glass-eyed and fangs bared; and a "Mama grizzly" politician who hates animal predators but is "pro-life" (whose life?), shaking hands with her fans.

I, who normally shun clustered humanity, once joined a rally in Fairbanks wielding a crude sign that said *Polar Bears want babies too. Stop our addiction to oil!* From the top dangled a plush white toy bear, a toddler I'd hung in effigy. Though wary of anthropomorphizing animals, I was not above playing that card. As we were marching and chanting and being ordered off the privately owned sidewalk, I checked the responses of passersby. A rattletrap truck blatting down Airport Way caught my ear, then my eye. The driver, a stereotypical crusty Sourdough, showed me the finger. Unbeknownst to him, his passenger—a grandmotherly Alaska Native woman, perhaps his wife—gave me a big, cheery thumbs-up.

The more things change, the more development and heat scarily spike here, the more they stay the same. Our current guv'nor on a gifted hunt in Texas gunned down hogs from a helicopter, a chase you can also book as a corporate team-building exercise, with coyotes thrown in as an afterthought. I fear that, promising an insane stopgap measure, geo-engineering will be next. As our second governor, "Wally" Hickel, pointed out, "You can't just let nature run wild." (Followed by the equally inane, pro-logging statement, "A tree looking at a tree really doesn't do anything.")

My favorite T-shirt ever? *I Support the Right to Arm Bears.* The slogan, next to a griz' brandishing a rifle, stretched across the belly of a Diomede Islander who resembled its subject. I naturally ordered one, a smaller size. And on my favorite greeting card, a leering wolf looks for human prey with his scoped weapon aimed from a low-flying Cessna above the motto: Aerial Predator Control. The culling of bears and wolves in Alaska for almost four decades has not improved moose or caribou hunting. Yet the state continues its war of attrition. Still, chamber of commerce figures show that potential visitors believe Alaskans to be more environmentally inclined than the nation on average. In truth, even Democratic governor candidates here have to espouse pro-drilling, anti–gun restriction agendas to get elected.

On this occasion, I was hoping a wave of Anchorage's human surge, perhaps the part that sloshed north from the Lower 48, would reach bookstores between the ceremonial race start—a "fake" one, in the eyes of hardcore mushing aficionados—and the magical hour when the bars would get busy.

The luncheon at a posh hotel seemed an auspicious beginning. My choice of reading, about my friend Bart raising his kids on roadkill, elicited gasps, eye rolling, and even laughs, but might have curbed book sales somewhat. The audience, professionals with silver manes, looked as if they knew their *coq au vin* from their *bouillabaisse* and which fork to use on which course.

The campus bookstore looked deserted; even students who read beyond their curriculum had left for spring break already. The museum was being renovated, and foot traffic through the echoing lobby, behind the owl's back, made her nervous and incontinent. I'm an inveterate owl fan, yet far from being an "owlaholic," member of a nonsectarian online cult that caroms from "mental illness" to "worship" of over 200 Strigiformes and back. *Striga* is Latin for "witch," and the order's name is a beautiful if unintended homage to persecuted women. I'm entranced with strigine secrecy;

the noiseless swoops, and dish faces with can-opener beaks below brimstone or inky stares that swivel for up to three-fourths of a circle to fixate on prey; faces that amplify sounds hidden ears briskly triangulate, even as the source scritches in tunnels under the snow; faces that, like the voices, have awed humans for at least 36,000 years. The earliest image, likely of a long-eared owl, which fingers traced onto a muddy cave wall at Chauvet, France, remains mute. We must picture its Paleolithic creator, who may have *whoo-whooed* as if blowing across the lip of a large, hollow gourd, affirming social bonds and home ground in the gloom, like this kindred hunter would have. The tune resonates in the Eurasian eagle owl's German name, *Uhu*, and its Linnaean one, *Bubo bubo*. The wingspan of this plumed phantom straight from a Grimm fairytale can reach over six feet. In May, at our cabin, a mated pair of equally tufted, slightly smaller, though no less impressive great horned owls booms back and forth, their *cris d'amour* contrasting in pitch. I love how these archetypal night prowlers have adapted to life under the midnight sun.

At the museum, a guy on crutches, not giving a hoot about owls, parked himself in front of my table. "Glad they didn't put you upstairs," he said, as if he had come to see me after reading one of the flyers. He launched into his lengthy medical history and then limped away without buying a book or so much as looking at one, or indeed the owl. Each signing appears to attract one of these attention hogs, and I'm convinced they are taking turns.

The chain-store branch manager put me in a prime spot, at a table facing the entrance, where I could make eye contact with customers as they entered. Light from the low sun made me squint like a shortsighted bookworm, not look vigilant as a wilderness guide and auteur should, or, when I tried to remedy that, glower like a sunglassed Mafioso. With each gust from the sliding doors, my poster swiveled on its stand, causing the printed grizzly to scan the room as if in search of prey. Management forbade raptors inside, for liability reasons. I was rather lonely without a feathered companion.

The large independent store downtown had advertised a panel discussion of the book. Unfortunately, only one of my authors showed up—and didn't reveal her presence until after my improvised reading. Her friends made up the bulk of the audience, literally, as fishermen and fisherwomen are put together impressively. I performed in the kids' books section, first wrestling with a defective microphone. Trying to maintain eye contact while keeping close to a mike set too low, I felt like Quasimodo talking out of the side of his mouth. Book clerks shook their heads as electronic feedback squeals filled the place. The birds, as always, drew scores of youngsters and their cash-carrying guardians.

At the café, wired on complimentary caffeine and with my voice beginning to sound like a raven's, I worked hard to be heard over the coffee grinder and hissing espresso machine.

The next day, the action and masses moved on to the real race start at Willow, and we joined a snake of cars creeping north. The Eagle River Nature Center was an escape from urban hubbub, a birdwatcher's Zen oasis. The turnout was good. When I opened the floor for questions, a kid in the front row who had endured my reading, piped up, "When do we get to touch the owl?"

"We don't," the bird handler snapped. The owl was not in a petting mood. Halfway through the presentation, she had noticed a stuffed eagle with fully spread wings, mounted below the log ceiling; she went into a hooting frenzy and kept diving off the handler's leather gauntlet, flapping upside down because she was leashed. She had to be put back in her cage. No doubt, these birds remained wild; they lit up the indoors with their own kind of electricity, the white-hot spark that still zaps us.

At our final venue, a bookstore-cum-café north of Anchorage, the manager had expected a signing, not a reading. There were no chairs for an audience, and I found myself separated from the handlers and their birds by a shelf full of gewgaws. (Has anyone else noticed how these increasingly augment book sales?) In a last-ditch bid for buyer attention, I rearranged some books on a shelf, placing my brainchild between two local bestsellers—one, a biography of that pit bull-with-lipstick governor—hoping to profit through proximity.

After two hours of signing, or rather no signing, I had sold five books total, four of those to the bird handlers. Because each bed within a 200-mile radius had been claimed for the night and we had no reservations, my girlfriend and I hit the road around sundown, trying to make Fairbanks that night. Near Denali State Park, snowflakes caught in our headlights and, rushing toward the windscreen, became galaxies seen at warp speed. Black ice on the road glared like a disgruntled publisher. We pulled out near some trailhead and fretted for a few hours, cramped in the back of the Subaru between boxes of unsold books, waiting for dawn to come.

Descending the last hill into Fairbanks bleary-eyed from our drive, I let the trip pass in review. Perhaps I'd competed with myself, pitting wild animals against words about wild animals, a contest I can't ever and possibly shouldn't win. The timing could have been better, the audience more receptive, the arrangements with store managers and owners bomb-proofed beforehand.

But in a strange M.C. Escher effect, like two hands drawing each other, the book had spawned more animal and people moments, encounters around which one could build whole new stories, and that had made the trip worth our while:

The gap-toothed teenager from Anaktuvuk, telling us about the wolf that bit his grandfather.

The grandmother, mother, and daughter trio—diligent bird-watchers all.

The bird handler and airplane mechanic who cleans cages and shows birds after work and talked about going back to school to become a raptor biologist.

The reader who complimented us on the book's cover and typography.

The naturalist-volunteer at the nature center, unwrapping a copy of *Walden* that Edward Abbey had prefaced and signed, as if it were an icon.

And, just as impressive:

The merlin that had helped its presenter to overcome her fear of public speaking.

The great horned owl, mesmerizing kids with her golden gaze.

The northern saw-whet owl, blind in one eye, elflike on the handler's gloved fist.

The red-tailed hawk, having suffered gunshot wounds, learning to trust humans.

Regardless of how many or few books were sold that time around, I could hope that our stories, like these birds, would touch someone's life, somewhere.

I later heard from a friend who used my essay from the book to teach nature writing to students in China. What did they make of grizzly–polar bear hybrids in the Arctic? How did the unknown creatures quicken in their imagination? Strangely, my words traveled farther than I ever did, spiraling outward, released from my care like bold, salvaged birds.

CHAPTER 10

F IS FOR FALCONRY

Critics knock falconry as a cruel, anachronistic blood sport. Proponents see an exalted practice upholding medieval traditions. For Randall Compton in Fairbanks, Alaska, it's "an expensive form of birdwatching," the chance to witness up close what few ever will, a privilege and a lifestyle, really. He also equates it with dog-mushing, in that "The longer you do it, the better it gets." The bearded, white-haired master falconer got his first bird, Guinevere, in 1969 and flew that red-tailed, a versatile, forgiving beginner's hawk, at Illinois' pheasants. Repurposing a barbecue glove into a gauntlet, the frugal teen devoured English falconry manuals, decoding the lingo and paraphernalia through their illustrations. Like his peers, Compton now tracks any defectors with fancy hardware.

We've claimed a picnic table under a blue-and-white striped pavilion glazed with rain, at the Creamer's Field Migratory Waterfowl Refuge. Paul Stitt, treasurer of the Alaska Falconers Association of 60-odd members, with Compton considers favorite birds and esoteric training and upkeep techniques. "Dirt-hawking" austringers guide their broadwings to snowshoe hares, ground squirrels, and launching, chuntering ptarmigans. Goshawks are psychos with hair's-breadth attention spans, both friends agree; glowering hulks with ember eyes, each as big as their brain, that spend most of their day ruffled or "bating," trying to hightail but ending up fluttering topsy-turvy, hanging from fists. They charge mountain bikers, tear after rabbits and into burrows. One goshawk harried a woman I knew when she walked by a nest in Denali National Park, marking her face, forever after reminding her of her transgression. Many goshawkers, also boasting facial scars, themselves suffer fits frequently. Some mesmerize their crazed bungee jumpers with strobe lights.

Compton likes Harris hawks, which course in packs, for their staid character and canine smarts. Alas, frostbite hurts the talons of this Southwestern desert denizen, so it's a poor choice where people put birds under hundred-watt lights in January, triggering molts early enough to hone aerial blades for the September-to-October hunt. Compton confesses to having an allergy to excrement, adding that "Paul's the word man" who will tell you the term for the chalky peregrine squirts. Stitt does: the word is *mutes*. "Only falconers whose birds get banged up a lot know as much about imping as you do," he teases Compton, referring to the grafting of molted feathers onto damaged ones. Compton counters that Stitt no longer hawks, since his wife abhors messes.

Their exchanges tatter my brain like rackets shredding a badminton birdie.

With his drum belly and a faint scar bridging a boxer's nose below a reversed ball cap, Compton projects iron heft, the grit of a Falstaff or Polo, mined from more than his former profession, that of a railroad-track maintenance worker. On his clad fist on the table rests Tinker Bell, a five-year-old peregrine the size of a cat but weighing one-fifth of one. He addresses this pixie as "Toots," in a voice surprisingly mellow for someone of his girth. She was rescued sick by the roadside, and he'll soon loose her at pigeons, or at mallards or pintails flushed from a Creamer's Field pond, his "special fishing hole...in the middle of town." (The ducks he snagged there with avian help—as a starving artist—marinated in orange juice? "My god!") Convalescents often become hunting birds, the lastingly handicapped, school and wildlife center ambassadors, just as the birds that stole my book-tour thunder had. Compton has bred falcons "naturally," pairing them, and truly artificially—one is tempted to say *unnaturally*—crowned with a dimpled "love hat" that looks like headwear from a Breughel painting. For a term paper his daughter had to write, they coaxed sperm from a tiercel (a male, always smaller) who was imprinted on him and inseminated a female, which yielded a viable egg.

Falcons also are lifted from cliff shelves as fuzzy hatchlings ("eyasses")—sometimes runts that would otherwise not survive, ensuring the rest receive extra food—or caught during maiden peregrinations from North Slope tundra to Chilean pampas. Three active licensed falconers as familiar with the Interior's flyways as they are with its nest sites reap two- to four-month-old "passage birds" of various species. They set spring-loaded clamshell nets that pop shut over tethered pigeons, or rig monofilament snares to jacketed decoys released on a string, or to chicken-wire cages confining mice. "You're doing those falcons a favor," as Compton puts it. Though wild ones can live for two decades, up to two-thirds die in their first year. They starve, freeze, drown, or topple off bridges or into smokestacks. Immature peregrines crash into buildings and power lines. They're shot, illegally; eaten by foxes or eagles; maimed by panicking prey; struck by lightning or planes, or by cars while scavenging roadkill.

Compton has pulled off Tinker Bell's leather hood, and she shivers and wails, anticipating a snack. He stokes her by keeping her hungry. It's a tightrope walk. An underfed hawk lacks the energy to hunt; an overfed one a reason to do so. Weigh-ins on the tailgate before each sortie help in gauging her *yarak* (a Persian word), her mental and physical fitness—or, some would say, the level of her rapaciousness. Like any athlete after a two-month break, but unlike bird dogs, hunting falcons need re-conditioning.

Hooding calms and aligns the winged missile. The ex-body-builder will tone its flight muscles for the famed 200-mph "stoop" dive with a drone. Like a bolt from a crossbow, the weapon her flight shape resembles before it contracts in the final approach, she will hit the target and clamp onto meat dangling from it at "700—hell, 1,000—feet." Falcons enjoy this, believing they're robbing a rival. A parachute opening upon impact sends them tumbling earthward, locked to a skydiver quail, in simulation of an actual kill. I'm close enough to admire the ergonomic nostrils with which Toots breathes at Formula I racecar speeds, and the beak serration for snipping a victim's spine. If a peregrine misses on its initial plunge, it and the duck will be matched evenly on the ensuing tail-chase at a more moderate, horserace velocity. Peregrines have fast vision, not just fast flight. We perceive 25 frames per second as a "movie," while for them no fewer than 130 create the same blur.

A chrome shoulder speck, like a single canary plume, contrasts with Tinker Bell's black-barred belly and thighs, blush breast, and bluish-slate back that the feathers' pearly edgings trace, an imitation of scale armor. The bright, incongruent splotch is acrylic. Toots surveils Compton where he portrays native fauna—his 14-foot canvas of Pleistocene beasts drifting into a valley that glaciered mountains rim hangs in UAF's Museum of the North. In another, a gyrfalcon squats on the curve of a mammoth tusk still half buried. Compton has traded a painting from his studio for Gimp, a "gyr" worth ten to fifteen grand, promised to be the rarer dark variant he'd wanted, but which—*shazaam*—after the first molt fledged dove-gray, her back the tone of weathered wood-shingle roofs. Why color variations crop up within raptor species remains a mystery. Like Alaska's three peregrine "races," gyrs, who bathe in snow, ultra-adapted to cold, are startlingly beautiful—the pale kind tessellated in black foremost to me. Inland Inupiat who fletched arrows with gyrfalcon feathers for preternatural power and traded them with coastal peoples had three names for the bird, depending on its age. *Okiotak*, the adult, was "the one that stays all winter." A fuzzy pre-fledgling, *atkuaruak*, is "like caribou mittens." Gyrs conveyed magic. A sixth-century effigy carved from walrus ivory in Canada's Arctic combines the head of a polar bear with a falcon's body. The gyrfalcon is the North's signature flying predator, and this amulet empowered its owner with the strength and agility of both animals. A giant white gyr initiated the Inuvialuit shaman Kublualuk, who had survived the Spanish flu, by grasping his chest and bearing him aloft during a storm. In a Greenlandic myth, a falcon spirit overwhelms evil giants and drives them off.

Gyrs impress with great nest-site fidelity, which reaches back even farther in time. The bottom layers of their foot-deep guano in Greenland are 2,500 years old. Norsemen procured these blasts from glacial realms and epochs, wraiths haunting vast spaces in Iceland, too. The *falcones albi* roosting in Renaissance maps sometimes were diplomatic gifts for Europe's kings and emperors—as recently as the 1970s, when an oil embargo threatened many economies, an Icelandic gyrfalcon Denmark presented to King Faisal of Saudi Arabia smoothed the waves of disruption. A gyr guards Iceland's coat of arms; another appears on Anne Boleyn's. Minstrels praised the falcon queen: "Of body small / Of power regal / She is / And sharp of sight." As in Europe, so in Asia: a gyrfalcon nourished a Mongol boy who had escaped from his captors into the mountains and years later made the known world tremble at his name, Genghis Khan. His future standing had been foretold in a dream in which a gyr clutched the sun and moon in its talons.

At the age of 21, Compton's regal trophy, White Bird, is retired.

These largest of falcons, outgrowing their "duck hawk" cousins by one-third, mate in Arctic-type settings exclusively. Between 700 and 1,500 do so in Alaska. "Outside falconers dream about gyrs" from a deeper than captive-bred gene pool, Compton says. Catching rare migrants is difficult, and the gyrs' stick cribs on vertiginous ledges in Alaska are so remote. On the other hand, breeding stock, jetting south caged, doesn't do well. X-rays at check-ins can depress fertility, while too many stimuli stress the birds.

Compton fists a dead quail from a coat pocket after twisting its head off, one of dozens ordered in bulk, frozen. A fellow falconer, a retired wildlife cop and commercial pilot, traps pigeons at a Fairbanks parking garage; the charter-school teacher Bennett Wong partakes of his birds' meals as if in communion, though he cooks his Canada geese.

Tinker Bell pins the carcass with one yellow reptilian foot, briefly mantles it, wings arched possessively, and, crunching twiggy bones, proceeds to devour it piecemeal. Feathers blow through the pavilion. A few stick to the short neck of the master's bottle of

Mickey's malt liquor. In a grand finishing flourish, Toots yanks out the gizzard with her meat hook and flings it onto the table-top. Bird-of-prey dining is not for the squeamish. But one rarely encounters such laser-beam focus, hunger so primal, or bodies so fully inhabited. Bloody handouts bind saurian to human once she is unleashed, though it's a link snapped as quickly as overstretched rubber. Out of sight, out of reach, out of luck—if they're full, sidetracked, or keen to migrate, falcons will ignore the glove that provides. For Dave Lorring, who has hunted with longwings since the age of twelve, "A successful day of falconing is when you come back with the same number of falcons as you left with."

Sated, Tinker Bell fluffs and shakes her coat from bill to obsidian toenails, announcing contentment with a *kek-kek-kek* less fierce than expected. Her dark mahogany orbs, bundling photons more efficiently than ours, can track three moving things simultaneously from a mile. If she were a fullback, she would spot multiple pigskins bobbling across the far goal line 17 ball fields away, with eyes big as light bulbs. Compton's, screened by hazel irises, will soon undergo cataract surgery, an irony for an artist-falconer. Aficionados quit if they can no longer follow their birds up hills and down dales, even just visually.

I next meet Tinker Bell for a walk in the park. She's being manned, planted on a novice's arm, carried through a Creamer's Field clear-ing to become acquainted and balanced. Compton, who recalls no women flying falcons in his youth, quips how "Mary, Queen of Scots must have been the last." Men still dominate the sport, so it's refreshing that one of Compton's four students is female. Jesica Lawson, 40, a mother of six, self-styled bird nut and military brat, first saw rehab eagles at an air force base where her husband was stationed. When Tinker Bell represented her tribe in a booth at a 355th Fighter Squadron—the "Fighting Falcons"—airshow, Compton met Lawson's spouse, who now is apprenticing too. State regulations prescribe which raptors and how many one can own, as well as the requisite setup. Graduating to falconry's "general" rank can take years.

For two weeks, Lawson has been nudging Tinker Bell toward flight on a leash. The object of her fascination rouses her as she morphs into a shaking, rustling feather duster, thereby sleeking her plumage. The journey from feral to semi-tame affects the falconer as it does their charge. Helen Macdonald, in her bestseller about wrangling her goshawk, *H Is for Hawk,* describes "thinking, seeing, imagining hawk all day long." For her, "Surprising things come to light, not simply memories, but states of mind, emotions, older ways of seeing the world."

These creatures are individuals, not Cartesian machines, which we overlook easily in our moments with wild ones.

Lawson's hours with Tinker Bell have been profound, a partial re-wilding. "A little of the bird's attitude rubs off on anyone who flies a hawk for a while, be it a gyrfalcon or a redtail," writes Steve Bodio, the tribe's New Mexico scribe in his classic *A Rage for Falcons.* Wide-eyed, breathless, clearly infatuated, the blonde in jeans, owlish glasses, and flowered ditch boots, a soccer-mom coach with lanyard and whistle garlanding her sweatshirt, speaks of the trust bonding handler and bird. "I'll probably cry the first time she returns to my fist."

Compton stresses responses to gestures, whistling, body positioning, or commands linked to food—for a joke golden eagle photo, he held up his infant son like a rabbit. Yet he distracts kids before beheading quails. And mocks Renaissance fair re-enactors adorned with live falcons. If folks want to parade a bird or scratch its neck, he grumbles, they should get a parrot. Lawson owns one.

The septuagenarian, fond of emojis, answers his phone when its gangsta-rap ringtone cues him.

Dog-lovers strolling on the meadow's trail repeat the same questions: "What kind is it?" and "Are you going to let it go?" But thankfully not the silly, "Is that thing real?" That would be insulting Toots and Compton, but in a way one can understand; her clean lines and bearing *do* make her appear statuesque, hewn from some older, nobler, rarer material. Airborne, conversely, she will be hard to cage up close in a camera's viewfinder, glimpsed only in part or as a smear. Raptors *enrapture*—"seizing by force," as the root of both words reminds us. You can't fly them without onlookers gathering. Or even walk, apparently. Compton enlightens bystanders opportunistically, boosting his métier's reputation. Some birders loathe raptors per se, because some species snatch dear songsters from their feeders. Raptors, for non-birders, incarnate freedom and majesty. Animal rights advocates seldom condemn defanged, domestic wildcat or wolf descendants. What about popular, increasingly hybridized, self-willed hobby raptors, though? Who's shaping whom; who bends to whose will? Possession is a dubious concept in this case. For falconers, "It is not the man who trains the bird, but the bird which trains the man." They mind their wards' weight, obsessively, more than their own. They foot vet bills, work night shifts, watch TV or nap together, buy them Pointers, trick out rigs with Astroturf, fittings, and build home aviary "mews." In season, they're out hunting, rain or shine, daily, neglecting their children, their spouses; truly zealous falconers settle where there's game and a job. Non-birders may be unaware also that breeders helped save North America's peregrine. By the mid-1960s, it had been endangered by DDT thinning eggshells. California condors, prairie falcons, and aplomados—larger kestrels with Zorro masks—have similarly recovered. Nowadays, pest abatement raptors scythe into crows raiding orchards and vineyards or scatter birds that could smash into jets; the DOT rejected Compton's proposal for a detachment of golden eagles at the Fairbanks airport.

Back at the pavilion, Lawson offers the ravenous shears chicken tidbits on a thumbnail, because, Compton says, "Some birds will take your finger off." The servant drops a morsel, and her highness *ee-chup*s impatiently, twice: "Pick-it-up!"

Time for Toots to hop into the Hawkmobile. Transferring her to her traveling roost demands finesse. Hooded again, she steps on herself, flapping nervously, risking broken primaries. Part of Lawson's challenge is to be deft with one hand, her other supporting the falcon. Proving mastery, Compton ties a bowline knot single-handedly, grounding Tinker Bell on her perch in the camper.

I myself took Toots for a jaunt into Creamer's Field, surprised at the muscle needed to keep this lightweight on an arm held akimbo. I don't know how Mongolians hunting with eagles on horseback do it. The fist, in a thumbs-up position, has to stay perfectly level, as the blindfolded bird feels most comfortable this way. All the while, you pinch her jesses, leather-strip ankle tethers, in case she decides to hop off. If your hand starts to droop, she might climb up your unprotected forearm, to roost on your shoulder like a pirate's parrot. Blimey, matey, is that blood on yer sleeve? It is thus with many falconry details—what strikes you as effortless grace, in truth stems from long practice.

As Randall Compton regains his sight, Bennett Wong prepares Chimkee, a four-year-old gyr, cadet-gray with boldly flecked underparts, that reasons "as much as a falcon can," to hunt geese before those head south. Wong often enlists students of his as game drivers at Creamer's Field. When I first saw Wong carry Chimkee—a portmanteau of "chimp" and "monkey"—his smile split a face between a strong jaw and a sable helmet of hair threaded with silver. He was also pushing a buggy, a black bear of a Newfoundland in tow.

He now clips Chimkee to a 50-yard "creance" safety line.

"Are you gonna fly it like a kite?" an observing boy asks. "No, we're just training her," Wong replies. The kid turns to his mom: "He's gonna fly it like a kite!"

After I un-hood Chimkee, and Wong's whistle shrills, she leaps off the short utility post, strokes low across the lawn toward him, two-foot sickle wings soughing, climbs, loops back, dives, stalls briefly like a dragon torching a walled city, and then nails the quail parts Wong spins on a cord.

We chill afterwards in a northwesterly breeze at the split-rail fence near a pond where Wong lets his bird survey her future hunting grounds. She blossoms in such conditions, all eyes, bobbing her head excitedly, though from my perspective brittle reeds hide any geese that might be there. Gyrfalcons have been known to monitor moving foxes and trucks that rousted game from its cover. Our conversation, skipping-stone-style, touches on ethics, respect, the environment, trends, as conversations will when discussing wildlife. Wong, who was born in Malaysia and came to the US as a toddler and once owned a baby yak, thinks that certain falconers care genuinely for their birds and the species. Others merely regard them as tools. "Might as well use a gun," he says, which is much more efficient. He's hunted with a "cast" of peregrines, perhaps the country's only falconer to have done so—twins he took from an aerie near Salcha, a river settlement south of Fairbanks. One absconded with hundreds of dollars in electronics. Tandem flying was tricky, because "They would have liked to eat each other." He synced their orbits, playing air traffic controller, cat herder with a pole lure for a whip, torero of bantams, juggler of porcelain angels with dagger claws.

Unlike their flexible cousins that dwell in skyscrapers, highly localized gyrs, some of which attack helicopters, soon could be struggling. Rain alternating with freezes kills rock ptarmigan, a staple of breeding gyrfalcons and a climate change sentinel. Against expectations, snow loss baring willows better conceals winter ptarmigans from predator eyes. With global heating, advancing diseases and parasites will afflict gyrs—already, avian cholera grips St. Lawrence Island; worms common in British Columbia can be found writhing in Norton Sound spruce grouse flesh, shocking Inupiaq residents. Birch, alder, and more combative peregrines will encroach on the gyrfalcon's niche. South-facing nests will be sweltering and spring storms will doom additional clutches.

Beholding the shrunken pond at Creamer's Field and the glowing scrim of fall vegetation, Wong, a Compton alumnus with a master's degree in biology and the director of Creamer's Field's Camp Habitat for youths, marvels at how many Alaskan falconers deny the climate emergency, despite being alleged preservationists and subject to dire new circumstances.

It's showtime: the culmination of months of patience and toil before the daunting unfettering, the brink of free flight, for Bodio "the single scariest moment" with adolescent birds. Removing Chimkee's hood, Wong hangs it on his convenient ear, which it cups like half of a headphone set. Wong doesn't toss Chimkee; Chimkee unfurls when she's ready, always into the wind, encouraged by Wong, who raises his arm as if to broaden her prospect, with her firmly poised on it.

Swish, swish, swish...

She scopes out the pond first, but, alas, all wildfowl have departed—the forecast calls for flurries. Ascending, she then sails the hayfield's far edge. Wong, worried about the flaneurs' dogs, twirls the lure, a rod featuring quail wings and breast bait on a steamrollered catcher's mitt instead of a Woolly Bugger. Swinging the fake to hook his partner's attention requires dexterity. A sloppy style can cripple a darting inbound bird. Chimkee, heeding the whistle, deciding the beakful in the craw beats the feast of her inner search image, boomerangs in, a scrap of the overcast hurtling earthward.

The day of the actual hunt is anticlimactic, riddled with slapstick à la Keystone Cops. Wong had considered putting a few duck and goose decoys on the pond to attract Arctic stragglers headed south. But four pintails and two swans have lit on the still surface, unaware of the nearby threat. Students of Wong and their parents are present, and he enlists them as drivers to spook the ducks, which Chimkee will only take on the wing. The swans, 30 pounds each, are too much to bite off for a gyr or any raptor besides an eagle. To ensure he won't be accused of harassing fairytale animals in a refuge, Wong calls Fish and Game. The warden tells him that swans becoming collateral damage if Chimkee takes a fancy to them is an acceptable risk and not against hunting regulations but to let spectators know that *he* is not going after the big white birds. Such are the vagaries of a suburban hunt.

Before we can even ring the pond, with Chimkee still blind, two ducks decamp for a different one. Because there are no swans there, it becomes the new center of attention. We all hare toward it, but the ducks, afloat in the middle, fail to rise despite the ruckus. So, it's back to the swan pond.

Caught up in the excitement, trying to keep up with my eyes on the prize, I trip in the bumpy field and, hitting my head, see stars—I never before realized how apt that image is. At the first pond, Chimkee, coming to the call of the whistle, strafes the unperturbed swans while those pintails escape. Wong, deciding to end this wild goose chase, waves the pole lure, which promptly breaks, but he still brings down the gyr to be hooded again.

The main point of refinement, cresting within minutes, at least for Wong, was never the kill. It's the display of stalwart drive, aerobatic flair, and above that, connection with an alien life form. Still, I can attest that livewire pursuits steep even non-falconers in awe and adrenaline. A gyr in flight is a crystal shard piercing your heart.

While her radio-GPS leg transmitter and trailing antenna may present her as a remote-controlled thing, she is anything but. Seeking the vital Darwinian instant that determines the quarry's fate, falconers elevate uncertain outcomes to an art. The wisest, doubting surefire loyalty and being aware how quickly raptors can die, embrace non-attachment. They sometimes free birds permanently, deliberately. Brass ankle bells once signaled their partners' doings and whereabouts. Between those relics' tinkles and more recent telemetry beeps, the sport's mystique spans three millennia. In an earlier age, Wong might have ridden in the Great Khan's retinue with a chocolate-brown saker primed for hunting herons and stoats. Compton would have worshipped Freya, who shape-shifted by donning a falcon-plume cape; or peregrine-headed Horus perhaps, the sky god whose glyph was the eye. As it stands, Compton, currently teaching a goshawk he has trapped, lives where the "grand species of birds for falconry" live. He's "fooling around with an addiction," yet, he insists, not fully consumed.

Steve Bodio characterized hardcore game hawkers thusly: "individualistic to the point of anarchism"; "committed to the point of obsession"; "sometimes paranoid"; and somewhat arrogant, as, "Like all self-made men, they want others to pay their dues."

If, as reasons for toxic pride, you replace raptor-flying with Alaska's qualities—its size, wealth, frontier toughness, and separateness—that depiction neatly sums up the state's Conservatives, who represent the vast majority of its constituents. Many Alaskans listened to the late Rush Limbaugh, who scorned the Covid-19 pandemic as a politically hyped "common cold, folks." Wong revealed, during our Creamer's Field fence chat, that in a Fairbanks Fred Meyer store during that time, an unmasked man had wordlessly harassed him by pulling his own eyes slantwise. After 28 years in the US, not wanting his son to grow up a target of hate, Wong contemplated emigrating again, thinking about quitting this land of the gyr.

CHAPTER 11

TAKING THE WATERS

Harbingers of spring, piebald snow buntings scatter in front of the truck's grille like confetti. A few miles farther on the Elliott Highway, a ptarmigan sails off into the sky's glacial blue. Its mottled plumage shows the brown these hills soon will display.

It's the end of March, one week past the spring equinox, when day and night hang briefly in balance. It is also the weekend of Seward's Day, and this year marks the 150th anniversary of Alaska's purchase from Russia. Though the acquisition proved to be a windfall for these United States, in 1867, Secretary of State William H. Seward was mocked for wasting government funds. The Republican press called his acquisition "Seward's ice box," "Walrussia," or President Johnson's "polar bear garden."

Seduced by sunshine and eager to shed surplus pounds and the season's lassitude, my wife, Melissa, and I are headed for Hutlinana Hot Springs, about 120 miles shy of the Arctic Circle. We've tunneled through three minus-50-degree spells in Fairbanks this winter, the last one in January.

A severe climate and Russian steam-bath heritage make hot-springing a favored Alaska pastime. Unlike coastal Alaska, the Interior has no volcanoes. Most hot springs here form when water seeping through cracks in the planet's dermis finds rocks closer to Earth's blazing heart. The named thermal springs in the state—more than a hundred of them—range from spartan to decadent, from tranquil to buzzing, from tepid to hot enough for boiling eggs. At the remote Selawik Hot Springs, separate bathhouses accommodate Athabaskans and Inupiat, and people warn you to exit quickly to keep from getting cooked if you see small hot-air bubbles rising in the water. On the Okpilak, Brooks Range hikers build rock dams to create a primitive tub. Chena Hot Springs, near Fairbanks, boasts a geothermal greenhouse that produces restaurant food and, until the fire marshal shut it down because it lacked sprinklers, had an ice hotel in which even the beds and martini glasses were made from that stuff. In the resort's outdoor pool, Alaskans float whale-like, with frost thatches that would give hairdressers migraines. Japanese tourists fond of winter and bathing culture join them in busload numbers. Contrary to a widely held belief, the Japanese do *not* think children conceived sub-aurorally will lead blessed lives—that urban legend arose from the TV show *Northern Exposure*, which spread similar fictions that had Alaskans in stitches.

There are lukewarm Alaska mud wallows known only to moose, muskox, and mosquitos. And there are spas where history lingers like a vagrant. Pilgrim Hot Springs, 60 washboard miles north of my former hometown of Nome, is one of those. In the early 1900s, during the gold rush, it was a spa for miners with sore backs, complete with a dance hall, a roadhouse, and of course, a saloon. The roadhouse and saloon burned in 1908, and the property (in an act of penance?) went to Father Bellarmine Lafortune. Seizing his luck, Lafortune turned it into an orphanage. Famished children found a home of sorts at Pilgrim Hot Springs. The Spanish flu epidemic of 1918 struck Native Alaskan communities especially hard, leaving behind an army of dependents housed in the Catholic mission that Father Lafortune had established. The hot springs kept indoor plumbing from freezing and the ground thawed early, and with summer daylight around the clock, food grew there successfully.

Melissa and I founder and flail—she on skis, I on snowshoes—for an hour under heavy backpacks in corn snow up to my thighs, unable to locate the trailhead. Ready to call it a day, we run into a group of snowmachiners who point us in the right direction. The trail is packed hard and skirts Hutlinana Creek, twisting in its bed between squat basaltic domes clad with spruce. I clomp along on the crimped vehicle track, which I could do just as well without snowshoes.

The creek owes its name to the Lower Tanana Athabaskans, subarctic cousins of the Navajos and Apaches. The original name *Khutl-'onh No'* translates as "He-or-She-Has-a-Structure Creek." No longer visible, the structure in question was likely the cabin that in 1915 stood on a small meadow near the spring. Someone grew vegetables and potatoes there, and placer miners from the Eureka Creek district stopped by to rinse the dirt from under their fingernails.

In my experience, built additions to hot springs often bring inconvenience. On a fly-in trip with two clients to Serpentine Hot Springs in western Alaska's Bering Land Bridge National Preserve, we found that the Park Service occupied half the bunkhouse. They were fixing the bathhouse, but the pipe that should have siphoned cold stream water into the tub didn't pipe. It dribbled. The hot water spigot, however, worked fine. The tub's content could be 170 degrees, and the only way to make it bearable was to haul five-gallon buckets—about 20—from the creek. I couldn't just wait for the hot tub to cool, because it leaked faster through cracks between the floorboards than it mellowed with cold influx from the pipe. My clients were shy, and after laboring with my coolant, I had the bathhouse to myself.

Serpentine is an extension of the Interior Alaskan Hot Springs Belt, whose outlets sit within or along the margins of granitic plutons—gigantic bodies of magma that slowly rose through fissures and ballooned like aneurysms before cooling near the crust's surface. Radioactive decay of uranium and thorium in the rocks and the deep circulation of groundwater drive the heating. Granite Mountain Hot Springs, at the far eastern edge of the Seward Peninsula, with a maximum temperature of 119 degrees F has potential for geothermal power creation similar to Chena Hot Springs, though its remoteness precludes development.

Living where folks love to bask in wood-heated tubs below the aurora's sheen, I did not understand why they'd entombed Serpentine Hot Springs in a room. Beyond the fogged window-panes, stark granite tors and bald hills and steam curling from the creek harked back to a bygone, primordial world. I half expected mammoths to come rumbling through. As it happens, archaeologists have found fluted stone spear tips in the Clovis style on one of the crowding hills. They've also troweled up charcoal 12,000 years old, possibly from the fires Pleistocene hunters built while camped there.

The Inupiat people of Shishmaref, on the coast, maintain close ties to Serpentine Hot Springs. They call their Blue Lagoon *Iyat*, "Cooking Pot," or "A Site for Cooking." According to one of their legends, the basaltic tors are Deering women who were petrified when they approached the forbidden location. You can easily pick out another figure, The Drummer, seated, beating the skin of his wood-hoop *qilaun*. In the quiet, if you stay long enough, the air around him throbs. Each of these stone sentinels is said to exude specific healing powers. This place is a shamanistic training ground, a numinous boot camp, and in the old days non-shamans avoided it until called upon.

When Shishmaref residents plucked spear points or similar ancient artifacts from their eroding beaches, spirits that dwelt at the springs whisked the unsuspecting back there via out-of-body flight or underground for some harsh lessons. The initiates would enter Iyat, pulsing gateway to parallel worlds, diving through permafrost to the nether realm.

Drumming, healing, and shamans are intimately connected in this belief system. Neuroscience supports what the Inupiat have long known about the good vibes, the rhythms that steadily knock on the doors of the otherworld. The therapeutic in this case is psychosomatic. Resounding like beating hearts, hypnotic drums release endorphins as in a runner's high; they reduce stress, lower blood pressure, and enhance immunity. They boost alpha brainwaves linked to bliss that induce meditative states. Brains of patients ultimately tune in to these cadences. "The drum will heal your soul," says Nome musician Bryan Muktoyuk. Similarly, hot-water bathing stimulates overall blood flow. Psychological effects include comfort and relief, also expressed in alpha waves.

Shamanism is no longer practiced in Northwest Alaska, supposedly. But through its Tribal Doctor Program, the Maniilaq

Association, a regional nonprofit, has arranged visits to Serpentine Hot Springs more recently for Inupiaq healers who, arriving by small plane instead of trance flight, uphold this curing tradition.

Those in the know not only consider the past at these springs, but also peek into their future. A mukluk's leather ties dipped into the seething water augur either a long life or impending death for the wearer. If your laces curl up, make sure your will is in order.

Serpentine was, and still is, a precarious place. Avoid visits while menstruating or with your mind or emotions on edge, elders advise—just when you need a soothing soak most. They caution against going alone or staying too long. A careless person may not make it back as herself or himself.

A third of the way to Hutlinana Spring, we pass through an old burn of spindly tree trunks, a skeleton forest. "In the sticks," makes suddenly sense. Somewhere downhill, two great horned owls are wooing, lusty with spring juices flowing. In the afternoon sun, our shadows have grown gaunt; those of blackened spruce striate the trail like so many sundials.

When we arrive at the springs late in the day, only one other couple is there, ensconced in a wall tent with woodstove. They hauled in their load on a sled, not like pack mules, as we did. After we set up our tent and start a fire, we cross the creek for our treat. The hot spring wells from a chink in the base of a cliff that braces the steep hillside west of the creek. Stacked rocks ring the pool of knee-deep, clear, bubbling water.

As flesh melts off my bones, I zoom back mentally to a bedrock pool in Yosemite's high country where, eons ago, a black bear had joined me for ablutions. I assure myself that at this time of year the bears still hibernate. Just in case of an early riser or insomniac, I keep my repellent handy. Next, I ponder the amoeba that prowls hot springs and lakes, which devours brain tissue and sometimes kills people. But I'm just as likely to catch that nasty bug from a Vegas motel room's air-conditioning duct or from decrepit plumbing on the Fairbanks university campus. (I no longer frequent saunas, developed hot springs, or public swimming pools because of COVID and human contaminants.) I then wonder if the locals long ago parboiled mammoth steaks at Serpentine. Did the Koyukons tender caribou venison in Kanuti? The scant records leave it unclear whether they just camped near the wholesome well or used it as a kitchen appliance.

Inupiat and Athabaskans have taken the waters at thermal springs in the Arctic and Interior for generations. The mineralized pools promised relief for hip and back pain, for headaches, arthritis, skin rashes, and other ailments long before there were HMOs. Greens for curing stomach problems, ulcers, and sores grow year-round nearby. Preparing the body, people drank from the springs and consumed medicinal plants beforehand. Some collected spring water and greens as home remedies. The pull was so strong that people traveled hundreds of miles to visit this spot. One elder recalled how in 1935, during the twilight days of western Alaska's reindeer-herding industry, a man brought his sick cousin from Cape Espenberg to Serpentine. The cousin rode bundled up in a sled hitched to four draft reindeer, on a journey that lasted a week. The patient and his driver stayed for a month, until they ran out of food. Compared to theirs, our round trip of twelve miles (not counting those in the truck), is but a jaunt in a park.

Like the popular Native Alaskan steambaths, hot springs offered a mental break as well a physical one. "It was way more complicated than they are doing now, just focusing on the physical body," a man raised near Serpentine once reminisced about the rites of immersion. Feeling the world's weight reduced—literally—or entirely lifted from them, people connected with their better selves and family, with their culture and the land. Such springs demarcated a neutral or even a sacred zone; conflict was not tolerated.

Lastly, there was hygiene, though sweaty travelers often leave such pools, scummed with algae and lined with mud, dirtier than they were when they slipped into them.

White as marble and shrunken from winter, my thighs turn to rubber in Hutlinana's silky embrace. The warmth triggers dim memories from the womb. It's like zero gravity, but down here on

Earth. Spirits, high-proof ones, cut some ice at this hot spring, too. I sip *uisge-beatha* I brought in a flask, and the Gaelic "water of life," a lovely single-malt, makes my insides glow. Shoulders uncramp. Then eyelids droop, and thoughts become fuzzy. No wonder someone drowns in a bathtub or spa somewhere in America nearly every day, three times more bathers in rural Western states and often under the influence. (Some who die, it must be said, are infants or senile or on blood-pressure medications.)

Once more, I toast William H. Seward and his beads-and-blankets bargain with the impoverished Tsar.

Without delay, I dress in the sharp night breeze and at camp heat a pouch meal for two. Some bears are moving about: Ursa Major wheels overhead in the clearing, backup to our fire's crackles and sparks. Melissa soon joins me, roasting socks on a stick over greedy flames and acrid smoke before marshmallowing her foam sleeping pad. Bands of aurora flank the state's signature constellation, phosphorescing neon green, rippling like the hem of a windblown curtain. Above the matchstick silhouette of forested hills twitches Orion's bejeweled belt. It all is almost too cliché, a centerfold from a tourist brochure.

Morning arrives with the feared symptoms of winter camping: stiff joints, frozen boots, cold campfire ashes, a sluggish gas stove, and a dehydration hangover.

After a last dip to preheat the engine—Melissa is taking her coffee in the pool, wearing only her pom-pom wool hat—we are breaking camp. Looking up from stuffing my pack, I glimpse a wolverine sauntering past the spring.

By the time we are halfway back to the truck, the light has thinned. Gray scud screens the sun. Winter has more in store.

CHAPTER 12

IN THE WAKE OF SKIN BOATS

With her engines cut, *Steller* idles inside Bear Cove, a crook in the coastline of Kenai Fjords National Park, while we unload our sea kayaks from the stern. A setting sun gilds the sea and shore with light thick as tinted glass. Where the high tide meets hemlock and spruce, not a foot of level ground is left. We don't know what the green wall conceals. But the coast that one Park Service historian called rock-bound and stern shows a friendly face on this summer day.

Initially the newcomers thought they had found a virgin world. When slender boats fashioned from animal skins crowded their ships, they quickly realized that this coast had been home to people for thousands of years. The Pacific Eskimos now known as Alutiit called themselves Sugpiat, the "Real People," though Russian fur hunters and traders considered them to be subhuman. Despite their disdain, the colonizers came to admire the native "leathern canoes" for their elasticity. They complimented their speed and considered them safer in bad weather than European small boats. With the help of Native Alaskan paddlers who powered these shallow craft with broad beams up shrouded estuaries and into lagoons, a foreign god's word spread as fast as the trade goods did. In a third, midship hatch of doubles especially modified, non-paddling passengers sometimes sat: priests; the buyers that eyed otter pelts; or the odd ethnographer.

A smooth three-hour ride delivered our group, two instructors and six OB students, into Aialik Bay. The boat ride spared us paddling nearly 40 miles up Resurrection Bay, around a promontory waves often lash, one with few landing places. *Steller*'s observation deck also gave us views of parrot-billed puffins clipping the spray, of mist geysering from the slick, glossy spine of some whale, and of a large sea otter—90 pounds of bewhiskered curiosity reclining in our wave train.

In days of yore, otters learned to fear humans. People closely related to the Alutiit have lived in the Kodiak Archipelago and Prince William Sound, and on the Lower Kenai and Southern Alaska Peninsula where it tapers into the Aleutian chain, for at least 7,000 years. They chased seals and sea otters in ingenious kayaks and lived in pit houses roofed with driftwood and sod. From the mid-18th century on, under Russian supervision, they served the demands of Asian markets, driving sea otters to the brink of extinction.

The rampage against this keystone species—sea-urchin munchers with the densest of all animal furs—surely spawned guilt in hunters who thought that otters had been people once. Traditionally, they gave freshly killed *arhnat* a drink of fresh water and buried or returned their bones to the sea. It was said that long, long ago, the incoming tide trapped a man out collecting chitons, marine mollusks that look like huge pill bugs. He wished to become an otter to save himself and, transforming, became the ancestor of all others. Another Alutiiq myth locates their amphibious nature: When the land and sea spirit divided all creatures between them, the otter was left behind. Quarreling over it, they stretched its stub into the long tail it now has. "Please let me go! I will stay with both of you," their victim pleaded.

Perhaps with heavy hearts, each April Alutiit assembled for commercial hunts in fleets of up to 500 *baidarkas* (a Russian term for Alutiiq *qayat* or "kayaks;" singular: *qayaq*). Fragile boats led by *promyshlenniki*—entrepreneurs more closely resembling mercenaries, alternatively described as "Cossacks of the fur trade"—traveled east from Kodiak Island, along the outer Kenai coast, to Sitka, enlisting additional hunters on the way. Crashing otter populations eventually made the hunt unprofitable, and with an international treaty that ended the trade and the pressure gone, the species recovered remarkably well.

Our group's excitement is almost palpable, and we suck in the long daylight and Alaska wilderness as if it were pure oxygen. Riding a wave of euphoria, I teach a brief lesson on campsite selection and leave-no-trace ethics before we tackle the gear piles on the beach. We are in our bags by 10:30, tired but still wired from the first day's impressions.

After breakfast and with the weather holding, we get down to basics: kayak anatomy, paddle strokes, and the much-dreaded wet exit and reentry. The water is cold, though not by Alaska standards. A few of the less motivated students try to talk their way out of the drill. But after a reminder that it is not negotiable and an instructor demonstration, they all follow suit. Two students, Chris and Jake, take several attempts to flip their double kayak. Upon reentry they capsize again, because Chris, already back in the cockpit, forgets to lean to the opposite side when six-foot-three Jake crawls onto the deck. My co-instructor Josh and I grin at each other. Before this trip is over, all of us will be forced out of our comfort zone. These two students have just been introduced to one of Outward Bound's pillars: teamwork.

As I watched the tandem struggle, memory flashed back to my own sea-kayak introduction, a trip, funnily, down the Noatak River. The craft was a fancy fiberglass number I'd borrowed from a friend. It came in three pieces that could be screwed together and separately fit into a Cessna. (External loads, including boats rigged to the belly of floatplanes like small whales, were no longer legal.) Missing a slot in one of the upper Noatak's shallow rock gardens, the river pinned me against a boulder and swamped me because I'd forgone the sprayskirt that day. The current started to fold both kayak ends around the pivot while sundry gear escaped from the cockpit, Bering Sea-bound. By the time I managed to wrench the beast off, the boat's shell had cracked—nothing half a roll of duct tape wouldn't fix. I aborted that trip, flying out from Noatak village, when a raincoat I'd tailored from a garbage bag into which I cut three holes proved to be ineffective.

The education of Alutiiq kayakers, unlike mine, began early, at age 14. On calm days, boys would travel into the bays to catch fish or kill birds with throw darts. A game of skill improved their hand-eye coordination. Sitting on the ground as if in a kayak, one youth would throw etched, metal-tipped miniature darts at an animal carving that another swung in front of him on a string. Elders encouraged the neophytes to harden their bodies by taking dips in the ocean at dawn. Calisthenics kept them balanced and flexible. Pull-ups on the roof rafters of their homes padded their shoulders and forearms with muscle. At 16, having undergone cleansing rituals, they joined uncles and other maternal kinsmen on sea-otter-hunting excursions. When they encountered a raft or single otters, hunters slapped the water with their paddles, forcing the animals to dive until they were exhausted and breathless. They sometimes clubbed otters meant for the trade, to prevent damage to the hide. Pearly air-bubble trails betrayed their prey's movements. Speed and accuracy mattered; an otter belonged to the first man who wounded it.

Hieromonk Gideon, an Orthodox official whom Empress Catherine the Great sent to report on Russian America in 1803, paints a vivid picture of methods and skills Kodiak Islanders used in hunting sea otters from double-hatch boats:

> The first man who sights a sea otter signals the others by lifting his paddle. The others try to encircle the place at a distance within range of their spears. Only those in the forward hatches throw the spears, everyone at will, before each other, while those in the rear hatches maneuver the *baidarkas*. Sometimes, the sea otter is hit by two spears, and in such a case, the carcass belongs to the hunter whose spear struck the animal closer to the head or above the other spear.

A lone hunter caught in a storm could steady his *qayaq* with inflated seal bladders he tied to its sides. Perhaps he had learned this from otters, which, caught in a gale, wrap kelp tubes around their middles to ride out the turmoil anchored and buoyed. Or he might implore Great Crow to take him on his wings and set him down safely on the shore. This spirit lived in the clouds. His flapping whipped up storms; his eyes in anger flashed lightning bolts, just before immense wings beating against his body rang over the whitecaps as thunder. The hunter also might buck Crow's commotion by lying down in the hull, whose hatch he sealed with his *kamleika*—an intestine sprayskirt–paddle-jacket combo equal to our Goretex and neoprene and tightened with hood and wrist drawstrings that he cinched around the cockpit's coaming. The hermetic capsule's design anticipated that of modern trans-Atlantic rowers, and one can only imagine the acoustics inside. Boys were taught early to Eskimo-roll, righting capsized *qayat* while their *kamleikas* kept them dry. Unfortunately, with only twelve days on this course, our students won't master this advanced self-rescue technique.

Assured that our pod can travel safely, at least under present conditions, we head out for the day. While the students work on staying in formation, we cruise past several sea caves, dark mouths in the land's escarpments. Closer to shore, the barely perceptible swell becomes animated, the ocean's rise and fall resounding in rock cavities like wet deep-breathing and pounding. An offshore breeze bears the scent of fecundity: a wreath of salt, fish, forest, mud, and decay. Wary of rebounding waves, we keep our distance from barnacled boulders and the kelp beds that hide them.

Later, at camp, we inventory our food supply under much joking and laughter. We stay up late telling stories and, rehashing the past, shape the present and forge bonds that we hope will weather the future.

The next day turns drizzly, as is typical for this stretch of coastline. We paddle ten miles to Abra Cove. A student captain and two navigators lead, trying to keep the group tight. How strange, I surprise myself thinking, for land creatures to travel this smoothly this far without gaining or losing elevation. Paddle cadences propel our boats, whose bows slice the slate gray with the verve of Roman galleys.

Our double-bladed, concave, and offset "feathered" paddles optimally transmit muscle power to water; they also prevent one-sided exertion. The Alutiit mostly used paddles with a single blade shaped like a spearhead or leaf. This blade—thinning at the edges, and often decorated with black and red ocher—was specifically engineered for windy conditions and quick stabilizing maneuvers. Beyond mere means of propulsion, the paddle served as a kind of sonar: hunters would clench the grip between their teeth, with the blade in the ocean. They could sense game moving underwater through the wood's vibration, as if reading land animal tracks in fresh snow.

Like their Aleut neighbors to the west, the Alutiit targeted even young minke, humpback, and fin whales feeding near shore in the summer. For that, they dipped slate javelin points into aconite, a neurotoxin mashed from the roots of monkshood, also called "wolf's bane" for its Old-World use in killing wolves with laced meat, and "devil's helmet" for its looks. Whales lanced with the alkaloid from this showy, blue-purple alpine flower lingered for days before dying, and only a hunter's deep knowledge of tides, currents, and wind patterns allowed him to predict the place of their stranding. A beast twice the length of his single-seater could feed a whole village for weeks. Retrieval rates approaching four whales in ten may seem surprising to us. Since kills required not only skills but also a great deal of mojo directed through rituals, whalers always were shamans. They'd dig up the bodies of powerful people whose fat, mixed with the plant sap, boosted the latter's potency. One whaler told Aleksandr Baranov—the Russian American Company boss on Kodiak and in effect Alaska's first governor—that he would disinter him after his death to turn him into poison. This breach of European etiquette was a statement of utmost respect.

Beyond being rocking seats for a hunter, *qayat* served as family vehicles, forerunners of skiffs and pickup trucks, in which to haul food, dogs, belongings, children, and later, chickens to camps at the summer fishing grounds. Crammed inside the slim boat filled with camping essentials, 50-mile days could feel longer yet.

In a cove gliding by on starboard we notice three black bear cubs. They are engaged in a wrestling match, now standing on hind legs, now dropping on all fours to chase each other across the beach. Mom is nowhere in sight. Bald eagles scrutinize us from trees bearded with mint-green moss. Harbor seals raise their heads from the sea like puppies eyeing a parade. Our pod travels through moon jelly galaxies. In a flurry of fins and tails, salmon prepare for their inland migration—strange to think we live above the roof of their home, in their firmament. A creation myth tells of the first Alutiit falling from the sky in their kayaks, and I understand how they must have felt: travelers between worlds, released from physical limitations.

The tide's broad back carries us into the cove.

We pitch our tents on a storm-built gravel dam that defends marsh against ocean. A cliff a thousand feet high lines the back of the bay; cascading waterfalls have stained it rust red. Splashes of burnt-orange lichen complement the minerals' blush.

During dinner we watch another black bear. This one is grazing in the meadow behind camp. It forages just a stone's throw away from the tents, absolutely unconcerned with our presence. That's a little too close for comfort. Shouting and waving, we announce ourselves. Without hurrying or altering its course, the bear contin-ues its evening rounds and eventually dives into the bushes. The students are awed. Most of them have never seen a bear in the wild.

Fueled by a pot of hot oatmeal, we shove off again the next morning. Soon, brash ice signals the terminus of Aialik Glacier. Tinkling, like ice cubes in a drink, mixes with the fizzing of air bubbles released from the vise of the eons, each one a tiny time capsule. Bergy bits migrate from the bay on the tide, sculptures of blown glass, stately Pleistocene beasts bound for oblivion. Growlers, like beer kegs, jostle our kayaks with deep *thunk*s and force us into a line. The point kayak as icebreaker clears a channel for our flotilla.

A Kodiak myth explains the Gulf *qayaq*'s lopsided design. Two cliffs closed on the boat of people traveling from the north, breaking its tail off. Ever thereafter, Alutiiq *qayat* featured one "sharp end"—the upturned, furcated bow, knifing through headwinds and swells—across from the blunt end. Icebergs formed the vise that pinched a hero kayaker's stern in a Greenlandic tale. The "Clashing Rocks" motif also found at the Bosporus better befit ice-free southerly seas. In swirly, tight Kenai Fjords passages, walls that can eat boats indeed seem to press in on you.

A salvo like an avalanche or volcanic eruption rolls across the water with each glacier calving. We slip behind Squab Island, about a mile from the interface of the sea and Aialik's tumultuous front. Shielded from rogue waves and from collapsing ice towers, we grab a quick snack rafted up in our boats. Thousands of kittiwakes protest our presence. The mob lifts in a vortex of wings and piercing cries but quickly settles again.

We notice ice floes in the bay, haul-outs for harbor seals, in particular mothers and pups. Remote video monitoring has shown that seals flee the ice when tour boats approach, or even kayakers. The animals experience stress, and more disturbingly, pups can get trampled in panic. In Aialik, Glacier Bay, and Prince William Sound, harbor seals are in decline. With the recent recession of many tidewater glaciers, their resting, birthing, nursing, and molting platforms have diminished. Forced onto shore, seals and especially pups become easy meals for wolves or bears combing the beaches.

To the Alutiit, harbor seals, and Steller's sea lions, were as bison to the Plains Indians; and the *qayaq* was their horse. The finfooted mammals nourished Alutiiq hunters and their families with meat, blubber, and oil, and kept them clothed and their houses warm and lit. They inspired song, story, dance, and ritual, totemic connections for an entire society. Human and other animals' lives merged in the bottleneck of survival, in an existence veined with taboos and mutual obligations. This relationship shaped the material culture, as in oil lamps sculpted from beach cobbles, lit during ceremonies. Seal heads joined to men's faces peered up from the lamp bottoms as oil was burning off, symbols of shared fates, of porous boundaries, common origins. In more mundane, though nevertheless miraculous transformations, sealskins became vehicles in which to trade, visit, and hunt. Five or six large skins of spotted seal or young sea lion sheathed a single *qayaq*. Boat-builders valued the hides of female sea lions, which were thinner and more pliable; they also have fewer scars and holes compared to the hides of the more combative males.

Beaching our crafts near the glacier's southwestern flank, we find that the closest campsite lies about 200 yards from shore. It takes all hands to haul the fully loaded double into the moraine's moonscape of grit, beyond the sea's reach.

A short hike along the stair-stepped glacier leads to benches spangled with flowers and further rewards us with a bald eagle's view across the bay and into ranks of mountains. Skee Glacier caps solemn heights deeper in the bay. Aialik is merely one of over 30 named ice-worms that inch down from the vast Harding Ice Field—most rather hotfoot it now in reverse. McCarty Glacier has yielded 15 miles in the last hundred years. "Glacial pace" no longer works as a metaphor. The ice field itself has thinned about 70 feet since Fats Domino sang *Blueberry Hill*. It's difficult nevertheless to imagine this crystalline weight at the peninsula's heart: 700 square miles of ice 3000 feet thick.

On our return to the foot of Aialik, we don't see any berries bluing the heather, but I still find my thrill contemplating the bay full of ice from up high: this one still reaches the sea.

Back at camp, we build a rare fire below the tide line. Half a forest of driftwood lies scattered about, like bones of some Brobdingnagian race, and the evening promises to be cool. Already, winds that daily fall from the two-tone waste at our backs spin glacial rock flour between the tents. Perhaps these flames, despite their pale puniness, will help offset the chill of a flint-skinned hermit coast.

Local trees, though never driftwood, furnished the skeleton of a *qayaq* in an elegant welding of the land and sea's bounties.

Native artisan craftsmen preferred hemlock for the frame, and spruce for the stem, stern, and crosspieces. They knew their materials as well as they knew the sea. Hemlock cracks or breaks easily; spruce is drier, and ribs from it can be bent after steaming. Besides de-hairing and tanning skins that covered many a frame, women gathered and split spruce roots or braided dried kelp, which could replace sinew as the boat's lashings. Several got together and tried to fit the irregular skins "the best they could without waste," and with special waterproof stitches would "sew all the seams together and sit here and chew on the seam, and all the sewing was done with the porpoise [tail] sinew," recalled Bill Hjort, a woodworker and boat builder raised in Chenega. According to the Alutiiq artist and seamstress June Simeonoff Pardue, men often made their own boat covers, because their life depended on them. If their craftsmanship lacked, their seams leaked, they had no one to blame but themselves.

Due to the suppleness of its joints, a *qayaq* could absorb the ocean's thrashing; rather than bounce atop wave crests it slithered over them, a piloted snake. Such boats also were lighter than dugout canoes, and paddlers shouldered them effortlessly to and from the surf zone. Alutiiq woodworkers still fashion kayaker bentwood hats from thin spruce planks. Now largely works of art, these duckbills on steroids once were essential headwear. Like our visors or baseball hats, they kept rain off cured faces and cut the glare from a low sun. Painted with bright geometric designs, sprouting feathers, seal whiskers, or puffin beaks, they not only conveyed status but also hid the hunter's identity from his prey—important when spirits retaliate for breaking any taboo in a maze of so many.

Throughout a night of twilight, we hear the glacier flex in its stone trough; distant skirmishing—cracking rifles, booming cannons—invades our dreams.

On day six, we emerge from our tents into a world of fine rain. The forest has become one dripping grotto. All peaks have been blotted out. On my way to the kitchen for coffee, I run into Josh, his cheeks red as apples, flushed with glee. "Come here," he says. "I have to show you something." One of the kayaks has been moved. A life jacket has been tossed aside and left on the ground. Hatch covers have been smeared with mud. My co-instructor points to the deck, to a paw print with five toe pads. Black bear! Fortunately, all our food still dangles from a rope strung between two trees. "Look at this," Josh says, finally sputtering. My boat's mascot rubber chicken has been decapitated. (It must have been damaged already, extruding a gum bubble—one of its air sacs?—from its behind instead of squawking when you squeezed it.)

"That's not funny," I say. "It was brand new."

Reverence for the kayak stemming from the fact that you entrust your life to it, connects us to the Alutiit on some deeper level. We personalize our polyurethane tubes with hand-painted names and lucky charms; they daubed their boats with red bands, adorned them with trade beads, and tasseled seams with seal whiskers and dyed bits of wool or wove human hair into them. (The meaning of those strands remains obscure. Were they mementos? A fount of protective powers? Animal hair for this decor would have been plentiful but evidently wouldn't do.) They strapped tools of survival onto their decks—seal clubs, bailers, lances, or harpoons, throwing-boards, bone darts, bows, and quivers bristling with arrows—all within easy reach, as crucial as our map cases, compasses, bilge pumps. Like us, they carried spare paddles and patch kits to mend tears in the hull.

After wrestling soaked tents and tarps into our kayak hatches, we enjoy the crossing to Verdant Cove. Sun dispels the clouds, turning the sea a tropical blue and Verdant Island's bulk jungle green, a perfect hideout for mutineers. On the cobble beach, we pull out our wet gear to dry. The scene reminds Josh of a yard sale. "Looks more like a shipwreck," I say.

After we've weighed down our stuff securely with rocks, Josh leads a short hike. The foreshore resembles an old burn site, its silvery trunks stripped of bark, the standing dead cushioned by billowy grass at their feet. Surprisingly, there is not much downed timber around. Ghost forests like this also haunt other parts of Southcentral Alaska's coast, reminding locals of one of the state's most dramatic upheavals, the Good Friday earthquake of March 27, 1964. Lasting less than five minutes, it registered 9.2 on the Richter scale, which at the time made it the second-strongest quake ever recorded. Swaths of destruction spread from the epicenter near Unakwik Inlet, leaving despair and 143 killed. Buildings in Anchorage cracked open like eggshells, spilling out panicked residents; streets buckled before ripping and swallowing cars; a massive underwater landslide sucked the Port Valdez docks into Prince William Sound. Old Chenega, the sound's longest-settled Alutiiq site, ceased to exist when a 27-foot tsunami killed a third of its residents. Until that day, they'd had a good life and a reputation as great sea-mammal hunters. They were "soaked in grease," as their neighbors put it. Here in Aialik, waves from submarine slides surged a hundred feet up the slopes at the bay's head, snapping spruce trees as wide as basketball hoops. Tidal pulses reached even Hawaii and Japan. Earth hiccupped, and tremors rippled worldwide.

When the convulsions stopped, the topography had been rearranged, a repeat of a similar event in 1170 CE. This time, some areas around Kodiak had been pushed up 30 feet. Others, southeast of Anchorage, at the head of Cook Inlet, dropped as much as eight feet. In many places where shorelines subsided, as in Verdant Cove, roots siphoned saltwater from the ocean and trees died soon after. But the brine also preserved them, keeping them upright for these past 40 years.

The drowned forest, however, is not the true destination of our hike, and we continue. Beyond the spiked perimeter, green envelops us in varying jungle shades. Leaf shadows dapple the forest floor, quivering in the breeze. We march silently, following Josh on an overgrown path. The matted decay of the seasons muffles our steps. Barely glimpsed songbirds flit through the canopy. Inside this arbor: the sea's gentle rhythm, like exhaling.

The trees, mostly alder and birch, tangle with berry brambles and mosses. Their girth, from wrist to bicep thickness, indicates second growth. It seems no people ever lingered here; but we've come to a halt in an old clearing—a former village site.

Only when Josh points them out do we notice house pits, shallow depressions in the ground. They once held single-room dwellings roofed with sod and dug in partway to insulate their inhabitants from high winds and wet cold. With little effort, I picture earth mounds doming the homes' sunk living spaces. From one such hillock boils a white cloud, sign of a steambath session. A nude man with a bowl haircut crouched near the roof hatchway takes a breather. Dog barks cut through the glass-bell joy of children at play and through murmurs of working adults. Between racks hung with rosy cod and maroon seal fillets for curing, nets woven from sinew cord stretch, being mended. The view is that of the Cossacks, who walked in on similar scenes.

Josh worked on an excavation here, as part of a joint project that involved students from both Alutiiq villages and the University of Alaska. With input from tribal governments and Native Alaskan corporations, the Smithsonian's Arctic Studies Center designed a unique blend of oral history and archaeology research, combining it with outreach and education. Since the 1880s, no Alutiit have lived on the Kenai Peninsula's outer coast, but elders who foraged there seasonally until the 1950s visited the dig for a taste of the old homelands. One such tradition-bearer, a subsistence hunter and well-known kayak builder, helped to interpret finds at the site and thereby to assess Aialik Bay's ability to support his ancestors.

In the context of Alutiiq sites in the park, which are close to 1,800 years old, Verdant Cove brings the past into sharper focus. Josh remembers that glass trade beads were unearthed here, and a pair of rusty shackles. The Smithsonian's archaeologists dated the settlement to around 1790, when Russian, British, and Spanish vessels made first contact along this coast.

The shackles across centuries darken the day. The Alutiit were pawns in the Russian fur venture, mere tools for acquisition.

Both oral tradition and European written sources attest to Alutiiq headmen or family members kept hostage to coerce villagers into joining the sea otter–hunting fleets. Far from the oversight of imperial officials, *promyshlenniki* brutalized the population and levied tributes payable in pelts. They shanghaied women and men, taking them as far south as Fort Ross, a Russian outpost in California, where the captives tried to survive as company hunters, cooks, workers, or concubines. The Alutiit, in turn, were not averse to bloodshed. They raided (and traded with) Yup'ik, Aleut, and Dena'ina people, taking slaves, or prisoners for ransom.

Overall, though, they got the thick end of the cudgel.

By the mid-1800s, introduced diseases, indentured servitude, and starvation had reduced the Kodiak Islanders from 10,000 to 1,500. The Russians, after landing on Kodiak, repaid an act of Alutiiq resistance with musket and cannon fire. They cut down 300 women, children, and men who had fled to Refuge Rock, connected at low tides to Sitkalidak Island by a spit. "When our people revisited the place in the summer," the Alutiiq elder Arsenti Aminak remembered, "the stench of the corpses lying on the shore polluted the air so badly that none could stay there." The island has been uninhabited ever since.

Despite its tranquility, Verdant Cove speaks of outer-coast dynamics to the attentive visitor; like the reach of an empire, glaciers and earthquakes routinely disrupted landscapes and lives, fracturing the terrain.

There is more to be gleaned from these lonesome pits. Middens at Verdant Cove and other nearby locations include bones from harbor seals, sea lions, porpoises, cod, rockfish, and various seabirds. The Gulf of Alaska's cold, fertile upwelling offered a banquet for those who knew how to set the table. Consequently, on the Kenai coast, archaeological sites mark every place where a kayak can land.

When sails first flocked on Aialik's horizon and trade beads trickled into the villages, the sea and air in the Gulf had cooled significantly. The peak of a period commonly known as the Little

Ice Age (ca. 1250 to 1850 CE) saw glaciers advancing to their most forward positions in recent times. Like earthquakes that dragged down stretches of coast, these glaciers depressed shorelines, even submerging some. Around the same time, epidemics scoured Alutiiq villages, sometimes ahead of the Russians. (Trade goods or middlemen could be carriers of smallpox and other diseases.) New illnesses, cannery jobs, climate change, or a combination of all three may have caused the late 19th-century abandonment of villages on the outer coast that remains so vivid in Alutiiq memory.

Verdant Cove's belt of dead forest provides an eerie flashback but also a warning, a preview of more gradual but no less scary sea level rises from melting ice caps and glaciers. A Bering Strait largely free of ice and thus more storm-prone already saps Shishmaref, forcing its relocation to higher ground. In addition to taking a physical beating, and perhaps more painfully, Alaska's coastal residents are losing faith in the knowledge accumulated through the millennia. As hunters on snowmachines sink through slush into black waters or vanish or get marooned on slivers of ice no longer shorefast, while sea creatures ail or die off, people no longer trust that which nourished them, the element that linked their forebears to landfalls in a new world. One can only hope that, once more, skills and resilience will let Native northerners steer a true course.

Today is a big day. We plan to round Aligo Point, the headland wedged between Aialik and Harris Bay. Because of the raw nature of the outer coast, only half of all OB kayaking courses make it into Northwestern Fjord, a narrow appendix on the far side. For beginners and even intermediate boaters to succeed, conditions need to be nearly perfect. Today they are. We launch early, with Gina leading the way. Chop causes the kayaks to corkscrew, and there is momentary confusion about certain landmarks, but we clear the cape without incident. After paddling up Granite Passage on an incoming tide, we huddle briefly downwind of Granite Island. We are making excellent progress. Fire Cove, Ripple Cove,

Crater Bay, Cataract Cove—each place brims with stories, stories we will not have time to learn on this trip.

Halfway up Harris Bay, combers in the main channel put us on edge. They break on the terminal moraine of Northwestern Glacier, now largely flooded at high tide. These shallows divide the bay from Northwestern Lagoon, barring large vessel traffic. We veer east and camp at Long Beach, where the sea took a bite out of Harris Peninsula, leaving a scimitar beach with sand the color of graphite. Its full sweep is impossible to fit into the frames even of film: white peaks and granite scarps, clouds like Baroque wigs, rivulets leaping from snow fields above hanging gardens, sapphire curlers collapsing exhausted on shore.

The night brings rain, rain, rain, some wind, and more rain. Even our eggs, reconstituted from powder, are soggy this morning. After breakfast, Josh and I string out the students along the beach, widely spaced to ensure privacy for their 24-hour solo, an OB tradition. Time alone with minimal distraction is meant to facilitate clarifying or adjusting goals, while the eremites are confined to small, individual blue-tarp shelters. Because of the bears, they are not allowed to bring food. For many, solo is the most challenging part of a course.

Wind gusts kicking up whitecaps dismantle some of the student setups, but hardship is the currency of every OB trip. The investment almost always pays off. At the very least, this demonstrates why knots should be tied properly and tarps weighed down with driftwood. I hit the sack early, listening to the rain *pitter-patter* on my tent.

While we enact our program's traditions, the first people on this coast seek to revive some of theirs. The comeback of the *qayaq* is a good example. Worried that the lore and construction methods might fade together with Indigenous languages, some elders have been initiating a new generation of boat-builders. They hope to pass on the essence of a seafaring culture, to remind the world and their own children of a proud heritage.

Gregor Welpton, a Juneau shipwright and former commercial fisherman, apprenticed in the time-honored ways of building *qayat*. For Welpton, the conception of a boat's design, as well as its manufacture, constitute deeply spiritual and intuitive acts, ritualistic gestures pleasing the ancestors and the sea. "I hear it in my head," he says, "I feel it through my heart, it comes out through my hands, and the boat is just completely born."

People who have paddled such craft comment not only on their comfort, but also on the boat's translucence, the sensation of merging with their surroundings. Alutiiq elders who rode in a *qayaq*'s belly as children mention the play of light and shadows on the hull and waves lapping like taps on a frame drum. Welpton compares this perfect communion, this best solitude on earth, to "slipping into the planet itself."

The low-pressure system has blown out overnight. Our soloists are happy to regroup, and we treat them to a big breakfast, including an instant-mix cheesecake. Along with a cleansing wind, strong surf has come up. With five-foot breakers thumping the beach, we brief the group on surf launching. A small lagoon in the lee of a spit lets us sit in our kayaks and get prepared before heading out. I lead to demonstrate, synchronizing my strokes with the incoming waves to avoid a drubbing as they barrel down. From the "green zone," a calmer area off shore, I watch Chris and then Brett battling up and over steep seas. The heaving water dwarfs their kayaks, and I realize that the waves have grown too big and threatening.

We dallied too long breaking camp.

Josh signals from shore. He is out of his kayak, looking sheepish and wet. Avoiding the breakers' pull, I paddle close enough to hear him above the commotion and learn that he got caught off guard and flipped—my turn to giggle. He thinks we should abort the launch or at least look for a better place. With paddle signals, he coaches the students already afloat for their approach to the beach. The landings need to be quick and perfectly timed to the sea's rhythm. Brett hesitates to exit and pull up his kayak before the next punch arrives; he gets trapped in the seething backwash, broaches, and swims. Chris and I land smoothly as gulls on a storm-battered crag.

While we scout for another launch site, two sea lions play near shore. They mount the big rollers seemingly without effort and shoot down the opaque wave faces, sleek and shiny torpedoes. We are klutzes in our plastic husks, next to these animals stream-lined by currents and tides. For good measure, a pulmonic *prfff* rises above the waves' crumping. We scan the green zone, where a vaporous blast betrays a humpback whale in the offing. It must be probing the estuary's nutritious outflow, which attracts salmon and smaller fish. We watch it dive shallowly and surface repeatedly, each time with an aerosol puff. Arching its back and waving its fluke in glinting slow motion, it eventually sounds, headed for the open sea.

We find a place farther down the beach to push off the students one by one, timed to the wave sets. Giving the mid-bay shoals a wide berth, we float above forests of bull kelp into quiet Northwestern Lagoon. Fish explode from the water around us; primed by the previous encounter and fooled by the grand scale of things, the mind mistakes their splashing for spouts from the blowholes of distant whales. Waves from our kayaks' bows fracture the light into myriad facets, shattering-mirror forests, glaciers, and fjords. Shedding gravity as if in an out-of-body experience, we levitate through liquid space. Seesawing paddles flash in the sun like helio-graphs that signal *Bliss!* With each stroke, my boat rocks on its keel like a cradle, from starboard to port, and back. Push—pull—glide. Push—pull—glide... I pause for split seconds between strokes to anticipate the water's resistance against my paddle blades and to better enjoy coasting. With my knees braced under the deck, I work my arms and upper body as levers of a machine well oiled. Soon, the rhythm becomes hypnotic, and I enter "the zone," where ego dissolves and, like the sea lions' play, movement is fluid, all-consuming purpose. The kayak has grown into an extension of my body, a means of ecstatic transport.

Not everybody reaches a trancelike state paddling. Our biggest student, Jake, rides in the double, as he has every day, because he feels unbalanced in a single and cramped in its smaller cockpit. Forced to synchronize his strokes as the back-man, he is paying attention to his partner, which takes his mind off capsizing.

Unlike our mass-produced kayaks, *qayat* were built to fit their owner like a buckskin boot does a foot. An Alutiiq hunter spent much of his life in such a boat, borne by and attuned to his environs, a hybrid being, part man and part dolphin. The bond between a man and his vessel even outlasted death. Alutiiq hunters were typically buried with their kayaks, so they could ply the calm waters of afterlife.

The last two days are finals for the students. They get to run the show. It's their turn to demonstrate what they have learned, and Josh and I will intervene only if things become risky. The group wants to explore Northwestern Glacier, recessed deep into the head of the bay. Bleak, bare, imposing, Striation Island guards the access, its granite flanks shot through with the quartzite veins that suggested its name. We look in vain for a place to land for a hike. As recently as the 1950s, the glacier held the island in an icy bracket, but since then it has shrunk, like so many in Alaska and elsewhere. Our captain decides that the forbidding shore is unsafe and changes course. The navigators keep the pod close together and far enough from the fjord's walls to avoid chunks that could carom off a hanging glacier, bombing us. We tack between jumbled facades, from Redstone to Ogive to Anchor, each one resplendent alabaster and azure. At this point we have almost become inured to beauty, suffering sensory overload. Nearly two weeks' worth of scents, sounds, images, thoughts, and conversations swarms in our heads like schools of sparkling smelt. It will take months or longer for the students to fully absorb the experience. On some, it will have little impact. For others, it will be transformative, opening new perspectives, life choices. Some will never comprehend their role in all this. Others will follow invisible wakes and forever remember that the sea shifts in their bodies also.

CHAPTER 13

A DAY ON THE ICE

The scene resembles one of Hendrick Avercamp's 17th-century paintings: Couples on skates hold hands, out of affection or to prop each other up. A pack of feral teenagers that two Labs chase dodges slowpokes. A father picks up his fallen toddler for another go. Hockey players hustle the puck while a grandma pushing her kick sled tries to sneak past them, afraid of getting body-checked. All that's missing from this frost fair are beggars, masked ladies, meat-pie vendors, or a hot grog stand.

This playground, however, is no Golden-Age Dutch canal, no ditch-y *gracht* or frozen river bisecting lowlands. In lieu of church steeples and oaks, 4,000-foot peaks frame the giddy milling-about. The sky is too deep, too blue to be anywhere but in Alaska. Rather than winter carnival, the setting whispers "ice giants" and "yetis," and this rink fits their size. The first time I laid eyes on this lake, popping out onto a ridge thousands of feet above it after a long, timbered summer hike, its color stole my breath.

Sheridan Lake marks the eponymous glacier's meltdown, 14 road miles, plus 10 minutes on a trail, from Cordova. Lacing my skating boots tight while sitting on an outcrop, I can see the blinding, fissured ice tongue descending to woods in the distance. I take a few tentative steps before I find my legs, remembering to push and glide, not to walk. It's like riding a bike. You never forget. But you do: the pain of crashing, the burning.

On this crisp, sunny day on the coast, the danger is wipeout, not whiteout. Breathless already, I wait for my wife, Melissa. Smarter, more cautious, she's witnessed many a train wreck before handing me dry clothes or the first-aid kit.

The first serious cold snap sealed off the lake a few days ago. A snow flurry since merely added an inch of frosting. The surface below is a smooth sheen, except for the odd sandpaper spot, which could stop and launch you from your boots Wile E. Coyote-style; stress lines can foul up things up, too, especially cracks paralleling your course. Bergs big as cabins lie grounded near shore, exhibits in a Dadaist ice-carving competition—though, as with the sky, the color is off. Instead of being transparent, the scalloped blocks glow with the impossible blue of curacao in a cocktail glass. Sapphire light suffuses glazed hollows, and caves deepen to aquamarine farther in. At the bergs' edges, lake ice thins and water is showing.

The clamor of the lake's outlet, ringing hollow like a flooded culvert's, signals open water somewhere close.

"Wild" or multiday "tour skating" in Alaska ranks high among the latest fads sprung from the wish to imbibe nature in innovative, costly ways. It's forest bathing on speed or fast-forward; ice hockey with a backpack, but without the stick and puck. Knee and elbow pads and a helmet are still recommended. So are ice screws, worn on a cord around the neck, for pulling yourself out of a cold inkwell if you break through. The wild-skating window, frustratingly brief, opens when serious freezes seal off lakes, lagoons, coastlines, and rivers and shuts once "termination dust" buries them. It may reopen during a midwinter melt. Devotees study satellite updates as the faithful do scripture, to pinpoint the marvelous transformation.

Few of these athletes on the sport's cutting edge realize they are not pioneers. A Dawson storeowner in the winter of 1900 rode a bike down the Yukon and up the coast into Nome, drawn by a new case of "yellow fever." (Not an outlier, but rather one spoke in a wheels-to-fortune migration, in the "Tour de Chance" previously mentioned, he pumped iron on standard tires and carved replacement pedals from wood—take that, you fatbikers.) Zipping full-tilt over glare ice, he passed a huge Norwegian who had skated right into an overflow, water that pools on top of ice and there sometimes freezes. The most famous of early Alaskan blade runners, "The Flying Dutchman" was really a Prussian: Carl von Knobelsdorff. Before leaving Nome for San Francisco in 1899, this uprooted Junker serviced camps mushrooming alongside the Kobuk River, inland from Kotzebue Sound, where a phony gold rush played out. He delivered newspapers and letters for one dollar each. Rumors and gossip he conveyed for free. One of his mail stops was Reilly Wreck, where the steamer *John Reilly* had struck a gravel bar and was stranded for the winter. Miners not quite living *The Life of Reilly* died from scurvy or "black leg" and overwork, drowned, or went missing. Some visited neighbor friends by skating on dulled whipsaw blades cut, chiseled, and filed to an edge. "I think I have traveled nearly eight hundred miles on my skates since I came here," one of them wrote. Army soldiers in uniform at Nome's Fort Davis in 1902 fell for this leisure trend.

A sepia photo shows Knobelsdorff, Blackbeard in checkered knee socks, a wool cap, sweater, and mitts, a pack with sleeping roll on his back, pistol and hunting knife on his belt. Neither snow nor rain nor gloom of night nor weak ice stayed this courier. The Germanic Hermes swung a metal-tipped pole for propulsion and balance and spread word about Nome's recent riches among the bipedal moles. At San Francisco, after giving some lectures, he disappeared into the white noise of history. His fellow stampeder Joseph Grinnell, an ornithologist who'd met John Muir on a cruise ship and would help establish Yosemite National Park, called the sailing mailman a "rustler" with "more grit than all the rest of the men on the Kowak [Kobuk]."

The only grit currently on my mind is grist from Sheridan's glacier mill, the kind that could cause me to tumble.

I dart through a narrows berg's flank, my blades now scraping, now rumbling, now crunching crystals underfoot. The ice chirps and pings with tension, as it does when it's young. On straight, wide stretches, I become weightless. I extend the glide phase on one leg before pushing off with the other. It's as close to flying as earthbound creatures without drugs can come, the fastest humans can run, a sensation akin to that of loping a horse at more than twice the top speed of Jamaican sprinter Usain Bolt. (The skating record holder, naturally, is a Dutchman.) For

Henry David Thoreau, an enthusiastic wild-skater on Concord's marshes, rivers, and ponds, "swift shoes" were "annihilators of distance." A lighter, more playful side came to the fore as soon as he cut loose and, in a tailwind, his coattails became bird wings. "A man feels like a new creature, a deer, perhaps, moving at this rate," he confided in his journal. Once, my strokes on another frozen lake answered to those of a pair of bald eagles passing overhead. In the winter of 1855, Thoreau skated 30 miles on one grand day, and on a different day, in a snowstorm. Aware of the danger of hitting open water, he could sail on a tack pretty well by adjusting the trim with his frock. Perhaps that is where he first found transcendence.

Even with thick ice, soaring above the abyss has an aspect of cheating death, of glimpsing an afterlife. Where snow is absent, veils of deep fracture seams hang arrested mid-flutter, white against black. "Looks like sea monsters down there," a kid on all fours told me once. "Is there enough room for the fish to swim?" a tot kept upright by a folding chair asked her mom. Ice can be a mirror of people's concerns.

And skating withdrawal may lead to grief and eroded identities. For the first time in over five decades, one of the world's longest ice rinks, Ottawa's Rideau Canal Skateway, remained closed for the season. Increased insulating snowfall and spiking temperatures were the culprits. For one man who'd pushed on "pristine glass" into the sunrise there, now it seemed "a part of winter is missing." Until this year, five skateable miles in the heart of the capital daily delighted thousands: tourists, racers in a triathlon, and commuters to school and work. As in the Dutch merrymaking of yore, skaters stopped at kiosks for fuel, in this case, frybread shaped like a beaver tail, and *poutine*—french fries and cheese curds topped with brown gravy. A "slush cannon" the city is currently testing helps the ice form, while "snowbots" sweep it in its formative stage. "We thought your frozen heart was there forever," an ex-journalist wrote, mourning his gutted hometown. "We were wrong."

Thin ice and old injuries have long been forgotten. Stepping like a classic speed skater with my feet crossing over, my center of gravity low, in an ape stance, leaning into the turns, and alternately swinging my arms like pendulums, I build momentum. The calligraphy of our sequined tracks spells pure joy. By now traffic has thinned. So have our shadows, which wax into the afternoon. In the past hour, we've passed only one other couple.

Taking a break with our skates on, we bank sunbeams and warmth and vitamin D, much needed, against the months to come. We sip hot chai from the thermos, passing the cup back and forth. Quiet reigns absolute. There's no sign of life besides us. A ringing fills my head, barely audible. It's the acoustic counterpart to the fugue of cobalt and white, the Delft-tile landscape enfolding us. The sun, now two hand-widths above the tree line, etches each snow crystal into relief; flowing and hatchet-mark grooves from our skates cast their own shadows. The glacier's terminus beckons from afar. Toes have gone numb and the hour is late, so we turn around.

Back at the outcrop, unlacing my boots where we left our town shoes, I am reminded that there is always a price to pay. Feeling returns to my imprisoned digits, and with it the pains of dungeon torture. I limp to the truck as if broken on the wheel, a geezer on needles and pins already dreading tomorrow's soreness in muscles I nowadays seldom flex. I comfort myself thinking that Sheridan is a top destination, on par with St. Moritz or Aspen, but even better, because we can arrive here after breakfast and be home before dinner. And we don't have to share it with multitudes.

CHAPTER 14

BERRY-PICKERS AND EARTHMOVERS

kneel on the slope below Newton Peak, four miles outside of Nome, where Melissa got a job as a public health nurse. With one hand cupped in berry bushes, I receive the land's gifts.

Sunshine massages my shoulders, while the spice of crushed Labrador tea rises from the warm tundra. Blueberry leaves tinged like claret; orange dwarf birch; and bearberry, crimson as freshly spilled blood, mingle in fall's luscious quilt. I strip berries from twigs, delicately, letting them roll into my palm before placing handfuls into a yogurt container. This late in the season, their flesh bursts easily, staining my fingertips purple. The fruits' signature hue, a pale, dusty indigo rarely encountered in nature, surprises and then reels you in; their scattershot growth pulls you farther and farther as hours slip away unnoticed.

I've lost sight of Melissa, lower down on the slope. Though meticulous, a "clean picker" who minimizes chaff in her pails, she leaves some fruit on each bush for the plants' propagation and the animals.

Lulled by the meditative activity, I pop a few berries into my mouth, where tartness explodes like insight between my tongue and palate. Most blueberries sold in stores pale in comparison; bloated and engineered into blandness, they betray an obsession with quantity, disregard for season and place. One Fairbanks friend crushes such cultivars to dye skeins of wool, which hard-core gourmets consider the only use for them.

Not a good berry year, this one—few sunny days in the past months. My bucket fills very slowly. People have flown up from Anchorage, because throughout Southcentral Alaska caterpillars have been shredding berry bushes. More than usual, information about productive patches has been guarded like insider-trading tips, shared only with friends. Blueberries are selling for 20 dollars a quart through our town's online exchange network, often to locals too busy or impatient to pick. Regardless of the shortage, I shun berry combs, the "bear claw" gadgets, knuckle rings made from plastic and steel, because they bruise berries and branches and collect much debris. They prevent handling the plump velvety spheres that hold trace warmth from the sun, and their efficiency strikes me as semi-industrial, inappropriate. Berry picking appeals to me for its humbling pace, its quiet thrift. It requires no fancy implements—no fishing poles, four-wheelers, high-powered rifles, or outboard motors—and no logistics or permits, just an old bucket and a strong back.

Two miles from here, four Cold War "White Alice" parabolic antennas crown Anvil Mountain, Mordor-type towers in the network formerly spying on the fiend to the west. Diesel-powered, nerved with miles of wiring and cable, it and 70 other installations throughout Alaska aimed at preventing Armageddon. The citizenry voted to preserve their beloved "Nomehenge" of antennas—"the last ones standing"—which were slated to be demolished. Sheathing on the back of the five-story-tall billowing sails contained lead paint and asbestos, and the Air Force, during Operation Clean Sweep, shipped over eight million pounds of contaminated top soil for treatment to Oregon—but some berry-pickers still will not harvest near the druidic assemblage that cups peachy light late on sunny days.

"Will your shields bedarken me?" the Inupiaq poet Joan Naviyuk Kane asked in "White Alice Changes Hands," composed apropos of the site's eleven acres reverting to Nome's Sitnasuak Native Corporation.

In 1958, one year before statehood and one year after Western Electric built Nome's "billboard" antennas, the Atomic Energy Commission hatched a scheme that makes the White Alice landscaping appear as child's play in the sandbox. It proposed the excavation of a coal-shipping harbor at Cape Thompson, 250 miles to the north, with a near-surface chain of six hydrogen bombs. Beating some post-World War II swords into plowshares, some spears into pruning hooks, the government's "Firecracker Boys" considered geographical engineering, the remolding of "a slightly flawed planet." Elsewhere, "peaceful" titanic technology was to fast-track fracking, reroute ocean currents, turn the Mediterranean Sea into a freshwater reservoir, or gouge a second, Israeli-controlled Suez Canal.

The economic and military benefits of this Project Chariot—a port designed to faze the Soviets—were dubious. Still, touring Alaska, the "Father of the H-Bomb," Edward Teller, who'd suggested nuking the moon with the harnessed sun "to observe what kind of disturbance it might cause," hawked it as a windfall. The *Fairbanks News-Miner* called Chariot "a fitting overture to the new era" dawning for the 49th state. His was really a sales pitch to convince other countries that this was efficient and safe.

Alaskan conservationists, Point Hope Inupiaq caribou hunters and whalers, Russia, The Wilderness Society and the Sierra Club, plus three contract biologists researching the likely impacts objected. The ex-bronc rider and Korean War vet Peter LaFarge's song "Radioactive Eskimo" on air rallied support:

> My wife can't suckle our babies,
> The milk must come from cans.
> My wife's too radioactive,
> Say, we're real atom fans.

Fallout from can-do-will-do attitudes—nuclear testing on the Aleutians' Amchitka Island and Novaya Zemlya poisoned lichen and, via reindeer, blossomed in humans and wolves, as it would again, decades later, after a meltdown in Chernobyl. Like one-third of the Nevada detonations, Amchitka's *Long Shot* sowed death when on October 29, 1965, the equivalent of 800 train-car loads of TNT flash-bloated half a mile underground. The military wanted to know how nuclear seismic signatures differed from those of earthquakes, to monitor the Soviet side of this arms race. Earth's crust split, lake levels dropped, mud geysered, and rocks cratered dirt two miles away. Krypton and tritium escaped.

Governor William J. Egan, worried Alaskans still shaken by the 1964 Good Friday quake might get spooked, had been reassured and was "pleased that we have been selected as the hosts, so to speak…"

Milrow, sparked during massive anti-Vietnam marches, sought to gage risks of an even bigger device, as domino-style tremors unleashing tsunamis were feared. It domed tundra two miles around 16 feet high, frothing the adjacent sea.

The last of this unholy Trinity, 1971's *Cannikin*, despite international outcry, a legal attempt at defusing it, and protests of a fledgling Environmental Protection Agency, became history's largest US subterranean nuclear test. Outgunning Hiroshima's *Little Boy* by a factor of 385, it registered 7.0 on the Richter scale, with 4.0 aftershocks. (The 1964 natural spasm had managed a record, traumatizing 9.2.) *Cannikin*'s pressure pulse crushed sea-otter heads, snapped bird spines, and ruptured fish air bladders and seal lungs. A creek vanished, drained into an aquifer, now polluted. AEC chief James Schlesinger, watching man's wrath with his family, thought it "fun for the kids."

How do our feelings about such destruction stack up against those of Alutiiq hunters who slaughtered sea otters under pressure to keep their loved ones alive?

Some Alaska Devil's dust was scattered at Cape Thompson to measure how it moved in groundwater and runoff. Ecological and technical concerns ultimately doomed the Ploughshare program. Funding evaporated; plans to pulverize caribou pastures fizzled. Chariot closed shop in 1962, the year Rachel Carson's *Silent Spring* revealed the creep of toxins up food chains. Point Hope–area Inupiat suffered beyond-average stomach and throat cancer casualties. Diesel-soaked soil and infrastructure debris was removed from the headland, but shallowly buried radioactive waste, ruled harmless, remains.

Far out, afloat on sheet-metal glare, dredges like barges sift ancient beaches, submerged when ice sheets melted and the sea repossessed land at the end of the Pleistocene. Belches and growls from heavy machinery waft up with an onshore breeze. A belt of scars girdles foothills below, outlining a much older interglacial beach and stream gravel rich in placer gold buried beneath glacial till. Earthmovers and caterpillars are scraping the lucrative layers, throwing up molehills of human industry. Dwarfing all present-day efforts here, long-necked, turn-of-the-century dredges wallow in marsh ponds like doomed coal-powered brontosauruses. Ancestors of even more monstrous bucket-wheel excavators elsewhere engaged in strip-mining, they bit frozen ground with iron teeth and shat tailings out at the back. A photo from 1904, of the tellingly named Miocene Ditch Company's operation at Glacier Creek, reveals the scope of destruction. A jet from a high-powered hydraulic water cannon blasting away the creek bank washes debris into the bottom of the pit, misting worker ants in the impact zone. The men seem redundant, an afterthought, just placed into this scene for scale. A similar shot from there is captioned "The 'Giants' at Play."

There is gold in them thar hills, but some of them hills are no longer thar.

By comparison, the local semi-nomadic hunter-gatherers, Inupiat and their Thule predecessors, traveling light, carried technology largely in their heads, in the form of skills acquired over the centuries. They fashioned tools as needed from local resources. The land provided wood, stone, bone, antler, and animal skins, if you knew where to look. Where wood was scarce, frozen fish wrapped in skins became sled runners, coated with moss to lessen friction or with an ice glaze from snow melted in the mouth, dribbled onto the runners. When missionaries turned them into herders, the Inupiat jerry-rigged fences of burlap, willows, or lake-ice slabs, behind which they corralled reindeer on the tundra. In the woodlands, Athabaskans could defy winter with nothing but an ax—building lean-tos, cabins, and deadfall traps, carving up game they trapped (including black bears), opening fishing holes, sparking life-saving fires, and probably even whittling toothpicks and dainty tobacco pipes.

Folly and felony as much as grandiosity tainted Nome's founding myth. A *Wild Wild West* steampunk gizmo on barrel wheels the miners designed to ease into shallows and plough and lift sandy seafloor was too heavy to move. A grander, more hare-brained plan yet proposed building a casino with a theater, hotel, saloon, and dance pavilions on the sea ice, a marine league from shore so as to bypass gambling laws. Burglars "mining the miners," meanwhile, slashed tent walls, pumping in chloroform and robbing their marks the moment they fainted. People stole entire camps and moved houses while the owners were out prospecting. From the perspective of arrivals anchored in Norton Sound, the foreshore's low ridges appeared littered with icebergs—the miners' white canvas wall tents. Along this cluttered waterfront stretched the "Poor Man's Diggings," called that because on the public beaches no man—or woman—had to stake or register claims. No permafrost ground had to be thawed out there, either. Green-horns broiled in the sun or, shivering under blankets, hugged the dirt. Some, not eating regularly, improvised huts with packing crates or boats flipped onto their sides. Latecomers marveled at damsels in flowerpot bonnets and ankle-length skirts over petticoat layers, feeding rockers and sluices with shovels of muck. Along the 30-mile beachhead, a US government official reported, "double ranks of men were rocking, almost shoulder to shoulder…passing jokes or singing as they worked." On slow days at his saloon, Wyatt Earp walked the cratered shore, plinking whisky bottles he threw in the air. Instead of streets paved with gold, five-year-old Klondy Nelson, joining her father (a Klondiker) on Ophir Creek, saw "an ugly blanket of soft-coal smoke hanging low over everything." Steadman Avenue ran the width of four men abreast between boardwalks, the only street with such luxury. Front Street, a dust bowl in the summer, became a "slough of despond" in the fall, swallowing wagons up to their axles and mules to their bellies.

Grifters and rumrunners connived to cheat the Inupiaq reindeer herder Changunak Antisarlook Andrewuk out of her wealth. They threatened and sued the imposing, curly-haired woman, harassed her animals, scattering them, and shot some they left rotting on the tundra. Desperados staked lots inside grazing ranges. They torched vegetation to clear the ground, thereby destroying forage, and, having eaten or scared off all game, rustled the antlered cattle.

Today's starry-eyed visitor imagines the town's rowdier, acclaimed days. Rudyard Kipling's lines, "For there's never a law of God or man / Runs north of Fifty-three" served Jack London as an epigraph to a tale set in this city where no tree could be found for a lynching.

For nearly a century, until 1998, when a miner in Ruby struck it rich, this crude circus wowed the world with Alaska's nugget record, a veined quartz chunk from Anvil Creek's No. 5 Bench, whose gold weighed as much as a classic cast-iron pan. To Jan Kralik, born in communist Czechoslovakia, dreams of a Bountiful West became reality four years after the Ruby find. While he was dousing on his claim northwest of Nome, the brass rods in his hands abruptly pointed at pay dirt. A slug fitting his palm unearthed the following spring was worth $25,000. The less arcanely gifted and those loath to muck, scrabble, and moil scan tailings with metal detectors instead.

Despite its scars and sores, Nome by far ranks as the most interesting of all my hometowns, for its eccentricity and star-studded past. I write more often about it than I do about Fairbanks. It once was the Tombstone of the North, with more peaceful Inupiat in place of Chiricahua Apaches. A city of 4,000 with a provisional feel, it keeps mesmerizing dreamers, schemers, misfits, and tinkerers. You may answer a knock on your door to find a neighbor in long johns (me), locked out of his home at 40 below, or discover the banging under your floor is the plumber who finally showed up unannounced to thaw out the pipes. People call a cab for a distance of three big-city blocks from their home to the only coffee bar in town (I hesitate to call it a "café") for an iced 24-ounce mochaccino. Or drive two hours just to see trees that look as if they're in pain. Ousting browned Christmas runts to the floe in January, celebrants plant a "Nome National Forest." In March, for the time being, while the ocean still freezes, they host the Bering Sea Ice Golf Classic, with bright-orange golf balls for visibility, though that fundraiser is a tad touristy.

Wildlife has a way of reclaiming turf in this town that can be charming. A nurse I knew, who scoffed when she heard that Alaska Natives had owned this continent for at least twelve millennia—Earth is only less than half as old after all—confronted a clerk at "AC," the Alaska Commercial Company. "Sir, you got rats in your store. I saw one running around," this public health worker said, appalled by the apparent lack of hygiene. "Ma'am," the man responded unfazed, almost proud, "that's an ermine." (That rat thing again. What is it with people?) Muskoxen, never distant, were plentiful. And in the AC parking lot you might meet Velvet Eyes, a pet reindeer, in the bed of a pickup truck doing errands with her owner. He said she loves blueberry pancakes.

Curbside dredge buckets planted with flowers passed for beautification there, and the world's largest gold pan, across from the Methodist church, resembled a UFO driven partway into the balding lawn. This burg was a lot like Cicely, the setting of *Northern Exposure*, only less photogenic, much rougher around the edges. It was as real as Alaska gets, a cocktail of quaintness and queasiness. At low tide, swigging oblivion from brown paper bags, the uprooted stood around driftwood fires behind the revetment where, despite the dike's granite boulders, the sea tries to steal the shore. Up-valley from wind turbines that flash with each revolution, some bright satanic mill disemboweled Mount Brynteson. With the economy's nosedive, the gold price had reached an all-time high, renewing the frenzy: a blueberry-size nugget was worth 1,200 dollars.

Before I discovered the town's substrate of berry bonanzas, culture, and history, I found the liquor too expensive, the missionaries too many, the constant wind too atrocious to like it much. We briefly lived on Lomen Avenue, where from a bay-window seat, feeling like a lighthouse keeper or ship's captain on his bridge, I watched 2011's "blizzicane" spit sea foam onto the street. A different kind of earthmover, that fall it tore off roofs and took bites out of the Nome–Council Road. It struck 43 communities. A storm in 2022 was even worse, I hear. Another rocked an earlier residence raised above the permafrost in the Icy View sub-division—its gusts made the toilet bowl hiccup. The Bering Strait, now freezing later, and added moisture in the atmosphere increase the likelihood of such events in western Alaska. And with brutal winters, repairs often must wait until spring.

Our house on Lomen was a block up the street from the Discovery Saloon, built in 1901, two years after Wyatt Earp's Dexter. The only false-fronted structure to weather fires and floods that repeatedly ravaged the town, the former palace of vice squatted sadly, disguised by aluminum siding and demoted to a private residence.

Fortunes made, fortunes missed, lives spent pawing the ground, and a few miners breaking even. Stuffy and dark as fox dens, the bars along Front Street stayed busy, as did Nome's only bank, handing out berry buckets with its logo as if promoting frugality. The payback as well as the scale of extraction differed, but diggers and pickers like Melissa and I equally fed a hankering, not a need. For her, the rattling of first berries in an empty yogurt container is a "sad sound"; happiness is a silent, short berry-drop. Secretive and territorial, we moved on when yields no longer warranted the effort. Quitting was hard. As the year tilted into winter, the berries turned mushy; earth and sea hardened to human intrusion, frost and ice put our ambition on hold.

Typically seen as women's business, berry picking lacks the excitement of prospecting or of killing a moose, except when blundering into a grizzly with a sweet tooth in your chosen patch. Berry size simply does not matter as much as nugget or rack size. As a rule, swamps, rivers, and mountain ranges need not be crossed chasing fruit. No guts, no glory. Not bringing home bacon. Men stalk—women stoop. Men navigate keenly aware of cardinal directions and distances, while women excel at locating landmarks. Surprisingly, in some hunter-gatherer societies, plants that women collect contribute most of the calories and prove more reliable than migratory big game. Notwithstanding evidence of women warriors and huntresses, the mental maps of both foraging sexes revealed different spheres. Weighed down with toddlers, women knew smaller, nearer places more intimately. Men, unencumbered, perhaps rushed to return while also using dead reckoning or "path integration"—a homing vector they compute by keeping track of distances and cardinal directions—excelled at memorizing long-range trails and trade routes, but with fewer details. Let us be clear: these are not biological givens but the results of culture-specific socialization.

It is tempting, from this perspective, to contemplate current domestic dynamics, attitudes toward the settled and the unsettled (or the unsettling), the bird in the hand and the birds in the bush. Melissa, for instance, loved combing the outskirts, looking for muskox wool, mushrooms, or chips of opaque beach glass from Earp's days, turquoise and cobalt, the kinds of hues no longer produced. Although she is an expedition boater and hiker, evening strolls through the neighborhood suited her just fine. She will pore for hours over seed and yarn catalogues. Not the homebuilder or handyman type, I've bunked in barracks, tents, monasteries, a guest ranch, log cabin, sauna, storage unit, stick lean-to, garage, various trailers, rock alcoves, the belly of a ferry, a houseboat on dry land, a survivalist's underground desert bunker, and a blue-tarp Tootsie Roll on the banks of the Rio Grande, all furnished minimally or not at all. Only half-joking, Melissa accuses me of ADD and of having become jaded about small things in nature, such as bird songs, snowflakes, or scents. It is true; I did inherit the restlessness gene, possibly from a great-grand uncle who sold the farm and joined a traveling circus. This, too, fits a gendered pattern: men less often than women return to places previously visited, like those berry patches. I crave a fresh view, forever following rivers, and piecing together new backpacking itineraries —big-picture stuff. Even the flat prospect of a topo map tickles me. Luckily, the rewards of wild fruit, culinary and otherwise sensory, prompt me to value the tangible and nearby, not just the abstract, faraway.

Back home, I carefully rinsed leaf litter from my loot before freezing the berries in Ziplocs. (Better yet, let them gently roll down a towel slide to catch crud, the same principle as that behind the miner's sluice box.) The local Inupiat stored their berries in skins ballooning with seal oil, avoiding spoilage and scurvy. Our stash likewise provided precious vitamins where produce, flown in, was expensive. In the bleak pit of December, when snow buried porches and winds moaned like errant souls, our berry-inked lips mocked hypothermia.

Cocooned in our kitchen, we relished summer's dense flavors, memories of the lush life, nuggets of wellness. We folded them into muffin, pancake and banana-bread batter, filled jam jars and piecrusts, or spooned them directly from a bag as a substitute for sorbet and lost daylight. Firmer than blueberries, cranberries store really well. Before the age of refrigerators, Kobuk River Inupiat dug pits they lined with moss and filled with berries before covering them with another moss layer and soil for caches of antiscorbutic. As barrels full of berries froze, one elder remembers, the ice crystals expanded and juice pearled from the seams and congealed like purple candle wax, interest on savings. These concentrate bumps she picked off and ate, and, "They tasted so good, but sometimes they were kind of strong."

Local blueberries, low-bush cranberries, and salmonberries (a paler raspberry) add sweetness to *akutuq*, "mix them together" or "Eskimo ice cream," the Arctic equivalent of Proust's *madeleines*. The cook beats caribou or bear fat and/or seal oil or bone tallow, or nowadays Crisco shortening and sugar, with optional whitefish eggs or flaked fish and the fruits, whipping the mix into a fluff silky as buttercream. Formerly, frozen and cut into bars, it provided high-energy pemmican travel rations. (Dr. Frederick Cook, the Denali sham-mountaineer, carried *akutaq,* and he certainly could not blame it for failing to reach the North Pole.) On a photo from pre-1930 reindeer heydays, three Inupiaq women with chin-stripe tattoos, burdened with full pails and buckets, face the camera next to two teens. It bears the same watermark as the "Giants" Glacier Creek image, of a Nome studio four brothers owned. Their corporation, which also held various stores and a newspaper—the *Nome Daily Gold Digger*—streamlined the region's herding, crossbreeding reindeer and caribou and shipping venison to the Lower 48, touting "America's New Health Meat" with Santa sleighs parading and Dasher, Dancer, Prancer, et al. tended by fur-clad "Eskimo helpers." (Rudolph had not yet been conceived.) He approached railroads and large New York hotels, asking them to put reindeer steaks on their menus. Photos of Inupiaq teamsters, of youths straddling reindeer, and of women in piebald reindeer-skin parkas helped to sell meat, along with the fiction that herding benefitted all Alaskans equally. Eventually, the Lomens, controlling the best grazing grounds, charged Indigenous herders a user fee and collected a fee for each Inupiaq reindeer that got mixed up with their stock. The Inupiat, many of whom were in debt to the company's stores, had no stateside connections, and no funds to build slaughterhouses or large underground cold storages—natural freezers that took advantage of the permafrost. Neither had they a warehouse, scows, barges, fishing vessels, or a gas screw-powered schooner for sending their prime cuts south.

The Lomen studio sold photos as postcards and to newspapers and scientific publications, and, with the berry-pickers' portrait and other E.S. Curtis-style pictures, may have tried to cash in on local color and the territory's new popularity. The Inupiaq women's smiles and frank gazes bridge a century; they clearly are happy with the day's harvest. One wonders if they were asked permission to have their likenesses taken. Lomen & Co. images featured bare-chested Siberian Yup'ik girls too, and one, a mother nursing two infants.

Nome's berry-pickers remain committed as ever. A 90-year-old Inupiaq woman proclaimed that she would never forsake Alaska for the Lower 48. She'd just visited Utah and found it crucially lacking. "They have no wild berries," she said, "only useless flowers."

Berry picking can be many things to many people: livelihood, recreation, fresh-air therapy, pause for reflection, or displacement activity, and sometimes, act of resistance. I distinctly remember a field trip with a Russian ethnographer, a dead ringer for Yul Brynner, to an Inupiaq village up the coast. He was grilling some grandmother in her single-room cabin, who had dressed in her best *kuspuk*, about his pet theory: the existence of Eskimo clans before first contact with Anglo-Americans. Repeatedly, patiently, she denied ever having heard of such kin groups. When the researcher persisted, her gaze strayed out the window. "It's such a nice day," she said sweetly. "I think I'm going to look for berries."

On one year's last fishing trip to Council, the place with the trees, I met Cassie Walker. An Inupiaq elder with silver pageboy hair, she suffered the piebald skin typical of vitiligo, a strange echo of the worn-out, ragged salmon thrashing in the river's pools. She was born there, in a cabin above the Niukluk, during the Great Depression. As her mind peopled the near–ghost town with spirits, she pointed out who used to live where. Many of her parents' generation perished from ills dogging vagrant fortune seekers everywhere: the newcomers introduced God, entrepreneurship, booze, and diseases. But berries kept bluing, in good as in bad years. In 1959, after boarding school in Sitka, Cassie moved to San Francisco, where she still lived. Now, perhaps for the last time, the old woman had come to this river to claim days long gone and the berries that mark vital ground.

CHAPTER 15

GOSSAMER GOLD

I step from the tundra into an alder thicket like a blind man off a curb into rush hour traffic. Although it is quiet in here, except for the vibes of mosquitos, my hackles rise. *Was that a branch snapping up ahead?*

In summery Nome, when the ocean's horizon blushes with midnight sun and shadows grow long and lean, this is one place you don't want to be—dense brush, where grizzly bears feed or nap and don't like being surprised. Unfortunately, this is where Nome's other gold, muskox underwool, too can be found. To relieve their June itch, shucking their shag to prevent overheating, muskoxen take to the bushes, where branches and trunks strip them of their winter insulation. The dark humps you glimpse now and again in the clearings can belong to one or the other kind of bruiser.

"I never was more astray in my preconcept of any animal," the naturalist Ernest Thompson Seton wrote about the first muskox he encountered, "for I had expected to see something like a large brown sheep." Thinking it looked "very much like an ordinary Buffalo," he undersold its uniqueness. With their own genus, undoubtedly bullish in appearance, muskoxen are closer related to sheep and goats. The scientific name gets it right: "musky-smelling sheep-ox." Its filigree fleece, *qiviut*, is eight times warmer than sheep's wool, keeping muskoxen cozy at 50 below. The name is also an Inupiaq word for waterfowl down, and in the 1960s a Vermont agricultural cooperative working with the University of Alaska got it registered as a trademark, to benefit Native craftswomen when an advertising firm was planning to use it for a synthetic yarn. In 1954, an Arctic ecologist had established the Institute of Northern Agricultural Research, and in the largest (and perhaps only) domestication experiment of modern times, endeavored to capture, tame, and breed muskoxen. He hoped their *qiviut* would benefit Alaska Native communities struggling to adapt to a cash economy. Today, with wild populations in decline, it is hoped *qiviut* from one Alaska nonprofit venture will find lucrative markets and perhaps inspire commercial breeding. The Musk Ox Farm in Palmer, just north of Anchorage, sets trends among the world's few muskox farms (including the Fairbanks Large Animal Research Station) with a total number of several hundred captive animals. Each May, in the shedding season, Palmer farm staff usher their animals into stalls, where they comb them for the underfur. They sell this *qiviut* in the farm gift shop to tourists, online, and wholesale to Oomingmak, a co-op whose owner-operators, Western Alaska Native women (and two men), process the fiber into yarn they then knit into high-end goods. Stoles in the Nelson Island Diamond Pattern borrow from a design on traditional Yup'ik parka trim. Nunivak Islanders developed their signature pattern based on a 1,200-year-old ivory harpoon head. Unalakleet contributes Wolverine Mask, while mukluk beadwork and woven grass baskets inspired other village-specific motifs. "My knitting is being bought by people from all over the place, and that makes me want to knit more," Katherine Charles, who grew up in Newtok, in the Yukon-Kuskokwim region, told the author of a book about *qiviut*.

Ranging from vanilla to beige, smoke-gray, and chocolate-brown, this "cashmere of the north," lustrous and soft as baby's breath, sells in stores for hard cash, a hundred dollars per spun ounce. As wearable art, smoke rings, cowls, hats, scarves, headbands, and shawls with their aura of fuzz bear even higher price tags. *Qiviut* does not keep a shape well enough to be made into sweaters. It's more of a feminine fiber, fit for lacy designs, I am told.

Wet feet or bug bites in the wilds are a small toll to pay for such riches. As browsers, muskoxen seek thickets that clog creek beds and ditches, dells into which melting permafrost drains; as suckers of warm life juice, mosquitos seek the same windless spots on their sorties.

My forager genes propel me along a trail of dung pellets and crushed vegetation, but I stay alert for surprises. Silky hunks and skeins snagged on branches are pennants leading up to the mother lode: a foot-wide mop, like a badly made wig. I am alert, fully alive, in tune with my inner predator. Yet with all the adrenaline coursing, this is still not considered a "masculine" pastime here. Real men go out and *shoot* the beast with the gladiator physique. I hear it's as challenging as dynamiting fish in a barrel. The firearms Yankee whalers introduced at the end of the 19th century quickly extinguished muskoxen in Alaska's Arctic. They just let you walk up close, and if they feel threatened, form a bulwark of curved, embossed horns in front of their calves. Marksmen were able to drop them one by one with the rest watching, like Plains bison, which, in Yellowstone, I'm glad to hear, are finally fighting back. Several muskox herds have hung around Nome in recent summers, wildlife officials say, to avoid bears. Hiding among us, as it were, as hunting them close to town is illegal. They rest and digest, or play King of the Hill on a vacant lot across from AC. (When they're not there, kids on dirt bikes practice bunny hops and wheelie skills or try to catch major air.) Wool gathered on that mound is no good though; it's dusty and matted like dreadlocks, trampled, run over by knobby rubber. It would be much easier to post an ad at our online exchange site, Nome Announce, or the grocery store, and buy a whole hide from a hunter. Then my wife or I, raking it, could separate *qiviut* from the unwanted coarse guard hair.

Melissa, my "wife"—I'm still not used to calling her that. We got married recently after grabbing a witness at the post office, in a bare-bones ceremony overseen by a walrus whose mounted skull hung on a wall in the courthouse. Like the tusks, our two lives henceforth would run parallel, tapering to their final points. We had met through the Internet, on a slicker version of *Alaska Men*, and our first date, you guessed it, had been a multi-day backcountry trip. This fiber scrounging is for her, really. She is a wildcrafter, converting the land's bounty into various products.

Increasingly popular in the Pacific Northwest, where ecosystems are generous, and in rural Alaska, where supply lines always have been frail, wildcrafting is fashionable once again, a bookend to subsistence hunting or paleo diets. On our windowsill sit Mason jars with dark, alchemic fluids, homemade lichen dyes for this kind of wool. Melissa has an Inupiaq woman friend, a healer with whom she picks stinkweed and arnica for cosmetics and ointments. One-gallon Ziplocs are taxing our freezer, berries preserved for pies, sauces, and jams. Driving through town, my wife takes mental notes on muskoxen hangouts to track them the minute she gets off work; we've already missed this year's salmon run. Competition is stiff. Wildcrafters always watch for cars parked on dirt roads. My wife has become a raw-material rubbernecker. Once, she pulled over on the shoulder of one of Nome's three gravel highways, and a deranged driver yelled at her—and she's normally not the inconveniencing type. She taught herself spinning with a hand spindle.

My spouse, clearly, is hardwired for gathering, whereas I lack any desire to hunt. But I cannot escape the "something for nothing" mindset, and being in nature brings its own rewards. A bird's nest cushioned with *qiviut*. White-headed ptarmigan flashing lipstick-red eyebrows. A weasel popping from its burrow like a furry Jack-in-the-box. And on a great day, bleating muskox calves or bulls locking horns. I get into the spirit of things, and dream of sneaking up on them with a rake to rid them of their burden, that downy, stifling discomfort. A win-win situation, I'd say. Collecting next to my wife, I indulge in some friendly rivalry. I once again feel the flush of our courtship, like a bowerbird or a tern bearing fish, when I offer to my mate a plastic bag bulging with *qiviut*. She never was one for flowers.

One could facetiously justify muskox hunting as a form of pest control, as, drifting through town, the beefy haystacks sometimes gore sled dogs tied up in people's yards. The cows, with slenderer horns, are not above sparring with each other or taking on a barker, either. In an outlier event, a state trooper was killed when he tried to haze muskoxen away from his kennel. Predictably, one headline shouting "mismanagement" averred that the beasts had "morphed from a novelty to a nuisance to a threat." Enchanters had turned into ogres. How quickly the magic of wild Alaska wears off. Some Nomeites won't let small children play outside when the muskies visit. Did they not know that wild animals live there when they made rural Alaska their home? Is this not what draws many of us to this state? Other grouches think muskoxen compete with reindeer or caribou, foods the locals favor. Wary of traffic hazards, Fish and Game wardens have posted inflatable grizzlies alongside Nome's small-plane airstrip to deter the archaic ruminants; these sentries sport a chest patch drenched with bear-urine repellent—sold through the Internet as "Predator Pee"—to up the scare factor. It's for naught. From a window seat during takeoff, I've watched bovine trespassers clip runway lawn. I love that animals assert their needs rather than blend in ornamentally with their backgrounds.

Riding my bike into town, gritting my teeth in the westerlies, I sometimes, too often, see muskox pelts rotting on the porches of people who don't make time for combing them out. In this place, taking voraciously from the land is an esteemed tradition. Gravel pits, tailings ponds, and rusty mining machinery scar the land-scape, drab reminders of past glories. Wool-picking might not be as manly as gold-digging or reenacting Pleistocene slaughter, but it clothes the family. I cherish its quiet luxuries and the thought that, this way, the beasts get to keep their hides.

CHAPTER 16

WEEKEND VOLCANO

Skookum's northeastern flank, abutting the snow-veined, somber gunmetal flat top, evokes Utah's canyon lands more than it does Alaska. Shouldering daypacks at a pullout on the Nabesna Road—an unpaved 42-mile spur into Wrangell-St. Elias National Park—my wife and I tackle this 7,125-foot telluric fist, the western Wrangells' only volcano with a trailhead reachable by car. Exquisitely ruined, dabbed with a Martian palette, it contrasts with the younger, ice-capped glory of its neighbors Mount Blackburn, Drum, and Sanford. Skookum repeatedly blew its top between three and two million years BCE, belching hot gas and ash clouds, tingeing vents around a collapsed caldera leaking magma. No walk for old men, the loop, cutting five miles through Earth's guts with an overnight option, bares the slipping of continental plates, molten upwellings at the planet's crustal seams.

Skookum has roots in the Wrangell Volcanic Field, a 2,000-square-mile arc linking the border and Glennallen. This hot spot along the Denali Fault thrust up a crop of North America's tallest peaks, including Mount Wrangell, a shield of stupendous bulk, over 90 percent of which perennial snow and ice cover. Also visible from the Nabesna Road, a groundswell drawing your eyes like a disaster in the making, Wrangell is twice Skookum's height. It's the continent's northernmost volcano and among the world's largest active ones. The Ahtna called it "the one who controls the weather" or, when it stirred, "the one with smoke on it."

Just as islands were for mariners, fiery mountains were for explorers "beacons by which to navigate," the historian Stephen J. Pyne observes, intermittent sources of heat and light. Lt. Henry T. Allen, leading "Alaska's Lewis & Clark" expedition on a five-month, 1,500-mile trek from the Copper River Delta to the Bering Strait's Norton Sound in 1885, reported Mount Wrangell's white vapor, together with permafrost and ice lenses in the soil. After the 1899 Icy Bay quake, epicentered five raven-flight hours to the south, the head guide of another mapping expedition noted that the peak emitted "smoke with unusual animation for the rest of the season," and in later years, ash falls on the summit icefield were photographed. Chitina residents on the banks of the Copper River watched a spectacular eruption throwing up huge black columns in 1930. They credited the spectacle to nearby Mount Blackburn, though Mount Wrangell was likely the one acting up. In 2004, Ring-of-Fire connections took the form of an eleven-minute swarm of local rumbles, repercussions of the big one in Sumatra that rang the whole globe like a gong and unleashed tsunamis that killed over 200,000 people. Mount Wrangell's depths still chamber warmth that sometimes escapes as steam plumes from vents rimming an ice-filled summit caldera so wide that planes on skis have landed inside.

Ashes that Mount Churchill spewed in the field's eastern reaches, near present-day McCarthy, blanketed parts of the Upper Yukon basin. One inch of ash can suffocate plants, and such a deposit 1,400 years ago perhaps forced Gwich'in ancestors into northern Alaska and farther east into Canada. The shocks echoed and radiated like "songlines," Outback origin stories from the "Dreamtime" that painted elders recite. Athabaskans to the northeast recalled a giant wrecking a mountain and voices inside remarking on burning smells before a blaze consumed the alp and its indwellers. A second tale mentions ground pirouetting, cardinal directions flip-flopping, a landscape instantly altered. In older understandings of the world, around the globe mythological and then-present historical planes overlapped or overlay each other like volcanic ejecta.

Contemplating tectonic fervor, we had to pry ourselves loose from the breakfast campfire. Ice clinked in our water jug; hoarfrost silvered the tents.

We now chase the trail through spruce bearded with mint-green lichen, through alders whose shed leaves I spear with my hiking pole. Windup-toy squirrels *churr*, firing bursts of their alternate name at us: chickaree. Jay hecklers alert the woods to our presence. Somewhere a porcupine bawls, disconcertingly like a lost bear cub.

Hopscotching back and forth across a rill that a curtseying dipper claims, we climb past the tree line. Skookum's name, a ranger said, rubbed off a brook plunging from its brow swift and brawling each spring, snowmelt on steroids. The word stems from the Chinook trade jargon spoken throughout the Pacific Northwest, which gave us such gems as "hooch," "muck-a-muck," "cheechako" ("newcomer" in an unflattering way), and "in the sticks." An adjective for hardworking folks, it meant "big," "strong," "brave," "excellent," or "impressive," while hinting at goblins, spirits, or monsters too, in the nuances "fearsome" and spiritually "powerful." It was a synonym for the Sasquatch and, as "skookum root," for the green false hellebore, a cure-all in the lily family that can stun or kill a person. A malamute could be *skookum*, or a drink or a feller, and jail, "skookum house," certainly was. Nowadays, even a fancy jacket can be. The volcano's most famous namesake (not counting Jack London's Skookum Bench king, who offered a thousand dollars for Buck), the Tagish-Tlingit prospector "Skookum" Jim Mason, or Kèsh, was part of the family group of four that sparked the Klondike rush, which unfolded across the border, an Alaska hop, skip, and a jump from here. In a land where men match the mountains, his stamina as a porter on the Chilkoot Trail earned him that sobriquet.

The sun struggles to tear the gauze overcast. When it succeeds, hills striped chalk-white, buff, sulfur, dove, and charcoal ignite.

A pass 1,900 feet above the trailhead separates Skookum's bulk from Theresa Dome. Swirls reminiscent of tie-dyed fabric or marbled bookend papers mark that outlier's barren slope, which loomed over us on our ascent. Frost-cracked basalt dragon-backs on the reverse slope. These pencil-gray dikes, spattered with lichens bright as safety vests, resist erosion better than the apron of pink and caramel scree and compacted ash. They are remnants of magma-filling fissures in older formations.

We follow the ridge past a pinnacle cluster to the dome's summit. Sips from the Nalgene bottle bring brain freeze. It's blustery, but my shadow shows. Variegated chevrons on Skookum's bottom two-thirds point at cliff bands the maroon of old blood and at the crown beyond. Rockfalls make me glass the slope for sheep—at day beds we earlier passed, pellets mingled with white hair and bones braided into wolf scat. We lounge vis-à-vis the panorama. Motley country at long last coheres. The Nabesna Road, a potholed gravel dead-end even seasoned Alaskans admit never having traveled (it punctured two of our tires in May), squirms between the Mentasta Mountains and evergreens like a flood breaking upward on the volcano's piedmont, where heavenly spotlights currently play. It leaps Jack Creek, whose steely flow fortifies the Nabesna, the Tanana, and the regal Yukon, all bound for the Bering Sea. Up-valley, near mile two, it bridges the Slana, which feeds into the Copper River and Prince William Sound. During the Depression, men wishing to apply at the mine the road serviced tramped a hundred miles from the Richardson Highway. We, seeking beauty, a different relief, drove 300 to hike ten.

After lunch, descending on ball bearings, we meet another Fairbanks couple recreating in the bubble the virus has imposed. We swap route details and pleasantries, keeping body lengths apart.

The return leg to the road, a ravine on the far side of the pass, taxes knee joints. Rockhounds, however, would swoon at its marvels. Scoria sponges mix with brick-red cobbles seemingly baked in a kiln and retaining some of the glow from the volcano's heart. Elephant skin coats one upright slab; ferns of iron oxide bloom across smaller, tan bits. We walk past lava chunks sintered into boulders big as dumpsters. Frailty survives amid such brutes: fireweed, flushed with the year's lateness.

We survey the riot of colors, of riches, drinking them in as castaways would sweet water. They're a boon to draw on when, in months to come, rebounding from shoulder surgery, I'll try to grow skookum again while Fairbanks hunkers down, cold, unwalkable, dreary, starkly gray and white, its residents dreaming of summer.

CHAPTER 17

LIGHT AT THE END OF THE TUNNEL

I lock the truck among 20 other vehicles, and within seconds, a mean Arctic wind comes at me like a bull terrier. Weather always funnels in tides through this bottleneck, one of the few gaps in the Alaska Range. My brow hurts with an ice-cream headache, and my hands are dead trout. I have forgotten the down jacket and so borrow floral fleece from a friend who drove an hour from Fairbanks with her family. I'm now wearing socks inside mitts and a skimpy hat topping bulky upper layers. The truck window reflects me pinheaded and fashion-challenged.

We chose a cold day on purpose, because shard forests sprout in Castner Glacier's guts only at freezing temperatures. Azure gloaming across the Delta River had bathed the snout of nearby Black Rapids Glacier as a low sun tried to part milling scud. My wife and I smiled when, igniting a lone summit, it succeeded.

The air calms the moment we drop from the pullout into the bed of Castner Creek, the glacier's outlet. Black water rushes under panes crashed at an overflow; tracks hint that a snowmachine foundered here. The procession spread out ahead of me features dogs, snowshoe enthusiasts, a kid towing a sled…bringing to mind the line of dreamers treading the "Golden Staircase" up the Chilkoot Pass. Walking the well-broken granular trail resembles plodding in sand, so I quickly warm up. Still, moisture from the balaclava stuck to my beard rimes my eyebrows and lashes. A fogbow fragment glows at the base of decapitated peaks at our back. Ptarmigan spoors hula between willows the birds fed on, past a boulder of rusty and silver layers, schist folded phyllo-like. Imprints of fingered wings show where the white birds took flight. Fox pugmarks flesh out the tale.

Fellow sightseers are elated yet subdued, the mood a mere ripple of solstice bonfires or winter carnivals. Everyone seems relieved to have escaped their dens and the doom cycle of the pandemic and rumors of voting fraud. It's mid-December, the year's gloomy pit, but we'll gain minutes of light, if not composure, before long, once the sun tilts higher again. Stepping off the trail for oncoming traffic, holding my breath while hikers pass, I sink up to my knees. We do chat with our friends, who, masked against frostbite and viral loads, these days live as shuttered as my wife and I.

The glacier's brow looms suddenly, around a bend about a mile from the trailhead. Its mouth is a whale shark's toothless yawn, larger than expected. Pinpricks of brilliance, stars unmoored, the headlamps of visitors exiting dance in the black depths. During the summers, snowmelt from a glacier's surface pours into cre-vasses, where its torrential milling in the depths undercuts the overlying mass, slowly forming such ice caves. They exist as long as the superstructure stays stable enough.

We get swallowed, northern Jonahs, and the maw turns into a shiny, scalloped dome in shades from aquamarine to lapis. It's a window, really, a lens telescoping dozens of winters, yet in its essence as a flow feature, a river, the Castner is at least twelve millennia old. Charcoal-colored grit veins walls encasing rocks and snarls of glass vermicelli. Though loess dusts the ice underfoot, it remains slippery. Milky discs dapple it, air pockets arrested till spring.

It's ten degrees colder here. My ungloved fingers fumble with the camera. When dusk yields to darkness, we click our head-lamps on. The beams slide across the glistening innards like trout over stream cobbles.

A sacral atmosphere reigns inside, that of a cathedral or a museum. "You must be quiet in the presence of the ice," Koyukon old-timers used to say. "You must show it respect." Tlingits and Athabaskans saw glaciers and river ice as both animate and animating the landscape. Glaciers housed fearsome creatures, giant worms or copper-clawed owls. Humbled, engulfed by it, the Castner cave makes perfect sense to me as some creepy-crawly's lair.

Crevassed, dangerous routes between the interior and coast, traversed while trading tanned moose hides and copper for salmon jerky and sea otter pelts, could be fickle. This of course reflects observable changes, "behavior." What John Muir called the "work of the ice-world." Willful powers, glaciers listen and will punish infractions. The smell of frying bacon or of cooking with grease offends them. Related beliefs persisted in Europe before the Industrial Revolution. There, villagers ventured into ice caves with drawn swords and erected crosses to halt the movement of glaciers that during the Little Ice Age threatened and sometimes razed villages. Muir, a geologist-deist with an animist streak, stood hushed before land ice carapaces, "gazing at the holy vision." He acquainted himself with glaciers and their work in the West and Alaska to come "as near the heart of the world" as he could. In the Andes, until recently, thousands of *campesinos* made pilgrimages to a special glacier terminus on an annual feast day, harvesting ice blocks ceremoniously. Peruvian peasants, who rightly implicated modern technology, blamed a drought on instruments that measured glacier-ice loss. Awe and the sacred in general always have carried notes of fear, the risk of being overwhelmed.

The ice harbors human secrets. The worm sometimes returns what it has claimed. Glaciers commit twofold sleight of hand: with their disappearance they surrender the disappeared, giving birth to a new branch of archaeology. Daylight once more has fallen on airplane-wreck parts, Roman coins, missing hikers, crossbow bolts, an Iron-Age wooden figurine and a horseshoe, plus manure, Bronze Age lederhosen, a Neolithic basket scrap, an Indian box full of gemstones, and a 16th-century pilgrim's or tradesman's rapier, dagger, wheel-lock pistol, and clothes, all released by glaciers and nearby ice patches. Life lay dormant in some buried things—seeds in hay bedding for World War I troops, inside caves blasted from bedrock and snow, one hundred years later sprouted into stalks.

In 1999, sheep hunters at the northern tip of the Alaska Panhandle discovered the mummified body of a 20-year-old melting from a glacier 60 miles inland. Nearby lay his finely woven split-spruce-root hat, an iron-blade knife, a throwing board with dart, remnants of a gaff or walking stick, and a beaver pouch holding moss, lichen, and leaves. He had traveled three days from the coast, carrying salmon and shellfish also, climbing steadily. Identified as Tlingit, possibly of the Wolf Clan, with several maternal relatives still living among the local people, he wore a cloak sewn from 96 ground-squirrel pelts. Hypothermia probably killed him, as no signs of pre-mortem trauma were found. He died in the summer, pollen revealed, between 1415 and 1445 CE, near the onset of the Little Ice Age. Could foul weather have caught him? Did his family think that the worm had devoured him in the flower of youth?

After a thorough examination approved by the First Nation bands that included his distant kin, Kwäday Dän Ts'ìnchi ("Long-ago Person Found") was cremated and his ashes scattered on the glacier.

As coincidental as his retrieval sounded, it was not, not entirely. The 1997 to 1998 El Niño had boosted the largest annual leap in global average surface temperature then on record. It helped to make 1998 the twentieth century's warmest year up to that point. With glaciation's worldwide breakdown, artifacts pop up faster and in greater numbers than researchers can survey and preserve. If those hunters had not chanced upon Kwäday Dän Ts'ìnchi's dissolving ice bed, scavengers and decay would have quickly erased him. His uncanny emergence connotes transience and resurgence, words ringing loud and clear across a great chasm.

Without meaning to, I lower my voice. Clusters *ooh* and *aah*, together but alone, each steam-puffing social bubble percolating separately. Pale beams pick out random details. Enchanted exclamations blur, at once muffled and resonant. One guy is ice-skating—it was on his bucket list, he tells someone. A thin ten-yard fracture has me questioning the rink's soundness.

Farther in, sprays of foot-long crystals above us fan out in stilettos. Elsewhere, serried frost sequins shine like translucent razor blades. This flowering in the dark is "crevasse hoar," which grows here only when it has been fairly cold. A boy knocks down a glitter shower. The father asks him to stop. Breaths in this walk-in fridge contribute moisture to the ceiling art, which is ironic. Access to some European galleries from the last ice age and Paleolithic is now strictly limited, since exhalations and body heat benefit mold that destroys murals of lions, rhinos, and bears. In a near, projected future, cloistered ice wonders could be history. Although the Castner shrinks much more slowly than neighboring glaciers because of our system's exhausts and exhaustion, it thins almost as fast. This isn't primarily an aesthetic problem, of course. Warm-blooded life in a glacial vault is as common, and as comforting a thought, as fallback Earths, last resorts in outer space.

The whale-shark throat tightens as the ceiling descends. I accidentally brush against dangling crystals. Gullies of water in some deeper, even less knowable, place boom ominously. Percy Bysshe Shelley, in his poem "Mont Blanc," ponders "The everlasting universe of things," their hold on our imagination, though his words fit the Castner's interior ice:

Now dark—now glittering—now, reflecting gloom
Now lending splendor...

Shelley wrote this in the Chamonix Valley, two-thirds through "The Year Without Summer," 1816, when ash and sulfates that Indonesia's Mount Tambora had spewed around the globe repelled the sun's photon storm and precipitated raindrops and snow crystals, intensifying that era's sunsets, chill, and sense of romantic ruin.

Time to resurface from the pit of glaciological past into the rays of a warm, living present.

With our perspective reversed, the blinding-white portal frames backlit human figures that appear as black cutouts. Step by step, Devil's Thumb across the valley materializes inside a royal-blue archway. The plunging afternoon sun pinks its ridge—light at the end of the tunnel. Until this year, this very instant, I never experienced or really grasped this metaphor, forged in an era of steam trains and gas lanterns. The image conveyed, predating the hopeful phrase by far, captures near-death perceptions. In one of four panels of his Renaissance altarpiece *Visions of the Beyond*, the Dutchman Hieronymus Bosch glorified angels lifting the naked, fragile departed toward the proverbial passage. He painted this in his twilight decade, perhaps in his final year, two generations after the "Iceman" journeyed through the St. Elias Mountains. Anecdotes based upon dying neurons firing mysteriously, on ebbing energy tickling the visual cortex, could have inspired Bosch's take on the dreaded transition. The physiology is that of asphyxiation, during which the heart beats faster initially and breathing speeds up and peripheral vision declines as the central nervous system shuts down. It's like the "iris shot" fadeout of silent movies in which a camera aperture closes slowly, with black decreasing the circle of what is seen, strangling brightness until it winks out. The phenomenon differs markedly from tunnel vision, an extreme focus and lack of situational awareness experienced under stress—during combat, for instance.

Pre-missionary Tlingit ideas of the afterlife also involved a gateway, a light source, and—how could it be otherwise?—a guide steering a canoe. "Man's shade," part of a person's essence freed from its shell, traveled a rocky, narrow trail tangled with brush and, with help, crossed a lake to finally sit by the central hearth fire in a house in the spirit realm, unless the deceased had not been cremated. In that case, he or she was doomed to stay near the door and endure chilly drafts. Before Kwäday Dän Ts'ìnchi was put to rest, for five and a half centuries, his shadow shivered in limbo.

Post-election, the physical climate notwithstanding, with a vaccine at last being issued, the promise of brightness and peace, and beauty, keep us going. Perhaps there *will* be a world like the one we already envisioned, one where people are not just disease bearers or faceless forms. One in which glaciers and kindness, wildness and refuge, pikas and civil liberties, can survive. We still have a choice: do we want Bosch's teeming if crackled *Garden of Earthly Delights,* or his burning cities and torture chambers, his animals punishing humans, *The Last Judgment*'s ruinous hell? Tellingly, recent research with eye-tracking glasses showed viewers to be foremost drawn to the triptych's dark and destructive panel.

In June 2022, with Alaska's Interior thick with smoke from wildfires and sweltering in temperatures above 80 degrees, the Castner ice cave partly collapsed—its front portion was gone, while the back remained. Hikers still ventured there but called it "super risky," hearing ice cracking and water and rocks raining from the ceiling. My first reaction upon reading about this was, "What if there had been people inside when it happened?" My second: "How can this crystal palace be gone?" Then, naturally, "Why now?" We assume landscape features will at least endure for a human lifespan.

Glacial topography, however, is a steady unmaking "through the silent working of immutable laws...ever and anon rent and torn," to quote Mary Shelley's *Frankenstein* (inspired by and penned during Europe's Holocene cold spell, while sheltering in a Geneva Lake villa with soon-to-be husband Percy), as if it were "but a plaything in their hands." Glaciers are rivers, really, but with their motion slowed, their waters arrested, layered like sediment. The ice charges and back-pedals, thickens and thins, leaving erratics, "wandering rocks," from pebbles to monstrous boulders. A glacier transports debris that could crush pickup trucks or cabins, which gouges bedrock flanks with striations. Melt-water dropping sediment while coursing through sub-glacial culverts builds eskers, gravel dams that snake across flats now bereft of ice. Caves widen and wither, and only a fool would try to link the Castner collapse, a single local event, to a global trend. Still, ashfall from wildfires, sooting ice and absorbing sun, speeds up the glaciers' demise.

A recent coinage, *solastalgia* is the grieving for dear places that progress has obliterated. It covers habitat destruction from development and flooded shorelines from melting icecaps. I never knew the Castner's crypt intimately; but I know snow and winter and ice, and I'll miss them sorely. How many things about which I have written over the decades will be gone when this gets published? In the pre-digital past, sand running through fingers of a hand or an hourglass was a poignant symbol. Snowflakes melting on a tongue would better serve our thirstier times.

News arrived, days after that witnessless rumble by the Richardson Highway, that an ice avalanche from a Dolomites glacier had killed eleven people amid record heat, following a drought winter with scant snowfall. Glaciers retreating in steep terrain bare weakened overburdens that rain and snowmelt freshets undermine further, priming scarps to heed gravity's call—cataclysmically. In 1963, at Vaiont Reservoir in northern Italy, a 300-foot impact wave from such a landslide overwhelmed the dam and in mere minutes killed 2,000 villagers. Glacier Bay has birthed landslides, always announced by rockfalls during the past three decades' warmest years. Thawing soils are to blame. Barry Arm, an appendix of Prince William Sound's glacier-rimmed Harriman Fjord, currently worries scientists. One 40-degree slope at this cruise and sea-kayaking destination sped up its creep in the past decade. A 30-foot tsunami from a slide, possible within a year, likely within 20, would batter the nearby port town of Whittier. Ten of the past century's hugest waves reared up in glaciered alpine places, many in coastal Alaska. Scientists predict that the risk and frequency of such episodes will increase. Fifteen million people worldwide live under an executioner's sword of glacial floods, many of them in Peru and around "the planet's third ice cap," the Himalayas. More than soil and deluges are loosed. A melting icecap on the Tibetan Plateau has been releasing 15,000-year-old viruses, many of which are new to science. Shelley's horror was human-shaped; today's horror as well is human-caused, but it comes in different guises.

It is too late for gestures of appeasement to the ice. It is too late to annul our sins and those of our fathers. A time to do penance has come. Light may greet us yet at the end of this tunnel.

CHAPTER 18

MARGINALIA

I put the maps of my Arctic traverse end to end, as I sometimes do, to relive the experience—all the wilderness I could ever want spreads across my living room floor. Cleaved by glacial valleys, shoaled by the Coastal Plain to the north and by boreal forest to the south, Alaska's stark Brooks Range spans the state's entire width, a thousand miles east to west, scaled down here to just 13 feet. To save weight on my 58-day trek, I had not brought notebooks but instead kept a journal on the maps' backs and in their margins. The dot-and-dash line of the Continental Divide, which I'd crossed numerous times, Morse-codes the mountainous spine, sorting waters headed north, to the Arctic Ocean, from those southbound for the Bering Strait.

The map sheets are battered, taped at the folds, as I consulted them often, and often in a drizzle, seeking advice from these silent oracles. Their backsides crawl with my densely packed handwriting, those journal notes I took against the fog of oblivion and to someday write about this. The map panels, too, are heavily annotated, with my route rambling through wilderness and my stretched I's for gravel airstrips—stepping stones of civilization—where a pilot had cached more fuel and food. Each camp shows as a mini triangle, like a tent a child would draw.

Uncluttered space, which I first encountered through maps and travelogues, was part of the attraction that had brought me north. Every named mountain seemed to huddle among ten anonymous peaks that had possibly never been climbed. Spoken like mantras, the names themselves rang with visionary topographies, from Plunge Creek to Mount Deliverance, Rumbling Mountain, Old Woman Creek, and beyond. Each was a haiku poem, pared down, a narrative in a nutshell. "Bedroom Pot" is a hollow whose dark water tastes "funny," and "Burns in the Mouth" is a sour, limey, very hard creek. "Always Windy" needs no explanation, and neither do "Place to Get Rock-Tool Material," no-nonsense "Breasts," mountains, or "Lonesome Sad Place," a camp. "Go After Seals with Spears" and "Piece of Coastland Where They Get Flounders" were important stops on the annual subsistence round. But despite my fascination with these details, I did not mistake the finger pointing at the moon for the moon, did not think this land could be understood through maps or names alone.

I had embarked on this territory more than two decades ago, as an anthropology student doing land use and subsistence research. The National Park Service wanted to know which areas of Kobuk Valley and Gates of the Arctic national parks Inupiaq and Koyukon hunters and gatherers had frequented in the past. If those tribes could establish prior claims, they would be entitled to hunt and trap there, an exception made for all Alaska Native groups that is unique in this country's national parks. An elder in Allakaket, a village of 90-some Koyukon that nuzzles the Arctic Circle, had shared his knowledge of the region's topography.

A dead beaver, half-skinned, lay sprawled on the kitchen floor, half-skinned on a piece of cardboard, to keep the meat clean and blood off the linoleum. The elder asked me to sit. Before I unrolled my maps on the table, we snacked on jerked caribou we dipped in seal oil, a delicacy of liquid amber that relatives on the coast had sent.

The meanders he drew on my maps with felt pens of various shades reflected the maze of animal ranges that wildlife biologists chart on theirs. Other ethnographers who worked with Inuit hunters noted that, although their collaborators had never before seen a map, they could easily read one, recognizing *nuna*, the land, even in its graphic abstraction. Through my interviews and the mapped data I gathered, I realized that, outside the purview of most people, a palimpsest of collective memory underlies our own, everywhere in North America. Landmarks, through their names and tales, express philosophies about sharing and owner-ship, about conflict and community. They hold knowledge passed down through the generations, circulating in families. The environmental philosopher Thom van Dooren has singled out naming by later arrivals as an act of colonization, a "reordering of reality": "New names and understandings are layered over the old, perhaps supplanting them or even coexisting, but inevitably changing the way in which people understand and relate to the world around them."

Before exact printed maps of the high Arctic existed, explorers elicited mental ones from the locals, who drew them freehand and could detail places they had not visited since their childhood. Sketches the Danish adventurer Knud Rasmussen gathered in this way on his dogsled trip through the Northwest Passage impress with great detail. The landscape, larder and repast for the spirit, had been fully internalized. The distortions also are telling. Inuit informants depicted known settings, *their* bays, lakes, lagoons, and inlets, in a scrimshaw based on travel and toil. The periphery, foreign coasts and plains, appeared vague, diminished in size and detail compared to the homeland. Women knew areas near the camps more intimately, their turf for rabbit snaring, berry picking, digging up roots. Men knew distant trade sites, passes, and portages, furbearers' itineraries, and the trails generations of caribou had inscribed in the tundra as if drawing their own maps for others to follow.

Treading lightly, Indigenous northerners nevertheless had altered the land, revealing the fallacy of the Arctic as virgin country. Cairns, or *inuksuit,* rose like lithic thumbs scabbed with lichen, the sculptural architecture of nomads and original "land art." Verticals in a landscape composed of horizontals, whose only upright mammals besides humans were ground squirrels guarding their burrows, they truly stood out. Rivets in a landscape in permanent flux, they arrested drift. *Inuksuit,* honoring shamans' graves, acting as dummies that funneled caribou during game drives, and flagging meat caches or Arctic char spawning grounds, could equally signal the best or the only course home. Different designs fit different purposes. There were single upright stones, stacks, and rock pyramids. There were "pointers" and "deconfusers" and window-shaped types framing sightlines that linked what in this flatness passes for eye catchers or key features, the settings of mythical or historic events or current gatherings. Some tagged convenient river crossings; others marked deeper, difficult channels or places where evil waited, a snaggletooth rock in a rapid, for instance. Many had names. The singular of the word, *inuksuk*, can be translated as "acting in the capacity of a human." There were good reasons for such substitutions. One could not simply stop at a village or camp to ask for directions. Habitations were spaced far apart and outsiders greeted with caution.

Following my cartographic obsession into the rabbit hole of museum collections and historic exploration accounts, I had read about tactile Inuit maps of the Greenland coastline; whittled from driftwood, they could be fingered in one's pocket, in wet and whiteout conditions or in polar darkness. Plotting the island's navigable fringe, the artifacts' indents and prows, the inlets and capes of that jigsawed coast, ascend one side of this Inuit GPS and descend the other, suggesting north didn't matter. A man named Kuniit notched these lumps before his small, mobile band met the first European, in the 1880s. In their simplicity, tactile maps condense ingenuity, and touching the smoothed relief as one does worry stones, anchoring oneself to solidity, must have reassured any storm-tossed kayaker.

Because in most terrains, under most weather conditions, maps suffice, I no longer carry a compass. Which naturally has come back and bit me. On a guided raft trip down the Aichilik, we were scheduled for a charter-plane pickup on the barrier islands, a chain of low, migrating sand-and-gravel bars off the Beaufort Sea coast, plastered with driftwood and haunted by polar bears. My boss, she who would once swipe the mammoth tusk while overnighting at our destination, had tied and taped cutlery onto driftwood staffs, preparing to fend off the beasts that beleaguered her crew's island camp. While mine paddled out from the delta for our one-mile crossing, fog rolled in like a ghost tsunami, as it often does there. Within minutes, the people in the bow had become shadows. The murk was a bit lighter in one spot, from the hidden sun, which allowed me to at least keep my bearing. Still, I worried that we might hit one of the wide gaps between islands unknowingly and head out into the open sea, toward the pole.

Stopping frequently, fishing for clues, I at long last heard the sighs of waves breaking on a most welcome shore. Home was this sailor, home from the sea. (Well, after clearing logs off a beach runway and after a night by a fire blazing sideways.) For the anthropologist of the Arctic, Tim Ingold, to "dwell within a weather-world," to "inhabit the open," is "to align one's own conduct to the celestial movements of sun, moon and stars, to the rhythmic alternations of night and day and of the seasons, rain and shine, sunlight and shade."

While Indigenous travelers sketched maps into snow or wet sand or on paper to give outsiders the lay of the land—and what a gift it was, potentially lifesaving—they availed themselves of more sophisticated means. Planning longer journeys, they factored in weather, topography, food sources, safe rest stops, waypoints of historic or personal interest, and their mode of transport, rather than metric distances. Three days with a dog team on easy ground approximated 70 miles. One Inuit place name referencing dead reckoning translates as "a fjord of such length that a kayak cannot even in a whole day paddle from the mouth to the head of the fjord and back again." The images place names encrypted were multidimensional, and speakers were aware that a traveler's relative position or that of the sun could alter a landmark's appearance. This attention to detail must have made for rich, full days. A cultural geographer with the Inuit wrote of the trail as home, "a place where life unfolded," and they existed "as if both living or moving were part of the same journey."

Traversing pack ice and landscapes that the untrained mind perceives largely as featureless, often in days-long whiteout conditions or in darkness, is like travel at sea, and one can plot a course with similar methods. Yup'ik and Inupiaq hunters deciphered currents and triangulated constellations. They interpreted atmospheric phenomena, the migrations of birds, whales, and caribou, and registered the shapes, angles, and bedding of "land waves"—snowdrifts. Like Polynesia's transoceanic mariners, who sensed the information that wave sets carry by lying down blindfolded in an outrigger's bottom, they could tell the aspect of snow crests while sledding over them, even with poor visibility. In Inuktitut, a person who navigates well is *aangaittuq*, "attentive," as opposed to the unobservant or *aangajuq* who "travels blindly." More than being a mere survival prerequisite, attentiveness characterizes an Inuit approach to life and one's environment generally.

Traveling well was part science and part creativity. It required adjustments to unforeseen circumstances. Meticulous readings on their home grounds over the centuries uniquely equipped northern Indigenous peoples to gauge the changes that runaway heating has wrought. "Back in the old days," stated Caleb Pungowiyi, a St. Lawrence Islander from Savoonga, "they could predict the weather by observing the stars, the sky, and other events. The old people think that back then they could predict the weather pattern for a few days in advance. Not anymore!" The earth is indeed faster now: natural history has accelerated while becoming unnatural.

Navigation methods had to account for the changing weather and seasons. The waxing light of spring, for example, renders stars indistinct. And in winter, fixed Polaris, then visible at the Little Bear's tail tip, stands too high in the sky to serve as a true marker of north.

Auditory stimuli mattered too, as they did on the Aichilik. In *Arctic Dreams*, Barry Lopez describes how the racket of cliff-nesting birds on one side and surf on the other kept a sledder on shore-fast ice in thick summer fog properly oriented. A knack for such feats wasn't innate. In Nunavut's Repulse Bay, Jose A. Kusugak, snowbound as a child in his family's sod igloo, was told to look and listen intently to the outdoors as though it were a symphony merging land, ice, and sky into one. Eavesdropping on the elements, playing *aaqsiiq,* or the "Silent Game," young Jose heard "rolling snow, driving and building and shaping snowdrifts." A different sound and faster tempo spelled violent *natiruviaq*—"flooring snow" swaddling the igloo. The boy knew that this layer promised good nursery lairs for seals and smoother travel on sea ice for people.

Even voyagers seemingly lost had a shot at succeeding. They'd tune in to a landscape or seascape or access a mindscape—information ingrained in place names and their elders' tales. An Inuk from Igloolik recalled two hunters who drifted out to sea on moving ice. With the wind and the sun's position prompting him, one trying to reach shore directly headed south. His partner deployed a harpoon float instead, to check tidal currents. He knew that initially the ice would move seaward but that the incoming tide would soon after take charge. He therefore walked north, away from land. The one who'd headed south changed his mind, joined his companion, and eventually, the shifty mass delivered both men back to shore-fast ice and safety. Some wayfinding feats boggle the mind. A Canadian researcher accompanied one Inuk who retrieved seven fox traps his uncle had 25 years ago set across eight square miles of tundra, flat and monotonous. The traps lay buried under snow. The hunter collected them all in roughly two hours. Another hunter found his way home snow-blind, feeling a steady wind on his face and maintaining its angle.

Ample signs speak to those who can read minutiae. "Water sky" darkly reflects open sea off the underbelly of clouds; the opposite of "ice blink," the yellow-white sheen from jumbled pack ice, it guides marine mammal hunters to "leads," the lanes through grinding mayhem where boats may pass and whales surface to breathe. A common polar refraction, "looming" conjures up boats, ice-shelves, or land from below a viewer's horizon line. Temperature inversions cause these bent-light illusions, which hover above the object's actual position, distorted and sometimes inverted. A person who can read a *puikkaqtuq,* or "pop-up" mirage, might be able to home in on walrus basking on distant ice floes.

Prevailing winds plane corduroy snow ridges like a dune's contours and ripples, which helps in fixing the cardinal directions if the wind compass is known. In certain regions, snow-bearing northeast winds weigh down tundra grass and freeze it leaning in a southwesterly direction. The same gales tilt balsam poplar or scattered, scraggly black spruce that way, which grow most of their branches and leaves on the trunks' lee side. On a windy whiteout day, Barry Lopez noticed, the alignment of hairs on a parka hood ruffed with fur lets travelers steer true.

In a few communities, orienteering know-how has endured the arrival of fast, scenery-blurring snowmachines and TVs, though an unhinged climate makes much sea-ice lore obsolete. Almost every year now, somebody breaks through the ice traveling and drowns or disappears. With Arctic societies in transition, with language loss, handheld GPS, and with long-distance journeys overland and at sea diminished, navigational savvy is fading. Regular users of GPS form less complex cognitive maps. The science writer Michael Bond compares satellite navigation to "being led by the nose," that idiom one of disempowerment, evoking an ox with a muzzle ring. Wayfinding by natural means, through awareness, on the other hand, "becomes a kind of meditation." Amazingly, some blind people learn the skill of echolocation by emitting clicks and by organizing the resulting information into spatial maps of familiar surroundings, with which they navigate. They enlist their dormant visual cortex for this. A sense not used can atrophy, just as a neglected one can be trained. For young Indigenous hunters, artificial features like radar towers and radio masts have replaced drift patterns and stars as beacons. Where diverse cultures formerly integrated nature's components into mental models of sparkling diversity, another, monolithic and dominant one has fashioned tools that with each improvement weaken our bonds with nature. There no longer are scores of men in a valley who *are* that valley, Wallace Stevens lamented, men whose souls, like the poet's, are "composed of the external world."

Gems of lessons about paying heed to one's surroundings (and moral compass) lie in stories like the Upper Tanana Athabaskan tale about two sisters who chased a butterfly, which got them lost. To make matters worse, they ignored route advice from a chickadee. Such stories' directional adverbs and place names, many of them anchored to the Tanana, the region's main waterway, situated listeners inside virtual landscapes "just like being there." The linguistic scaffolding allowed audiences to follow the string of events as they would a map. Similar techniques benefit nature and travel writers and draw upon the archetypal heroic quest.

The Upper Tanana protagonists may have been girls only because the plot needed them to be, because girls were the target audience. (It contains a rape by a devilish monster.) Cognitive research, however, refutes beliefs that women are worse at route-finding and related spatial tasks, at least in countries with relative gender equality. We all know that guys are simply too macho to ask for directions. They try shortcuts in experimental mazes, while women stick to learned routes. (I almost died that way once, making a beeline in Death Valley.) All these phenomena had been my academic interest in pursuit of a Ph.D, but in the context of forager societies. And they were instrumental in becoming an accomplished wilderness guide.

From early adulthood on, I've shared the peripatetic streak of Alaska Native elders I had yet to meet. In lieu of their guidance, maps and books fostered my independence, nudging me to walk new terrain. Mark Twain, Karl May (an author of Westerns who never had seen the West), Robert Louis Stevenson, James Fenimore Cooper, and later, Hermann Hesse were my scouts. "I can drop you anywhere with a map, and you'll find your way home," a former boss told me. I do and, I might modestly add, always on time for the air-taxi pickup. This I rank among the highest of compliments, like a brain surgeon being praised for his sutures and steady hands. I wish there were similar aids for living my life, diagrams that recommend pathways from dream to goal, that warn of dangerous detours and dead ends. Seeing map contours, I envisioned landforms and watersheds and, like the writer I would soon become, built inner worlds.

My fondness for maps stands in a tradition predating Gutenberg's press and Han Dynasty silk maps from the second century BCE. A seven-by-five-inch incised stone tablet from northern Spain not only depicts mountains, river bends, and a home cave, but also a ford or pass and paths to ibexes, red deer, and young bovines. After 15 years of deciphering, it was interpreted as either the chronicle of a glorious hunt, or else a plan for conducting one. Its date: 12,000 BCE. By that point, the end of the last ice age, *Homo sapiens* long had replaced its Neanderthal competition. Neuroscientists credit the new hominin's success to brain developments that allowed symbolic thinking and the anticipation of different outcomes flowing from different actions. Wayfinding and mapmaking exemplify the earliest joint manifestation of these mental capabilities.

I'm aware that the popularity of Google Earth's panopticon makes my passion for paper maps oddly antiquated. As tangible objects, they're as printed books are to e-books. Or books compared to films, as a matter of fact. Crisply detailed, distilled, rarely updated, crawling with glosses, smelling of places they've been in, map sheets freeze places and time while leaving enough room for the imagination. And try starting an emergency fire with a GPS receiver. Of course, like roads and worn trails, printed maps leading the clueless were a step on the path to our cognition's pauperization. Yet, beyond all the differences, place names and maps share common ground as human tools in the symbolic organization of space.

Beholding the map set of my traverse, my eyes flick to the journey's beginning, 20 miles from the Canadian border. I'd hiked east for a day to view the line dividing what can't be divided, not for practical or even aesthetic reasons but for a sense of completeness— the hardest part of the trip psychologically, as 1,000 miles lay ahead in the other direction. There were bronze obelisks among a total of 389 waypoints to a polar sea that once cairned the cleared lane between the two countries. Streams cross this construct, as snow geese and caribou do, flowing for now undeterred between winter and summer ranges. A smart gopher living in a burrow beneath one of the monuments is poised for unilateral crises, I heard from a re-surveyor. It has dug exits to both countries, oblivious of passport requirements. First Peoples dwell on either side, kin by custom and blood, divided by politics, paying import taxes when they visit bearing gifts. On my easternmost map sheet, Canada—a country "not us"—had been amputated, flush with the longitude grid. An old atlas I own renders the neighbor pale gray, insubstantial. That boundary, part of which forms the longest straight line in the country, runs from Demarcation Point south to Mount Saint Elias, where it veers into the Alaska panhandle's littoral; for nearly 700 miles it matches the 141st meridian west, proof of failure to read or accept a region's natural flow. Crews with choppers and chainsaws faithfully groom the scar of the recent historical break.

As a warmup for all that monumental work, in 1902, the men of a summit boundary post built a Janus-headed snowman over 32 feet tall on this Yukon–Alaska border. King Edward's bearded face overlooked the British domain, Uncle Sam's the Americans'. The thermometer read minus 52. "Nowhere in the broad and busy world are the contributory elements of suicidal melancholia more in evidence," the *Vancouver World* editorialized. If a frost giant topples above the tree line and no one is around to hear it, does it make a sound? Both countries' claims on the empire of stone and serenity are as long-lived as the effigy's flesh.

Five weeks on foot to the east of my starting point, in the heart of Gates of the Arctic National Park, Anaktuvuk Pass straddles the Continental Divide. On the map, this enclave of 300 inland Inupiat is a cluster of flyspecks. The "Place of Caribou Droppings" rouses fond memories. I'd mailed myself a box of greasy goodies, one of six caches I'd arranged along the traverse, and devoured smoked oysters and salty potato chips sitting in the dirt lot of the trailer-size post office. The dinged pint of Ben & Jerry's from the village store to me was worth four times the eight bucks I had paid.

For Kenneth Brower, son of the conservation icon David Brower, "The knowledge that aerial mapmakers have is poor, shared with too many, and hard to take pride in" compared to that of a person who walks the backcountry. Or, put differently, every map is a treasure map, as it hides the real that will always surprise you. Tracking Brooks Range contour lines, as Brower did, with my feet, not my eyes, I quickly wised up to the cartographers' code. Bunched, nut-brown hairlines meant steep climbs or descents; "hedgehog" silhouettes promised abysmal swamps— could those be stylized tussocks? Azure stood for lakes, ponds, and rivers or, finely striated, for snowfields and glaciers; the same hue spelled the same substance, also: wet crossings, creek-side coffee breaks, slippery footing. Black airplane icons, lettering, or cabin-squares betrayed human presence, which I could do without. Still, my throat tightened at the glint of the tube that siphons a nation's lifeblood and bane from Prudhoe Bay to Valdez. I was gazing down from a notch in the Philip Smith Mountains, the westernmost range of the Arctic National Wildlife Refuge. (People call it "ANWR," pronounced as one word, "An-war," but it's a sanctuary, not an acronym, not deadened bureaucratic land.) I knew then that, short of an accident, I could manage this trek, step by step and one day at a time. Roughly two-thirds of the hiking now lay behind me, and, strangely, the silvery thread in the distance carried the comforts of civilization, of my former home Fairbanks, near that same pipeline. And yet, my link with the world known felt much more tenuous.

I never fully foresaw the many hardships along the way. Maps are for fantasizing, for grappling with three-dimensional puzzles. Maps invite interpretation, the projection of difficulties and possibilities. Does this pass "go"? Is this mileage feasible? How deep and fast is this river? Reality, on the other hand, is measured in elevation-feet lost and gained, in tough days on the ground. It should have been obvious. The Brooks Range can't be found on even the best of maps. True places never are, Melville thought.

What my USGS quadrangles fail to show (besides the missing

route segment): Tussocks, those knee-high mop-heads through which I had storked, fright wigs of vegetation that taxed my knees, ankles, and spirit. Ekokpuk Creek, the trip's worst bushwhacking, not even hinted at by the usual mint green patches on the map. The depth of streams I had forded with hiking poles vibrating in the current. The opportunistic grizzlies that circled downwind for a rank whiff of me, which normally sent those bolting. The mosquitos that shadowed me—I close my eyes and I hear their flimsy wings still. Though I did not mark my encounters with wolves on these sheets, I can pinpoint each one to within half a mile to this day. I can raise each one from memory scraps, even without my dense notes. The maps do not hold the steel taste of spring water so cold it hurt teeth. They lack the perfume of crushed heather or Labrador tea, the soughing of breezes, peregrine shrieks, and the tang of August blueberries, as they do Indigenous history beyond the shorthand of names. They omit the fog that blotted out Peregrine Pass, the gusting in the Noatak valley, the rain that soaked me for 30 consecutive days. They can never convey the magic of puppy-eyed seals bobbing near my boat, of cranes' pterodactyl calls bouncing off the still river's skin. Nor do they include the small corner of the map quadrangle I chose not to buy, out of thrift, which, out there, sent me into a frenzy of cussing and scouting. You don't find in them either the image of me afterward, reduced by 25 pounds. Together with that weight, mental dross and routines had been stripped away. Six hundred miles walking and 400 rowing the Noatak River, all solo, had reopened my eyes to nature's small, quiet wonders. In addition to route choices, the maps inscribed with my entries, dossiers of topographic wisdom, offer advice: seize the day. Or better yet, let the day seize you.

CHAPTER 19

HONEYMOON FOR THREE

elow us, a tundra mosaic unfolds in a hundred pieces of green and brown, with unblinking blue splotches of melt-water ponds. Frost heaves or *pingos* blister the land, interrupting its polygonal patterns. Willow patches cling to rivers whose braids unravel with distance. Above the horizon, the peaks of northern Alaska's Brooks Range soar like long-held wishes come true.

Our pilot, Bob, is an old hand with the frame and facial hair of a griz'. He turns to me, nods. I can see myself duplicated in his insect-eye aviator glasses, dwarfed by the immensity outside the cockpit. A toothy grin splits his furry face.

My brother, his new wife, and I took the regular twin-prop from Fairbanks, where I was waiting for my summer guiding schedule to fill. On its way north, the plane crossed the Yukon River thousands of feet above the pipeline that sluices buried sunlight down from Prudhoe Bay. Whittling away at pale bluffs covered with spruce, the great one rolled placidly westward to its appointment with the Bering Sea. After a brief stop in Bettles, on the airfield that served as a way station for US warplanes sent to Russia during World War II, we switched to Bob's single-engine Cessna with floats, chartered through an outfitter.

"So, when are you guys gonna be at the Alatna?" our pilot comes in over my headset, between bouts of static.

I shudder and roll my eyes to get my brother's attention.

"What do you mean, 'Alatna'? We were planning to hike to the John, where you are supposed to drop off our boats and supplies for the river leg of this trip."

"Right. No problem," drawls the voice in my ear.

He pulls on the horn, the plane banks into a steep easterly turn, and gravity pushes me into the seat. On the instrument panel, the artificial horizon is tilting like unbalanced scales when the stalling alarm shrills. I catch a glimpse of my brother. His eyes seem to plead. *I hope you know what you are doing*, they say.

They are on their honeymoon—Andreas and Kerstin, my pert, curly-haired sister-in-law. This is to be the adventure heralding an even bigger one: a life spent together. I know the area between Gates of the Arctic National Park and the middle reaches of the Koyukuk River from my research in Alaska Native communities and agreed to be their guide—on the ground and water, but not up here. They are kin, and I hold myself responsible for their safety and wellbeing. Right now, I worry about the male gene pool of our family evaporating in a big ball of fire.

Before long, the plane loses altitude, diving straight for a chain of glacial lakes that separates foothills and plains from the gray granite of the Endicott Mountains. I crane my neck to scan the slopes on my side for wildlife. Bob zeroes in on one of the glassy surfaces. When the floats touch down, spray swallows our bird's shadow on the water. With the engine throttled, we taxi to shore.

As we unload backpacks and sort through piles of food, I notice movement from the corner of my eye. Turning toward it, I catch a stately caribou bull splashing into the shallows before throwing itself into the deep. It cuts straight across the lake, and the chevrons of its wake twinkle in the rich afternoon light. Only the head and sweep of antlers are showing, like forked driftwood. Not far behind, a grizzly comes crashing through the underbrush, desperate for a meal. The ease and speed of this bolt of taut muscle are breathtaking—at a short distance, it could out-gallop a horse. Without hesitation, Old Ephraim plunges in and streaks after the bull.

"I'll keep her running," Bob shouts over the engine's growling, "Just in case." Dumbstruck and momentarily frozen in place, all three of us think that this is a good idea.

By the time Andreas has rummaged through his backpack and pulled out the camera, the bear and its intended lunch are too far away for a decent shot. When I clip the economy-size can of pepper spray to my pack, it seems awfully puny.

"Got your hot sauce," Bob jokes, "to spice up his dinner?" I think he means us.

Before we part, I point out the rendezvous place to him on the map.

"See you guys in a week, then."

"Headwaters of the John!"

"The John. Right."

We shake his calloused paw, and watch as he folds his bulk back into the cockpit.

Too soon for us to feel ready, the engine's droning ebbs and dies, and the plane shrinks to a speck in the distance. The smell of kerosene lingers. Silence reigns again, and the insistence of mosquitos only accentuates it. Worn out from two flights and spooked by our introduction to nature's way of doing business, we decide to spend the night here. While Kerstin and I set up the tents, Robert Redford assembles his rod and reel and starts casting for grayling or trout.

"You might want to put on some bug dope, or better yet, gloves and a hat," I say.

"In a minute. Just a few more."

We end up having good old mac-'n'-cheese, without fish, inside their roomy honeymoon suite. My brother's hands are almost too swollen to hold a spoon. His usually gaunt face looks puffy and flushed, feverish.

"Told you so, city slicker."

"Whatever."

Stretched out in my pup tent later, I contemplate our arrival.

Hard to believe that only this morning, I awoke in a bed in the city. Through my fly screen I watch a lazy sun grazing the world's edge without ever dipping below. Light dense and golden as mead floods the enclosed space. Shadows on the ground outside mimic the lengthening summer days. Then the horizon fades to lilac, unburdened by clouds, while famished hordes hit the tent, sounding like rain.

Our route to the headwaters is a treeless Via Dolorosa. Distance north of the Arctic Circle often is measured in pints of sweat and blood. We mostly hike resembling beekeepers, dolled-up in rain gear, gaiters, gloves, head nets, and hats, with temperatures approaching 90 degrees. The only alternative is an insect repellent with DEET, a chemical compound the Army developed after the Pacific War. Its side effects can include hallucinations, insomnia, mood disturbances, and seizures, a few of which have ended in death. It dissolves plastic zippers and leather and is probably a derivative of DDT or Agent Orange. People with PhDs worked on this Jungle Juice—the bugs do not like it. Tasting skin slathered with it with the receptors in their feet, they take off in revulsion like bats out of hell (about that size, too). Imagine having six legs, and tongues replacing your toes! There is no kissing with this bitter stuff on for the newlyweds, either; fearing weird consequences and planning to have healthy offspring, they stay chaste, at least to my knowledge. Athabaskan old-timers have told me that, to keep mosquitos away, they would carry a can of smoldering tree fungus in the bottom of their boats. But there's no tree fungus to be found here, as there are no trees.

In his two-part lecture "Walking" and "The Wild," Thoreau declared that he sometimes recreated himself by seeking "the thickest and most interminable and to the citizen, most dismal, swamp" and that he would enter a swamp "as a sacred place."

"Take a walk on *my* wild side," I'd like to tell him.

Boots are forever soaked in this marshy terrain. *Squish, squish, squish, squelch* goes the soundtrack for our hike. In some places, the ground is more water than land. Only surface layers of soil thaw under the 24/7 stare of the Arctic midsummer sun. Because the permafrost underneath, per definition, ideally, never melts, water pools on the tundra with nowhere to drain—perfect breeding grounds for the beasts. Atop this gigantic sponge, we barely find enough level, dry ground to pitch our tents. When there are no mosquitos, tiny no-see-ums ("much-fear-ums") or bullet-size horseflies plague us. Some people call the latter "bulldogs" or "stouts." The insects appear to be working in shifts. On a good day, there are nondescript gnats. Each night, before we slip into our sleeping bags, we check for mold growing between our toes.

Tussocks promise dry crossings of the soggy flats, but camel humps would be easier to balance on. Stepping into the lip-smacking mud pockets in-between is not a good option, either; it feels like post-holing in snow, and boots get soaked within minutes. Stepping dead center onto the mop heads seems to be the trick to avoid wet feet and sprained ankles. Still, every few hundred yards I need to stop, wheezing like an asthmatic.

With each step, a voracious cloud lifts from a tussock, and I am miffed that I have to take in the scenery filtered through a head net. (When Andreas developed the photos from our trip, he found most of them ruined, stippled with dots like black snow. Like pictures of grizzly charges, none of his convey the brutal reality.) I once knew a biologist, a snake guy and hardcore hiker, driven crazy by non-stinging midges even. It was the sensation of always walking behind a milling-particle veil, of so many critters wanting something from him. They didn't, or at least nothing they wouldn't also ask of a bush or a boulder: male midges swarm around any large visual marker to attract females, which join the fray.

Dealing with the stinging species, we've perfected the "cook dinner dressed to the gills and dive into the tent without spilling the beans" act, which by now has become routine. Before we sample the first spoonful of stews I concoct from dehydrated ingredients, we purge the tent of intruders. Mozzies sated already by *their* meal leave crimson smears on the tent walls when we squeeze the life out of them. We learn that the big, clumsy ones that survived the winter are not nearly as agile or vicious or numerous as this year's batch. In the mornings, we break camp in a hurry to get moving and escape our pursuers for a while, literally itching to go.

Occasionally, I try to dish out more protracted punishment through an apocryphal method of executing mosquitos. You can supposedly tighten a muscle to prevent a freeloader from with-drawing its stiletto proboscis from your skin. Your pumping heart will bloat the bug's abdomen until it bursts like a tiny bleb, a death fit for gluttons. After repeated attempts, I find that I am more likely to bust a blood vessel or suffer a hernia from the strain. There is no consolation either in knowing that I just volunteered nourishment for another generation of suckers.

Make no mistake; these are not your garden-variety vermin— some of Alaska's 35 kinds rank among the fiercest and most prolific of North America's 150 mosquito species. A fellow diarist described their predecessors in the Klondike goldfields, more than a hundred years ago:

> They are not like the usual mosquito. They light and bite in the same instant, never lose any time in feeling around… In panning, we sometimes have them light on the back of the bare hand so thick that instantly the hand is black with them and we scrape them off the same way we would mud or other so stuff. Plunging the hand in water will not dislodge those that have a good hold.

Gone are the times when we joked about Alaska's vampire state birds, or the leg-hold-trap key rings for their capture that Fairbanks curio shops sell. The single-strike kill record on our trip stands at 34. Overriding my Buddhist inclinations, I have become used to the sound of one hand slapping. This is nothing but good, old-fashioned revenge, an eye for an eye, a vendetta with the divine: "He sent among them swarms of flies, which devoured them"—*Psalms* 78:45.

In a place where storytelling explains the world and alleviates endless dark nights, people recall how mosquitos originated. An Inuk in one myth stabbed a cannibal monster after learning about its Achilles' heel. "Though I am dead," the giant said, "I will keep on eating you and all other humans forever." To prevent this, the man cut the body into pieces, which he burned in a fire. When he tossed the resulting ashes into the wind, each flake became a mosquito.

Modern science does not tell creation stories about the pests, but it can give us a handle on quantities. An entomologist calculated for me the mass of mosquitos in Alaska, with equations that made my brain hurt. The annual crop of the devil's seed, his math showed, weighs roughly 96 million pounds, the equivalent of human biomass in the state. I know that carbon dioxide I exhale attracts them. But holding my breath would not save me; they also follow the breadcrumbs of my body's heat, odor, and perspiration. There are people, mosquito magnets, whose aroma makes them a hundred times more attractive as targets, as if they had bull's-eyes on their foreheads. The only way they can lose their tormentors is to die.

I always thought it counterproductive that mosquitos announce their intention with an enthusiastic *wheeeeee!* that grows louder, more irksome, the closer they come. Are they testing their prey's alertness? Would a sneak attack not be far more efficient? Could it be a means of psychological warfare, like the whistling bombs designed to instill terror in World War II attacks? It turns out mosquitos can't help but whir. The cricket leeches stridulate when they're airborne, through a special structure rubbing on their wings. And the kicker: they find mates that way, since they can hear with their antennas, and females and males hum edgy love songs at different frequencies.

This John River trip, then, is a honeymoon not for three but for thousands.

Over dinner one evening, I wonder aloud what the stinging masses eat when we are not around. "Caribou," my brother says. And he's right. Feasting mosquitos draw up to a quart of blood per week from a hapless animal, and backpackers find rotting carcasses that have been completely drained. A bush pilot I know gives graphic accounts of mosquito rapaciousness: surveying large caribou herds from the air, he's seen engorged swarms spatter his plane's windows like blood rain. Increasing in numbers as the climate ramps up, mosquitos even drive breeding birds from their nests and assault their naked feet, which, to one researcher, made them look like "fur slippers." But at least we are spared botflies and warbleflies, whose larvae digest the tissue of nasal passages and upon maturation wiggle out from the backs of living caribou.

Scratching my bites till they're raw, it helps to remember the good even in mosquitos. Without them, and without winter's dark moods, Alaska would be as crowded as Colorado or Wyoming, playgrounds for the newly rich and eternally bored. Like grizzlies, those largest predators on the tundra, the smallest ones keep us humble. They remind us that we are still part of the food chain, and not necessarily at the top. In a beautiful democracy of predation, mosquitos feed on bears as well as on us but, as major pollinators in the Arctic, repay both hosts with berries; their pond-born larvae, myriads of wriggling question marks, in turn sustain thousands of shorebirds and their chicks.

The nearly featureless landscape that harbors mosquito eggs throughout subzero winters keeps unfurling, doing its best to deny us progress. With nothing but lackluster hills around, it is hard to identify landmarks for taking compass bearings, and the maps often are useless. We zig and then zag repeatedly, attempting to correct our course. At some point, Kerstin throws down her pack, sits on a hummock, and breaks into tears.

"Wilderness—I had no idea what you meant." "No trails—anywhere. I want trees!"

I feel sorry for her. At times like these, I feel sorry for myself.

For good measure, the only wingless wildlife we encounter after the spectacle at the lake is a lone moose. It's scrawny enough to act as a double for the one from the opening credits of the 1990s cult sitcom *Northern Exposure*, a moose Washington State University provided and that Alaskans would be ashamed to show on TV or to be associated with. (In fact, ours are bigger than theirs as a rule.)

More than a week and who knows how many miles later, we top yet another rise of the oceanic expanse. Below us, Paradise: stunted Christmas trees, the first black spruce since we left

Fairbanks. A lake tucked into a silvery crook of the John River. At last! The put-in for our journey's waterborn leg. We may be running a day or two late; we don't know exactly. The only watch we carry does not show dates. Time's fun when you're having flies. Close to shore, we come upon two canoes with the outfitter's logo, several bear-proof barrels of food, and, I hope, a shipment from the blood bank.

Here's to Bob. Long may he soar!

After a layover day at the depot, splurging on fresh veggies and fruit, resting sore muscles, and airing out feet, we take some practice turns on the lake. Neither of the honeymooners has ever sat in a canoe. We then portage to the river, load up, and shove off. By the time we join the main current, the bugs have let up considerably.

The honeymoon, however, is far from over.

Andreas and Kerstin share one canoe, while I paddle the other. Or try to. A few strokes out, I realize that the load is unbalanced, too far back in the boat and listing to starboard. The bow is too light, which becomes a problem when a headwind starts up. Gusts spin the canoe like a compass needle until it points upriver—due north. I curse and swear and keep turning it downstream, falling quickly behind. Upset, I paddle hard, uncoordinated, only to capsize. My breath catches high in my chest and the moment distends to contain—everything. I take a mouthful of John River that is half ice water, half glacial silt.

As soon as we've righted the boat and fished my sodden belongings from an eddy, we re-shuffle the seating arrangements. All three of us now ride in one canoe, with myself in the middle. In the Gulf of Alaska, this is known as the "missionary position." In the old days, greenhorns in black robes and clutching Bibles always rode mid-ship, while their straight-faced Indigenous guides propelled kayaks with deft strokes, biting their lips to keep from laughing. "People never stayed quiet," the Gwich'in elder Joan Nazon reminisced in Tsiigehtchic, in "Mouth of Iron River," about the floating nomadic life in Canada's Northwest Territories. "They paddled all the time—their arm was their kicker and their

engine." Lacking a kicker but having regained our pep, we hitch
the second canoe to our stern with its bowline, towing it along.
Here we come, three White Folks tugging down the river, grinning
like fools, one sopping wet. Luckily, nobody seems to be watching.

I am having a bad flashback to a solo trip on the Noatak River
the year before. Rounding a bend, I'd come face to face with a
grizzly and her cub. They were swimming across the narrow
channel, ears and black noses poking from the water. The current kept sweeping me onward, swiftly and relentlessly, despite
much frantic backpaddling. I was clearly set on a collision course.
The mother in a second calculated both bearings, and decided to
return to the side from which they had come. Back on the cutbank
she shook her massive head, shedding water in a halo of droplets
like an overgrown Saint Bernard. One last glance over her shoulder and she'd sauntered into the bushes, her fuzzy offspring glued
to her heels.

The scenario of a snarling mess of bear, rope, honeymooners,
and boats so far from help brings cold sweat to my brow.

Several miles downstream, we are well into the tree line.

Because we are no longer used to vegetation higher than knee
level, the sky appears pinched and somehow diminished. The
stream roils complacently under our keels, slipping across gravel
bars, wheeling around bends, weaving and murmuring, grabbing
clods of dirt here and there, unhurried, but preoccupied with its
destination. It leaves sandbars exposed, vibrates fallen trees as
it passes. Such strainers can be sudden deathtraps. *Whack!* The
sound of a beaver's tail feels like a slap in the face, asking me
to pay attention. It almost makes me drop my paddle, but the
culprit stays hidden.

Days later, we pull out at the confluence of the John and the
Koyukuk River. Bettles, a village of 40, lies several miles upstream
from this junction. We could line our canoes along the Koyukuk's
brushy banks, but I decide to forgo the ordeal and blow a wad of
cash instead.

"Let's call a taxi," I say.

"Have you been drinking?" Andreas asks, concern rumpling his face. He knows I don't have a satellite phone or even a cell phone or landline.

Near a meat cache on stilts and a log cabin, I locate the weatherproof box I knew would be there, clamped to the trunk of a tall spruce. An antenna extends above the tree's top, and a solar panel close by fuels the contraption. Hi-tech has come to the bush. I open the box, lift the receiver, and almost instantly talk to our outfitter in Bettles.

"I'll be there in an hour," he says and hangs up.

"Another chatterbox," I mutter to myself.

"I wonder if you could have ordered us pizza," Kerstin chimes in.

Soon after we've finished unloading the canoes, a decked aluminum skiff rounds a bend in the river. With it, noise has returned. But we bask in the glow of accomplishment, ready for beer, a shower, and a bunk bed, in that order.

"Guess you found the boats all right," our chauffeur greets us, throwing me a line.

We strap both canoes to the skiff's cabin roof and cast off. As the boreal forest zips past in a blur and the wind musses my hair, an emotion like regret washes over me. It could be a long time before I find myself up north again, if ever, as life has a tendency to intervene in even our best-laid plans. Despite two weeks of discomforts, I feel that something profound has ended. But for the lovebirds reclining on the front deck, wrapped up in fleece jackets and conversation, this is just the beginning.

CHAPTER 20

ARCTIC SAHARA

Time slipping, a tabula rasa. Footprints erased, slopes advanced, ripples un-sculpted. A whole world the whims of weather have recast. Besides snowfields and foreshores, few landscapes appear so clean-cut, so refined. Here, emptiness is the main attraction.

I'm perched on a gear pile at the lip of a sand dune adjacent to boreal spruce—a latter-day Lawrence of Beringia. The two Guatemalans I'm shepherding on a weeklong sampler tour of northwestern national parks busy themselves snapping farewell photos of Ahnewetut Creek, whose braids skirt the Great Kobuk Sand Dunes' scalloped smooth bays. The whine of our scheduled plane, which I hear repeatedly, is revealed as a mosquito or simply the high pitch of silence in this place. The bugs have been pesky, and my clients wanted to camp on the flat, hard-packed sand where the pilot dropped us off two days ago. That stuff would invade every crevice, I told them, and it's too far to water, but even so, they took to eating their meals on top, in the herb-scented breeze, drunk on the views, safe from bloodsuckers and cranky moose.

The Sierra Club calls this "America's most obscure desert." I call it an awesome freak of nature.

Thirty-five miles north of the Arctic Circle, just shy of the Brooks Range, Kobuk Valley National Park ranks among America's least explored gems for an obvious reason. To visit, you charter a Cessna in Kotzebue or backpack an hour from a river loop after beaching a raft or floatplane or motorboat.

This region holds special meaning for me. I spent my first summer of ethnographic fieldwork in the inland Inupiaq communities of Ambler (upstream) and Kiana (downstream), about equidistant from the dunes, recording place names and subsistence patterns for a Park Service study. In essence, the university paid me to shadow Alaska Native tradition bearers, many of which had been born in seasonal fishcamps, to travel, sometimes around midnight, in outboard-powered skiffs and catch pike, whitefish, grayling, and burbot, a cod impersonating a catfish. This was the fun side of anthropology, which, I would soon discover, was thoroughly blighted by the slog of pie charts, data entry, airless libraries, windowless seminar rooms in ivory towers styled like Soviet-bunker housing blocks, and by theorizing and department infighting—"internecine warfare," in our lingo. We were trained to dive into foreign cultures but often could not tolerate our own kind. Still naïve with respect to and for academia, in Alaska's northwestern river villages I quickly learned that among the Kuuvangmiut ("People of the Kobuk") "upstream" and "downstream" crop up daily in conversations as cardinal directions that orient lives. This orientation is even more pronounced in their first language, Inupiaq. *Qikiqtaqpak*, or "Big Island," for example, refers to a feature above and to the right (upriver) of the speaker. The worldwide ubiquity of similar prepositions, such as the English "under," "above," "behind," "across," and metaphorical modifiers—*heightened* awareness, *broadened* horizons, *close* friends, *distant* memories, etc.—leads some neuroscientists to believe that language as a whole might be based on a spatial framework; that it sprang from the need to convey crucial information about the environment.

I'd caught my first glimpse of dune fields slightly larger than Manhattan and snow-covered two-thirds of the year from the window of a prop plane returning from Ambler to Kotzebue. Including their Little Kobuk and Hunt River outliers, the continent's largest active dunes in high latitudes smother 30 square miles in a mini-Sahara. Summer temperatures can hover around 100 degrees, fooling you with mirages: heat waver; peaks flared like anvils; and sprawling, coalescing lakes. The park's terrain is an absence birthed by retreating glaciers. Easterly winds carried rock that Pleistocene ice had finely abraded, dumping it along the Kobuk Valley. As the climate seesawed, the Aeolian conveyor belt slowed or sped up, and the dune field shrank or expanded ten-fold. Encroaching grasses and trees now claim 90 percent of the underlying sand. The dusty void was aligned into serried heights, separated by troughs ten stories deep. If the Statue of Liberty stepped off her pedestal, only her head would poke out between the tallest mounds. There are parabolic dunes and crescent barch-ans in the field's southern part, with two horns pointing down-wind, and steeper, slip faces on that side. Some dunes migrate as far as the length of a football field annually. From the crown of one behemoth, our gaze had roamed lone, heaving sands to a suddenly broadened horizon scored by the Baird Mountains' powder-blue silhouettes.

The dunes override soggy sediments whose moisture percolates through the superimposed sands. Ever wandering, they release and inter ice-age bone fragments once in a while. Plant succes-sion shows with textbook clarity. Sedges, sparse grasses, dwarf lupines, wild rye, the purplish-pink Kobuk locoweed, thriving nowhere else, and forest islands all struggle for toeholds, resisting live-burial, anchoring into the substrate with root feelers, tapping reservoirs frozen solid for part of the year. A pale population of tiger beetles lives here, apart from the bulk of this Northern Plains subspecies. These are the cheetahs of the insect world, with reactions as quick as those of houseflies. One Australian species can scurry a distance of 120 times its body length in one second, which for a human runner would equal a speed of over 400 miles per hour. Moving in spurts, these ambush hunters are so fast they have to stop to avoid losing sight of their prey. This, too, is a trait of the desert: its openness highlights the minute.

Signs of larger wildlife abound in and near the dunes. Loons wail insanely. Wolf paws twice as big as a dog's shadow the zip-per tracks of Western Arctic Herd caribou, ending at vertebrae scattered like ghoulish dice. Moose nuggets and bear scat nest in lichen and moss pillows below the sliding, granular cliffs. Willow sticks dam Ahnewetut amid alders that porcupines girdled. Beavers push V-wavelets through its shallows on constant repair errands. Miners and trappers had extirpated them along the river in the late 19th century. And when I'd scooped up buckets of water for yesterday's dinner from the creek, black, beady eyes gleamed from a root hollow in the bank—yet another ermine?

"You should not see the desert simply as some faraway place of little rain. There are many forms of thirst," the pilot and journalist William Langewiesche writes in his travelogue *Sahara Unveiled*, and I never met a desert I didn't like. Stripped of the superfluous, parched lands resemble good writing and a desirable life. Like Saint-Exupéry, air-racing toward Saigon above the Libyan desert, I succumbed to the first sand waste I saw, three decades ago, during a Death Valley shortcut that almost killed me. This glaring sea is a harsh mistress, strict and serene—it's hard not to wax philosophical in her presence. Life and death balance on the scimitar edge of her swells. Lines from "Ozymandias" reverberate. Hermits and prophets dwelled in her furnace, forging messianic religions. Eons unspool in streams of grains running through your fingers, cycled through deposition and weathering's mill—not once, but over and over again. Each rounded quartz bit is a world unto itself, and with each, William Blake observed, you cup infinity in the palm of your hand. Each dune, then, must be a universe. Early-Holocene satellite hunting camps fringe the Kobuk field. One wonders what a sea-ice people thought of the restless golden crests. The people of Shungnak, a village 50 miles upriver, as laconic as the locale itself, called it *Qaviat*, "Covered with Sand."

Like tourists and wilderness guides, scientists rack up days there, though they seek explanations for distant worlds too in these blank fields. Astrophysicists, comparing satellite images of the same Martian scene periodically, discovered dune fronts marching across the red planet. With a remote-sensing technique they had developed, they estimated the speed of the Kobuk dunes, finding those progressing slower than their counterparts near the equator. Strangely, the data also suggested huge northern dunes inch forward faster than dwarf ones. Drilling boreholes in March, taking the dunes' winter temperatures, and scanning them with ground-penetrating radar, researchers learned that unfrozen ridges of giants towering above their neighbors bear the wind's brunt, which increases their momentum. Lee sides and sinks ("interdunes," technically) and smaller surges under snow, in comparison, remain fairly static. Our sibling planet's polar dunes, coated with carbon dioxide and frost, behave in a similar manner. Liquid groundwater, the boreholes showed, persists year-round beneath the dunes, with permafrost absent.

The Kobuk's enigmatic reach compels us to toe sharp divides, to weigh lines between risk and annihilation. Sand in the gear we unpack at home makes an exquisite memento. With Mars here on Earth and a chance to see ermines or wolves, who needs to colonize space?

CHAPTER 21

CONVERGENCES

Encounters with wildlife can feel like payback for karmic points earned and keep some of us buzzing for days. Perhaps more than in its weather or plants, the land's life force concentrates in its creatures, sharpened to poignancy, similar but foreign enough to our own to be captivating. To a few people, it, or a thing closely related to it, becomes audible. A fellow wilderness guide describes it as a low-frequency sound, "like a didgeridoo," which she has come to expect in certain places and greets as an old friend. Of course, the humming just might be tinnitus, or a hallucination hunger brings on, or our mind wanting to hear something, anything, beyond sub-polar silence.

One fall day, on a Canning River raft trip I guided, at the western boundary of the Arctic National Wildlife Refuge, will always remain special to the trip's participants for what the land offered up without asking for anything but our attention.

Sipping coffee in the morning's quiet, looking south from the top of the bluff where we had pitched our tents, I noticed a white blob on the bench below, muscling toward camp. I did not believe my eyes. A polar bear! The clients popped from their nylon cocoons like ground squirrels from their burrows when I alerted them—one clad in boxer shorts and a down jacket. My co-guide Cyn, the one who perceived the land's droning, insisted on getting the shotgun from its waterproof sleeve by my tent. We stood and watched the bear sniff and root around. To the marine mammal-dependent carnivore (the largest on land), ground squirrels, foxes, or birds could have been the only morsels of interest there. But as mere ashes in its metabolic pan, they would never provide enough calories for this blubber-burning powerhouse.

The bear's wedge head swung on its pendulous neck, snake-like, gauging god-knows-what. Thirty miles from the coast, radiant against heather and willows, the bear looked as displaced as it would have in a zoo. The previous year, sea ice, a haul-out for seals, hunting base for the bears, and highway for the Inupiat— the Canadian novelist Murray Lee calls it "a crucial piece of traditional Arctic infrastructure"—had shrunk to the third-lowest extent ever. Hunger or curiosity could have driven the bear this far inland. It appeared healthy and fat, but if the spring ice had broken up early again, it would be in for a long fast. It needed to grub for 12,000 calories every day, five times the amount people who aren't Olympian swimmers or cyclists need. On the bear's meal plan, that meant almost 40 quarts of blueberries, or six ground squirrels, notoriously hard to dig up.

In the spring of 2008, a Gwich'in hunter had killed a polar bear near Fort Yukon, 250 miles south of the Beaufort Sea coast. Its inland excursion was the longest on record for an Alaska polar bear. Normally at that time of year the animals would be ambushing seals on the ice. I only found out after our trip that our sighting qualified as the farthest inland sighting of *Ursus maritimus* in the Arctic Refuge. In 2011, a scientific study reported a polar bear marathon feat. A GPS-collared female with her yearling cub had churned 426 miles across the Beaufort Sea, from east of Barrow to near the Canadian border. In search of an ice floe on which to rest, she spent nine days straight in water barely above the freezing temperature. Her cub did not survive. And in January 2023, in the first fatal polar bear attack in Alaska in three decades, an older male killed a young mother and her baby boy right outside the school in Wales, an Inupiaq village at the tip of the Seward Peninsula. The bear was described as being in "poor physical condition." A climate connection may be hard to prove in some of these cases. Clearly, though, as far as northern species and their behavior go, we now should expect the unexpected.

Without a care in the world, the bear we'd been watching lay down for a nap halfway up the bluff's slope. What was there to fear?

We sat, with our binoculars trained on the pile that could easily have been mistaken for a limestone boulder. Occasionally, the bear lifted its head to sample the air. We crouched downwind from it, and it remained unaware of our presence.

Before long, a golden eagle stroked past. Some gulls mobbed it, but, regal in its bearing, it scrutinized the bear, which did not wake up. Then another bright spot heading downstream caught my eye. A cub? But the gait differed: a trot, with a mission more than an ambling, the mark of canine determination, not of the larger carnivore's easy opportunism. A scan with my glasses revealed a white wolf.

Animals congregating near us for no obvious reason leave us mystified and in awe, more so when they are "charismatic" or rare. They stand for connections we've lost, evoke life ways and lineages once familiar that now seem arcane. They appear as sudden emissaries, omens, or uncanny messengers, although most of us no longer speak their language. At our layover camp, caribou, wolves, moose, bears, foxes, and a wolverine had stamped the mudflats with coded messages. Breezy flyways for geese lined the sky, and taste tracks and the current's fibers textured the river for Arctic char, as fleetingly and invisibly as words an index finger scrawls into wind. The day after, we had observed a black Arctic fox, a moose built like a bulldozer, and a peregrine striking a ptarmigan on the fly and passing it off to a juvenile bird, all within one hour. The char finned in beryl fishing holes, otherwise still, resting, olive backs above orange bellies, each one a scaly muscle as big as a thigh. Every third cast or so snagged one. Even Cyn got in on the act, while I just stood down and gawped.

Animals sought contact with us on occasion, mirroring our curiosity. Mew gulls escorted the rafts, screeching blue murder and sounding like rusty door hinges. Caribou stepped closer, curious, eyeing us nervously. Waving my paddle overhead, I baited them onward. A red fox, non-native like myself and likely to cannibalize its smaller Arctic cousins if it came upon them, investigated our dinner setup. In the continent's outskirts, the ways of animals had changed. *We* had changed them through our mere presence.

Sure, there were explanations for such meetings, for the over-lapping of agendas in space and time, or at least the beginnings of explanations. Caribou are nosey, and gulls and terns peeved about intruders, which they pursue. Mornings and evenings, mammals tend to be more active, avoiding mosquito peak times or heat, fueling up for a cold night or the day ahead. In part, our encounters signaled the land's abundance, the narrow seasonal window for blooming and birthing, maturing and mating, that winter too soon slams shut. We also had to account for selective perception, our minds' tunnel vision. The more we yielded to our surroundings, and the better we learned to look and listen for clues and shed our civilization's blinders, the more animals rewarded us with sightings. When our attention strayed to daydreams or to each other, wildlife must have slipped past unnoticed. Despite our desire, the landscape lay lifeless for hours at a time and miles around. We frequently surveyed it from a hilltop or standing up in the rafts, finding no movement except in the river's slippage beneath scudding clouds.

What orchestrated animal transects that measured this land? What tangled pathways at greater than random frequency? Did life glom onto more life, beyond caloric or reproductive necessities? Was there some faunal magnetism, some orbiting of terrestrial bodies about which we knew nothing but which encompassed us?

Watercourses, by their very nature, attract life forms other than river guides. They promise a continuum of easy travel and cover in dense vegetation, as well as thermoregulation, building materials, and sustenance. Even in its reduced, domestic, stagnant form, water exerts its pull upon humans. Bathers lounge poolside, or in tubs, far beyond the point of cleanliness, hobbyists stare into goldfish bowls, and sailors once crowded around the scuttlebutt—an antecedent of the office water cooler—for gripes and rumors of omens and land. "If there is magic on this planet, it is contained in water," the philosopher-anthropologist Loren Eiseley wrote. Students of the evolutionary psychologist E.O. Wilson have noted a cross-cultural preference for semi-open landscapes with a water source, an attraction they credit to our species' savanna origins. Imagine roasting on the African veldt, newly bipedal, newly less hirsute, having abandoned tree shade and finally kneeling in yellow dust by that stream or waterhole, each sip a prayer answered.

Backing up Wilson's disciples and Eiseley, environmental psychologists found that time spent in blue spaces—near coasts, rivers, lakes, waterfalls, even fountains—boosts people's Vitamin D and energy levels and their mood and social relations, while also reducing stress and anxiety. Worldwide surveys ranked shades between blue and deep teal as the most popular colors. And the medium does not have to be water. Blue lights installed at subway stations cut suicide numbers drastically. The benefits of blue spaces surpass even those gained from green ones. As components in this spa package that improve wellbeing, researchers list the motion of waves (including rapids!), sounds, reflections of light, and the vehicles of classic activities: swimming, fishing, boating, surfing, and so on. Children who enjoyed all this are more likely to revisit blue spaces as adults, and will be healthier mentally later in life. Aquaphiles notice a distraction from inner turmoil—such as, ironically, "the blues"—and transition toward thinking about the environment and timeless patterns, "putting your life in perspective, if you like." To engage in the pursuits mentioned, one researcher explains, "You have to understand the motion of the wind, the movement of the water," and are thereby "getting back in touch with our historical heritage, cognitively." Unlike green spaces, blue ones, more dynamic, can be truly immersive. Unsurprisingly, swimming as a form of near-full-body touch—a sense still undervalued—helps us to connect with and care for the nonhuman world.

Unconcerned with attempts to make sense of the landscape and how we two-legged ones fit into it, fully present instead, *here* and *now*, the wolf approached the sleeping bear. Casting sideways glances and giving it a wide berth of respect, it then sauntered over a ridge, out of sight but already etched into memory.

Because the bear was not moving much and posed no threat, I had breakfast and broke down my tent. Then I acted as lookout while the rest of our group took their turn and loaded the rafts, screened by the bluff and prevailing wind. As I contemplated Sleeping Beauty with voyeuristic unease, I realized once again that, out there, who spots whom first amounts to a matter of safety. Vision, hearing, and sense of smell have been sharpened to various degrees in the tundra's denizens to ensure survival of the most sentient. Exposure and this landscape's spare natural soundtrack awaken instincts long dulled in us. Sudden unease once compelled me to switch banks while hiking along an Arctic creek just before I rounded a bend and roused a bruin with her two cubs right where I would have been stepping. Another time, I noticed Alaska boykinia ("bearflower") spiking a slope. Knowing that its petite white blossoms are catnip to grizzlies, I wondered if there were any close by. And lo, when I hollered, one popped from a ravine thick with alders I'd been about to dive into.

Alert, we become fully, if at times frightfully, alive.

As if to drive home that point, a camouflaged couple we'd run into below the Marsh Fork confluence came floating around the bend. Velvety caribou antlers in the raft's bow attested to their prowess as hunters. But they drifted past with their bloody cargo, oblivious to the predator outside their field of vision that had bumped them to a lower rank on the food chain. I shuddered to think how often I had courted disaster unknowingly, like this.

When we shoved into the current a few hours after the initial sighting, the bear was up and moving again, nosing and pawing through bushes on the bench. We snuck away like thieves, enriched by an encounter that luckily stressed none of the parties involved.

Over the next 15 miles, our course intersected with that of a northern harrier, a rough-legged hawk, more peregrines, and yammering, low-flying loons. Another Arctic fox popped from between tussocks and then sat on its haunches with erect ears, riveted by the bipedal transients.

Hours later, a tundra airstrip and a water flow gauge perched on a terrace on river right announced the end of our journey. They were the first manmade structures we had seen since we launched a week before.

After a dinner upgraded by fresh grayling and one final char, I dumped dishwater down the cutbank, scattering ground squirrels that had staked out riverfront property by tunneling below its lip. Straightening up, I faced a grizzly snuffling along the opposite shore. As we gathered to monitor its progress, furtive movement on our side caught my eye. A dark troll momentarily rose on its hind legs for a better view of us. *Bear cub*, my thoughts clicked into the familiar groove; but Cyn pegged the creature correctly: "It's a wolverine." Loping toward us flat-footed, it stopped repeatedly, as if considering a dare. This allowed us to check the bushy tail, burly legs, and brawler's snout characteristic of one of the North's most secretive animals. I stared in disbelief until my eyes watered. It was only my second face-to-snout with this weasel on steroids, and the first time, in Denali, it had been a mere glimpse. At roughly a hundred yards, the wolverine hesitated. Some kind of threshold deflected it, and it scampered, jumped into the river, and treaded water till it reached the far side. Onshore, it shook its backlit coat, sending a burst of droplets flying in all directions. By then, the bear had bedded down for the evening. The wolverine continued upstream, where it spied the bear. Like its wolf counterpart before, it detoured around the shaggy, sleeping mound. Then it clawed from the gravel bar up onto a bench and vanished behind a rise.

What a strange variation of a theme, like an *Animal Planet* rerun with a different cast. But to capture scenes like the ones we had witnessed in a single day, a film crew would have to spend weeks or even months in the wilds.

Sunset had turned the northwestern horizon into a garish smear. A string of geese sailed right through it, black cutouts which instinct was pulling to their fall staging grounds near Beaufort Lagoon. The river shone gunmetal blue, braiding and unbraiding into its delta, bidding us to carry on. What did it know about charter dates, about jobs and commitments and rat marathons back in the cities? It knew persistence, confident that its constant fretting and winnowing would wear down the hardest of rocks. It knew that movement is the only state of being, that transit is the only permanence. It thus knew cycles, eroding land the eons had laid down and dropped, grain by grain by grain at point bars, in eddies, or in its delta, destroying its bed while rebuilding it. The river knew paths of least resistance, through which, engorged, it sometimes pushed with blunt force. It knew that some creatures it harbored or whose thirst it quenched or whom it fed were diminished in numbers and health. And it knew that humans no longer respected its kind as they once had. The river *not* knowing certain things was just as important. It knew nothing about dams, powerboats, the Englishman that had named it, or the Englishman for whom it had been named. It knew not that its sinuous body divided what should be inviolate from that which was up for grabs.

Rivers keep reminding me that what happens upstream, be it flood, drought, upset, or pollution, before long will reach downstream. Dams and diversions notwithstanding, rivers bear the gift of renewal. They caution flexibility: be the boulder they move or the willow they bend or the boat they crush.

Rivers have taught me how to listen, and hold me under their spell—you can learn every essential thing from them. Each river, like Norman Maclean's Big Blackfoot, "has so many things to say that it is hard to know what it says to each of us." Increasingly straitjacketed, drained, lifeless, and poisoned, rivers have been warning the attentive of a future that we are narrowing. "The more you watch the river," any river, "the more you understand what it means to apply the adjective 'alive,'" Barry Lopez told a fellow writer during his 50-year residence on Oregon's upper McKenzie. I was born in a town by a river and rarely ever feel more alive than when I am joining one. Paradoxical as it may seem when speaking of things in constant motion, rivers have been my home.

Sea ice glowed in the distance, struck by oblique rays. The bear kept snoozing. When it got too dark to make out its shape, the clients crawled into their tents, trusting in our arsenal of pots and pans, pepper spray, and assorted firearms.

As evening stream sounds will, the Canning's monologue made me pensive. In my 52 years on the planet, much of them spent in the backcountry, I had never seen a federally endangered species. This summer, I had crossed the paths of two: the polar bear and a passel of humpback chubs in the Grand Canyon. Did the odds simply increase as more animals ended up on that shameful list, or had I, on some subconscious level, sought out the rare and the blighted before they could disappear? The fact that my clients essentially funded my wildlife viewing and that the pollution I left in my wake possibly outweighed any awareness I hoped to instill further complicated matters. But I consoled myself somewhat with the thought that remaining childless was the biggest contribution I could make to preserve Earth. The lifetime carbon footprint of one offspring alone equals emissions from over 600 transatlantic flights. Despite heading north every year, I had some miles yet to spare.

"A few recovered species don't compensate for the lost company of great beasts," the marine biologist Carl Safina writes. Sadly, he's right. But here there still were some wildlings, and we in their company, finding a measure of peace in these seamless days on the river. I knew that each time the refuge played big in the media, because yet another attack on it had been launched, more people would come. Many with whom I spoke confessed that they wanted to visit this place while there was time; though a haven for animals, we needed it just as badly. What, though, did it say about us as a species, or a country, if we could not guarantee the integrity of enclaves we'd set aside, not even for the duration of one person's lifetime? What we all felt, I'd like to believe, was a mixture of helplessness, guilt, and regret, rather than morbid, rubbernecking curiosity. Like conscientious criminals, we were drawn to the scene of the crime, witnesses and perpetrators rolled into one, forever haunted by our deeds and sins of omission. Perhaps, in the great beasts' presence, we were hoping to somehow be forgiven.

While the land already had drowned in dusk, the Canning gathered twilight into a gleaming band. Before I turned in, the realities of our streamside world dissolved into those of another, one by then almost forgotten. To the north, near the coast, orange gas flares and red strobes turned the night into a mad carnival. Flames split, fused and gyrated in the crystalline air, like some live, alien thing. They spelled the undoing of everything we had lived with this past week. They proclaimed the place where sanctuary yielded to busyness, where extraction passed for production, where the earth and its creatures took second billing. They hawked the stuff that became our gear and got us to the river: Prudhoe Bay crude.

CHAPTER 22

SITTING WITH CARIBOU

I have always been lucky on the Hulahula, except for one bear charge to be recounted farther on in these pages. Once, a wolverine pair gamboled on a hillside there; the people whom I'd led there had no idea what a remarkable sight that was. And I've witnessed the ageless throng of the Porcupine Caribou Herd thrice on that sinuous river.

The first time, we dropped in like party crashers. Approaching Old Woman Creek, a Hula tributary, on my wife's 37th birthday, our Cessna banked above the gravel landing strip, and we faced tundra teeming, oddly flecked. Momentarily spooked, dozens of caribou splashed through the shallows before climbing the loamy far bank. Hundreds milled about, or like a tawny blanket covered the foothills. While elk lope, moose stilt, and deer pogo, caribou tiptoe through tussocks at top speeds, ballerinas among the Cervidae. Think *Swan Lake* performed in a swamp but more scattered, less choreographed. As the pilot throttled the engine and swooped in for a touchdown near the river, a cow and calf cleared the runway barely ahead of the propeller blades.

By the time we had sorted our gear, the departing plane's drone had faded back to silence. Trusting the safety in numbers, caribou are less wary in a throng. The animals had settled down, attending to the matter at hand—putting on pounds. It was June, and the Porcupine herd was fueling up for its return to the woodlands in late July.

Having pitched tents on top of a knob that housed a ground squirrel colony, we observed the grazing crowd, when one of my clients spotted a griz'.

"What's it got in its mouth?" he asked.

Through my binocs, I saw. A bloody hindquarter so large it dragged on the muskeg. Just then, another bear on the opposite bank waded in to join this free-for-all.

Needless to say, I did not sleep well that night. Still, we'd clinked plastic flutes of champagne a client had brought, toasting Melissa's birth and the herd's humming presence.

I would remember that quartered caribou on my Arctic traverse a few years afterward. It might have been the slowest member of that Old Woman Creek herd, or else sick, old, or simply inattentive. The day after I'd left Anaktuvuk, weighed down by my excessive resupply, my Achilles' tendon acted up. Hobbling along with my hiking poles serving as crutches, I was close to tears, not from the pain or the thought that the visibly weakened or sick become easy prey but more so fearing that the handicap might mean the end of my trip. I'd already been spared once, weeks before, when I tumbled head over uninjured heels down a snow-clogged icy gully descending from a pass, without breaking a limb. Luckily, a rest day took care of my Achilles problem while it also lightened the load.

Roughly one hundred miles south of Old Woman Creek, 230 Gwich'in neighbors of the Inupiat live in Arctic Village. They call themselves the "Caribou People" and the Arctic National Wildlife Refuge's contested 1002 Area, a nursery almost as big as Delaware, *Iizhik Gwats'an Gwandaii Goodlit*, the "Sacred Place Where Life Begins." The Porcupine herd, migrating south beyond the tree line each fall, provides over half of all food for Gwich'in families, plus material for tools and clothing and for stories, dances, and songs. Residents of 14 more Gwich'in villages on both sides of the US–Canada border also depend on the 200,000 caribou—at last count—that will winter nearby at the end of their 2,800-mile round-trip annual journey. Since the near-extermination of bison in the late 19th century, no larger or longer land-mammal migration occurs in North America. Tides of furry backs wash across the tundra when the time is ripe. The Gwich'in believe that their fate is intertwined with that of the herd.

"We have a spiritual connection to caribou. They are everything to us," says Sarah James, an elder and board member of the

Gwich'in Steering Committee, spearhead of resistance against oil development. It's a social justice issue and an environmental one.

Unseasonal rains freezing can form glassy crusts, and caribou—from the Algonquian *qalipu*, "One Who Paws" snow, to excavate lichen—struggle and die. You can see scarring on caribou legs from having to push through that layer. In the summers, caribou seek windy areas, respite from mosquitos, and lingering snow on which they can cool off. Development could ruin their escape zones. Biologists and the Gwich'in worry about future declines of the herd that would mirror slumps in Canada and Siberia. As environmental conditions change, so do caribou highways. Hunters in Arctic Village remark that, as the region gets bushier, with willows and alders marching north in lockstep with climate breakdown, sighting game now is harder. The caribou's tundra biome is projected to shrink one-third or more by the century's end due to encroaching forest. Muskoxen and Arctic foxes also will suffer from this, while boreal species will benefit. On average, the Arctic greens two weeks earlier than it used to, and pregnant cows reach the smorgasbord too late for their calves to take full advantage. Consequently, more, weakened offspring succumb to wolf packs, diseases, lone bears, parasites, or the elements. Still, the herd's losses translate into carnivores' gains only short-term, until starvation catches up with *them*. If caribou numbers nose-dive, zealots will surely blame wolves and clamor again for drastic controls—the aerial shooting of packs and the baiting of bears.

Before satellite tracking or even maps of that country existed, savvy elders forecast where and when caribou would arrive, based on dreams and a life's worth of observations. Caribou-hunting songs, sometimes sung when a hunter encountered tracks, came to him upon awakening and were thought to please the animal spirit. A caribou sang through a hunter to either inform him that the herd was nearby or else that a taboo had been broken, which explained a landscape that stayed empty. Owls and certain songbirds could be messengers auguring a herd's location. The Gwich'in waylaid the animals at river crossings, spearing or shooting some with bows and arrows. Families, banding together, built brush-and-post corrals with mile-long fences of poles dressed with moss to resemble human drivers. Those funneled part of the herd into an enclosure or lake or through a natural bottleneck, where the prey could be snared or lassoed with braided-skin ropes and killed. Alternatively, young, fast men, howling like wolves, pushed caribou toward entrapment. Markers of such communal hunts remain on the land in physical form—rocks piled up as blinds—and in names like *Tthał Njik*, "Caribou-Fence Creek." While traveling and scouting for caribou, hunters, too, followed their trails. Once firearms had been introduced, caribou traps fell into disrepair.

Like the migrating caribou, on my trips I scan the tundra for threats—but also for beauty. And for antlers that have been cast off, which I seldom resist putting up against my head, impersonating The Other. Some of us just don't age gracefully, and I mean that as a compliment. Wearing such headgear, I look over one shoulder for hungry grizzlies. Beneath the silliness, my performance also connects me with hunters who painted antlered humanoids, shamans or gods, in Texas cliff alcoves 4,000 years ago.

Sights like those that blessed us on the Hulahula would have been familiar to Paleo-Eskimo hunters, who 6,000 years ago cordoned caribou within Agiak Lake in Gates of the Arctic National Park, west of the refuge. There, kayakers dispatched addled animals blowing hard. Crouching in stone hunting blinds, their Inupiaq successors allowed cows and fawns to pass undisturbed, as reproductive capital invested into an uncertain future. They had seen migration paths shift over time like the rivers' loops. "We don't like to change the caribou route," Ralph Ayyatungak Ramoth from Selawik recalled, "and this is rule number one. We have to let the first bunch go through, no matter what. Then, after the first bunch has gone by, then you can shoot and catch caribou, but only what you need." The weapons and tools may have evolved, but the principles had endured. Hunting, far from just being a pastime or even subsistence, was truly a way of life, a perspective on the world.

During fieldwork on the Kobuk River, I saw a caribou killed in the water with a high-powered, scoped rifle, from an aluminum skiff with an outboard motor. Air trapped in the fur buoyed the carcass, which was then towed to shore. I was with two Inupiaq elders at Onion Portage, when we faced the fear in that bull's bulging brown eyes. Eight previous cultures had stocked their larders there for a total of eight millennia at least, harvesting meat and the chives with the purple blooms after which that cutoff was named. Traces of their routines reached 20-foot depths below the sod on which we stepped when we butchered the animal. Blood and bone splinters enriched the archaeological record of appetites with evidence of our own.

The last time I ran into the Porcupine herd, or it into us, to be more specific, I heard it before I saw it. It was past midnight, and I had been soundly asleep on a saddle between the Hulahula and Sheenjek. I had only one client on a two-week hike with one air re-supply, a quiet, experienced German who once aborted a solo hike in Labrador's Torngat Mountains when a bear ate his supplies and who helped me setting up the kitchen tarp and doing the dishes. Grunts engulfing my tent woke me, and when I stuck my head out, an antlered throng was overrunning our camp. Whisper-shouting to Wilfrid, sacked out a few yards away in his tent, I did not even dress. It was chilly, despite the blush of midnight sun on the north-facing, Hulahula-side slope. Prone in my long johns, I had a unique, ground squirrel's view of the show. Wilfrid sat in his vestibule, entranced, his down bag draped around his shoulders. Neither of us spoke. It felt unreal, like having a front seat at a Cinemax capture of the Serengeti, except that there in the Arctic, large mammal aggregations were more sporadic, all the more to be treasured.

As I lay drowsily in my sleeping bag later, pressing bodies kept streaming behind my closed eyelids. I did not bother to count them like sheep. A few real caribou would end up in Arctic Village stewpots as a toll on migration. There would be, John Haines wrote, "long hunts through the wet autumn grass, meat piled high in caches—a red memory against whiteness." The herd's timing had been impeccable. Two days after its passage over the saddle, a foot of snow mantled our tents and the Sheenjek valley. It had probably infiltrated the sheltering tree line like a many-bodied ghost by then.

My own attempts to fill my belly and freezer with Arctic venison have amounted to nothing tangible. The first time, about to drive north on the Haul Road toward Deadhorse, Prudhoe Bay, with my neighbor and friend, all packed up and piled in, we never left the driveway. His truck wouldn't start. The second time, two National Outdoor Leadership School instructors and I, on a resupply mission in an old school bus, managed to get to the Brooks Range, where zero caribou entered our gun sight. Perhaps, the elders might have explained, we had bragged beforehand, voicing overconfidence, or our hearts were not pure, and the animals that we sought sensed this. Or we had moved too visibly or upwind. Sitting around the campfire, so much younger then, thinking our Ruger had to be put to some use, we took turns plugging a shirt I'd volunteered and hung from a spruce tree. I wore it for years afterward, displaying the bullet holes as if they were trophies.

CHAPTER 23

SMOOTH SAILING

The mood at Happy Valley is anything but that. Atmospheric shrouds drape this pipeline "man camp" at mile 334 on the Dalton Highway, the "Haul Road." Near Galbraith Lake, where we pitched our tent last night, the clouds briefly descended to tundra level, turning the coastal plain's rolling features into one formless, soggy, gray mess.

We are now parked in this graveled lot among trailers, Quonset-style shelters, camper shell husks, broken camp chairs, oil barrels—a postindustrial wasteland. Every 20 minutes, a tanker truck snorkels water from the Sagavanirktok River (the "Sag") to tame the Dalton's notorious dust at a construction site up the road. As if it needed that in these conditions. The truck bleeping in reverse; rain ticking on our windshield: the perfect soundtrack for gloom. Inside my wife's Toyota, she and I are awaiting Matt Thoft, one of Silvertip Aviation's two owner-pilots, an adventurous husband-and-wife team. No need to get wet when we still can stay dry.

Communications with Matt had been sketchy; summers, he's busy flying long days, and he's running his lodge in the Ivishak's foothills, beyond cell phone reception. It is after two o'clock and he's officially late. Could this trip be over before it has even begun?

With nothing to do, I sift through memories of our blond, clean-cut pilot. Born in Montana, Matt has piloted planes since he was 17. He and I once got stranded for two days at the airstrip in Bettles, hoping fog on the North Slope would lift. He'd shared his box-wine with me then and gave his emergency pouch-meals to my client, who decided the first evening that he liked none of the foods I had brought. Another time, Matt picked me up on the Canning, where I'd been guiding the Wilderness Society's national and Alaska directors. We'd cut short our rafting because headwinds had lashed us with snow squalls and water froze overnight in our buckets. We'd not observed any wildlife, either. After takeoff on the first shuttle-load out, we'd spotted ten wolves lounging outside their den, pups included. Were we being mocked? Matt circled once, for a better view.

Low-key buzzing jolts me from my reverie. The truck's rear-view mirror frames Matt swooping in low across the river. Bush pilots never arrive when or from where you expect them.

As the prop stutters to a standstill, we lug our packs, paddles, and bagged packrafts to the plane, an orange-and-black Piper PA-12 Super Cruiser built before the Berlin Blockade and "Air Bridge," modified for tundra landings and greater reach but with barely enough room for two backpackers and their gear. A pit stop to refuel his bird—Matt runs the pump off our truck battery—and we're on our way.

Matt skims a few hundred feet above the tundra, keeping below the cloud ceiling and looking for wildlife. I am wedged next to Melissa into a seat behind his, fragile as an egg in an airborne basket. Encapsulated by Plexiglas, next to struts as thin as a wrist that hold up the wings, I feel the urge to pull in my knees to brace for impact.

The Piper's bald tires touch down near Porcupine Lake, which feeds the Ivishak River, a 95-mile tributary of the Sagavanirktok or "Sag." A gap to the north allows glimpses of the Canning's corridor. Wolfish clouds rear up into hammerheads, about to devour the sun. After handshakes and watering a few tussocks, our pilot takes off. Seeing a plane's lifeline shrink before it disappears in an act of finality never has failed to move me. We watch the receding mote while silence and mosquito squadrons subdue us.

Eager to put in a few miles—twelve separate us from the river—we shoulder our packs. When thunder growls at us, we race to set up our tent, finishing scarcely before a drencher starts. After a delayed dinner, I brood, perched on my bear-proof food barrel, insects and rain pelting my hood.

In the morning, under steel-wool skies, we follow a brushy gulch and creek till we reach a dry bench camp overlooking the Ivishak. Time to unroll and inflate our packrafts. (Think six-foot-long donut, but synthetic and elliptic, with a rubber membrane for a floor, if you've never seen one.)

When we finally launch, sore shoulders relax, and we let the current take charge. The stream darts around bends, braided, and tinted aqua like antique bottle glass, each stone sharply defined at the bottom. Fishing holes with the glow of a glacier's core match the firmament, which overnight has been swept clean. Some channels demand deft maneuvering to avoid immersed willow "strainers" or "sweepers," drooping branches. Rarely do shallows force us out of our boats to drag them over polished cobbles. With such ease of motion and the water's Caribbean colors, this float is a yacht cruise, regardless of the rafts' tub dimensions. I truly sense "peace like a river" enfolding me.

Risk-taking fueled by hormones and a craving for "suffer fests" have melted away as I've aged. In my twenties, I could not pass a waterfall without stepping under it, or a lake thick with floes without playing seal, hauling out on one, barking butt-naked. Such acts are fads now in league with "forest bathing"—T.C. Boyle's "exercise in the obvious"—and known as "cold plunging" and "wild swimming." As is "stone stacking," though rampant so far only near Alaska's cities and in the Lower 48 backcountry. In this form of three-D *Kilroy Was Here* graffiti, hikers and floaters (I won't call them "river runners") build balanced-stone phalli, entire groves of imbecilic inuksuit that speed up erosion and evict rock-dwelling critters, from rodents to reptiles to invertebrates, and remind you that you're never alone anymore. US national parks already have outlawed this practice as malicious mischief on par with vandalism, punishable with fines and jail time. Nevertheless, volunteers in Acadia National Park dismantled almost 3,500 mountaintop stacks within two years. There are books, calendars, websites, video clips, "Gravity Glue" hashtags, and probably special shoes and T-shirts reading *I Stack Therefore*

I Am for fans of such meditative defacement. "Almost Zen," rock stacking, like many laid-back pastimes, has become competitive, with world championships, mine-is-bigger-than-yours matches, contestants racing the clock, and a barefoot medalist connecting with the ground. Pebbles that visitors place at Jewish gravesites betoken remembrance in a gesture more frugal than leaving flowers. And twelve men before the Jericho siege, one from each tribe of Israelites, carried twelve stones from the Jordan's bed to a spot on the shore, where they erected a monument to commemorate its miraculously parting waters, a replay of the Red Sea episode. I contrarily undo cairns to forget, acknowledging evanescence. With great glee, I kick over all less-than-crucial route markers wherever I find them. I should instead start a fad of "tundra lazing" but can't imagine any merchandise besides a bug swatter and Crazy Creek chair. And even those would be optional.

"As you get older and wiser," the translator and Zen expert Alan Watts wrote, "it is not just flagging energy but wisdom that teaches you to look at mountains from below, or perhaps just climb them a little way. For at the top you can no longer see the mountain."

Nowadays I'm content to sit on a boulder (making sure it stays put), soaking my bones in the sun, just watching the world go by. Now, when it's late and the summit tauntingly distant, I can turn around, glad to have made it that far. Now, not envying boaters in gnarly rapids, I contentedly sit on shore and, like Robert Frost, watch the hypnotic curl of a creek tinged with tannin, "The black stream, catching on a sunken rock / Flung backward on itself in one white wave," with the whitecap riding "the black forever / Not gaining but not losing, like a bird…" The bird that these lines evoke is an Arctic tern, bundled light hovering, waiting to dive and spear a fingerling fish.

Oh, the beauty of latter years. Nothing to prove, not even to myself, no monuments needed to show I existed. (Do not think books, with the shelf life of yogurt, qualify either.)

July Fourth finds us sunbathing nude, on a bluff above camp, where a breeze grounds the winged plague. It is less pesky on the river also, and with each northward mile, its numbers decline. The Ivishak wends down a valley that glaciers carved, the sole parade on display, not counting the sun's sluggish midsummer circumambulation. We are blessed with front seats, without noise or jostling from a crowd.

After days of this brand of la dolce vita, time jellifies. The campsites and day hikes are blending together. It's no surprise that rivers provide a metaphor for the life force and, on a smaller scale, for the progression of a human life—which can meet as abruptly as the Sag with oceanic oblivion.

Remnants from a plane crumpled in the Ivishak headwaters remind us of how quickly and thoroughly things can go wrong here. A twin-engine, amphibious Grumman Goose plowed into the mountainside below a saddle on the Continental Divide in 1958, killing two US Fish and Wildlife Service (USFWS) wardens and the son of one. Despite the largest search conducted in Alaska up to that point, backpackers only discovered the wreck 21 years later.

We glide past ranks of stark limestone fins, past tendril freshets, fuchsia mats of river beauty, slick jambs of cliffs, drunken strata, mountain flanks rainbowed, folded, and marbled. *Ivisaaq*, the root of the river's name, is an Inupiaq term for red pigment mined from iron-rich soils that blush this watershed here and there.

To gain perspective, we scramble up ridgelines into acres of scree and snow pockets. Perched on boulders crinkly with lichen, we assume as much as humanly possible the eagle's point of view. (Vistas outside plane windows do not qualify; the panes almost always are scratched, and wind cannot ruffle your hair.) From this vantage, the river suggests Earth's circulatory system, our rafts two brilliant blood cells temporarily stranded.

The eponymous hot springs announce their presence with the pea-green of balsam poplars—one of the species' northernmost stands—a grove nestled near the end of the stream's mountain section. We do not land, because the springs are merely lukewarm (39 to 46 degrees Fahrenheit), hot only compared to the snowmelt buoying us. Still, they keep this branch of water from freezing solid, unlike 99 percent of North Slope streams during the cooler months. The Ivishak therefore suits overwintering Dolly Vardens, which spawn in the main stem and whose fry thrive in its microclimate for two years before setting out for the sea.

A mile past the springs, approaching the portal to the plains, I spy a grizzly half a mile from the river, a bug crawling across a dog's coat, a moving dot a tad darker than the tundra. We see no other carnivorous carnivores and don't regret the lack of adrenalin moments for a change. As a matter of fact, recent research shows brown bears to be less carnivorous than previously thought. In late summer, they have been observed raking berry bushes for eight hours straight, ignoring nearby salmon swollen with eggs. But you just never know, from one moment to the next, if they have a sweet tooth or hanker for a hunk of meat.

On my two-month traverse from the Canadian border to the Bering Strait, I encountered, on average, one grizzly every other day. Occasionally they popped up in clusters of three or four. The first one, one of seven I'd sight that day, reared up at the airstrip where I'd been dropped off, watching me as I sorted my gear. From a slope above camp that night I called my wife on the satellite phone to say my farewell. I'd never felt lonelier. One bear dashed into the Noatak River, chasing me, or my boat. Another materialized uninvited during dinner at my tent. Several quartered downwind to check my edibility. I blundered into a female and her two cubs gnawing on Dall sheep remains—the worst scenario, wildlife biologists say. I was mock-charged, huffed at, stalked, ogled, seldom ignored. At the end of a hard day, I often hiked extra miles when bears showed up as I made camp. I lay awake many hours, clutching a folding knife, doubting I'd make it through the night.

On this outing, we don't find a single pile of bear scat. So, we have no idea if the preferred flavor of the week is sweet or savory, fruit or backpacker brisket.

At long last, the Ivishak pours into the coastal plain, inducing vertigo under a canopy sky. Each time I spin to look back at the

Brooks Range's solid wall, it has shrunk farther. Our days in the mountains already feel like a dream. Few landmarks now guide us besides uniform bluffs along this watercourse. The day we emerge from the foothills, we camp on a rocky shore facing an *aufeis* field, a river's shield of layered frozen overflows that lingers all summer. Meltwater drips from crystalline undercuts, and shelves collapse in the night with muffled thumps. A breeze crossing the miniature ice field raises goose bumps as we zip up in our sleeping bags.

Our last day on the river, we wend through scent plumes from dwarf lupine and northern sweet-vetch ablaze on cutbanks. At the confluence, the Sagavanirktok doubles the water volume. Incongruous boxes contour a ridge in the horizon's flickering heat—freight traffic to and from Prudhoe Bay.

We take out soon after Pump Station 2, where the Sag jigs closest to the Dalton Highway. I got here by sitting, I realize, with an idiot grin. A short tramp through bug-ridden tundra, a quick pipeline-photo stop, and we again stand on the road that a gravel dam buttresses to prevent sagging from thawing permafrost. The 414-mile highway was named for James W. Dalton, the engineer son of John "Jack" Dalton, a brawling pathfinder-entrepreneur who carved out a toll road for livestock supplying the Klondike claims. Exploring the Yukon's Kluane Lake in an Indian cotton-wood dugout with oars and a jury-rigged sail, Jack and a pal almost drowned, hypothermic and dashed against cliffs, when a freak storm capsized their craft. They lost irreplaceable stuff: Dalton's pocket watch, a compass and sextant, rifles, ammo, and cooking utensils. Another time, perhaps simply because he was young and could, he piggybacked said journalist with assorted camp gear across a stream, Christopher with a hogleg, patron saint of bush travelers.

Getting back to the truck at Happy Valley is the one stretch of our journey we couldn't plan, with some potential for boredom. It is 22 miles on the road, a long walk with loaded packs, but we're trying to hitchhike. "Truckers always stop," Matt had assured us.

The first few don't. Then Melissa slyly moves to the orange cones of a construction bottleneck a way down the road. Trucks have to slow there, and we figure a woman by herself will sooner be offered a lift. (Melissa can easily return with her truck, should the driver choose not to take me as well.)

We're enthroned high in a cabin free of bugs ten minutes later.

The trucker, another Matt, with a baby face and living in Fairbanks, regales us with stories and trivia at each milepost. He points to the spot where he shot a six-foot wolf around here one winter. He tells us that Gobblers Knob (a prime midnight sun viewing spot at mile 132) was named after a whorehouse that was hopping while Dalton's "Haul Road" and the pipeline were being built. Truckers also christened Sand Hill (mile 73), Roller Coaster (mile 75), and Beaver Slide (mile 110), for obvious reasons. Watching his weight, our gracious tour guide munches celery sticks from a Ziploc bag. Tattoos crawl on his forearms: a scorpion and, in Gothic script, his credo, *Family Is What Matters Most.*

Plane, boats, boots, trucks; switching between means of transport, we've come full circle. Seated on the Toyota's tailgate at Happy Valley, we pop two beers to toast a journey without glitches. The industrial junk no longer seems dreary.

Adventure often springs from poor planning or shoddy decision-making. Some people say it's only an adventure if you live to tell the tale. But who needs these stories? Who needs cold-water dunkings, blizzards of bugs, or a real one? Who wants to cringe in the fetal position at the wrath of a grizzly bear?

Sometimes, I think both Matts would agree, the best thing is a smooth ride.

CHAPTER 24

LEAST FORCE NECESSARY

There are thresholds we cross that leave us profoundly, irrevocably changed. They do not have to appear momentous, like an ocean, a border, a mountain range, but can seem rather commonplace—a traffic sign, envelope, door of a home. We may not even be aware of facing one as we approach. I'm not saying this was one of the big ones. But I can't say yet that it wasn't.

The second I step up onto the tundra bench I realize my mistake. I forgot to shout, "Hey bear!" like I normally do when beaching the raft, to avoid nasty surprises.

Right now, this slip of attention could get me killed.

Not 20 yards away, a grizzly stands up in the grass, fixing me in the crossfire of its stare. Next to it, two fur balls, jolly as piglets: cubs. It's a worst-case scenario come to life.

What a mess. I have two clients, brain surgeons, on a beach upstream, one wet and fiercely shivering—luckily, he was able to swim ashore after flipping in this no-brainer rapid, a boulder garden. I have his paddle, which I shed from the current after chasing it in the "mother ship," the big baggage raft. I don't have his $1,200 packraft; it lies wedged into rocks on the Hulahula River's far side. Nor do I have the pump-action shotgun, which I left strapped on top of the load in my haste to hike back to my packrafters and unravel this snarl.

Overall, I don't like bringing guns. We're in the bears' home and it is impolite to shoot the host. But the company I work for requires its guides to carry firearms, and clients are more relaxed knowing that we do. I personally prefer the least amount of force necessary to deter nosey or grumpy or pesky bruins, deploying a long-tested, effective escalation of choices. First, whistles, to make our presence known in brushy country (like the bright orange one tied to my life vest, the one I should have blown upon landing). Then pots and pans to bang together and thereby claim our turf with sound. And, most formidably, "pepper spray": a potent chemical aerosol pressurized in a can. It's the last-ditch of self-defense, also for women and policemen in urban face-offs.

I am a staunch believer in bear spray. No serious harm has come to anyone who has used it properly in a bear attack. People with rifles or revolvers, counterintuitively, have been maimed or killed, because a wounded bear is more dangerous than one that's only pissed off. We therefore weigh each of the slender black spray cans before the season starts to see if they're full. I keep mine on a backpack holster or in a side pocket of my pants, for quick access. However, as we caution everyone before each trip, your best survival tool is your brain.

Right now, mine is stuck after firing that mental blank when I stepped onto the beach. With my heart trapped in a freefalling elevator, reptilian reflexes take over. My arms go up. I mumble appeasement, apology. My legs move backwards, taking me down the bench to the rocky foreshore. I hope the bear won't follow.

She does. Like a hellhound charging after a fallen soul, she rumbles in my direction, a boulder trundling downhill. She's on all fours, bulked-up, center of gravity close to the ground, in combat mode. Her ears lie flat against her skull—a sign of her mood and to protect them from being bitten. As if I would.

In a motion that would do a gunslinger proud ("fastest can in the North"), I reach into my pocket, whip out the bear spray, thumb off the safety, and aim. Perhaps she is chuffing, growling, chomping her jaws—I couldn't say. My perspective has shrunk to needlepoint vision. I wish I were anywhere else.

But what I want or don't want does not matter right now. Chaos is calling the shots.

I am counting on her bluffing, that she will abort the charge at the last instant to test my resolve and send a blunt message: *Leave my cubs alone.* They say that most bear charges are mock charges, and I've weathered my share. If you run, bears will hunt you down. Standing your ground, though, is easier said than done. Every fiber in your body twitches to flee or curl up like a fetus. Experts "recommend" the prenatal position when a bear is upon you, to protect your vital organs, and no image better conveys your vulnerability under such circumstances than that naked, blind, unborn worm.

This is really going down, I realize, as she crosses the invisible line that would normally stop or deflect her. It is time to release a red-pepper cloud. I press the can's trigger and, with a dragon's hiss, a burning jet hits the bear squarely in the face. She zigs less than ten feet from me.

No! The can is empty. I pushed down the trigger too long instead of giving one short, fell blast. Now I'm left without reserve. But it seemed too short. *Did they weigh this can before sending it out on the trip?*

The bear, as if sensing my dilemma, bends the evasion into a fluid loop. She wheels about on her hindquarters, resuming the attack. I'm getting a bad case of déjà vu from this second round.

It takes longer to tell this than it did to play out, but while it did, I sensed time's elasticity, the trippy, simultaneous squashing and stretching of seconds that rides on adrenaline and speed-warps reality. I stood strangely removed, impartial to my own potential demise.

Some people experience flashbacks; their whole history unspools before their mind's eye like a time-lapse film. External motion congeals, except for your own movements, and you have all the time in the world to react. Maybe you won't. You certainly don't have all the time in the world. The quickening is also a slow-ing-down. The ultimate quickening can be complete standstill: the cessation of you.

I am not a religious person; yet in situations like these, pledges are made, bargains struck, conversions affected. Souls alchemize in the crucible of fear. When we witness death, in nature or else-where, we confront it indirectly, because it is not our own. With your own life at stake, stoicism evaporates in a jiffy.

To this day, I don't know exactly what happened next. I don't know if the soles of my hip waders slipped on cobbles slick with algae or if some archaic memory, some biological godhead, commanded me to prostrate myself.

The bear has left, or so I'd like to believe, still lying on the ground. I feel no pain. In fact, I have not been touched, I think. I don't know how close she came. Perhaps my eyes were shut. Carefully, without moving much, I scan the vicinity. Some people have been savaged, a few repeatedly, after standing too soon with a mad grizzly still hanging around.

I sit up, expecting deformity, blood, spilling guts. Soldiers and accident casualties can suffer short-term amnesia, and sometimes the Adrenaline rush in their system masks even the pain of amputation.

But there's no blood. Nothing. I'm untouched. And the bear has skedaddled, cubs in her wake. I still cannot believe my luck. With the threat to her young neutralized, she chose not to risk injury from this thing on the ground that had wielded some kind of stinger. In this hardscrabble place, health and survival are simply too precious to wager on a bet already won.

I take a few minutes to collect myself on the bow of the raft. My knees are shaking so badly I cannot stand. Questions flit through my mind like the proverbial sparrow, flying from darkness into the hall's light to exit again, too soon, into the night. Would my life jacket have absorbed some of this bear's anger? Would it have prolonged my life? Would my packrafters have been okay without me? I hadn't even demonstrated how to use the satellite phone to call for help; I never thought I might be the one who would be helpless out here.

Oh shit! The clients. What if she rampaged upstream, tearing into them as they waited for me at the river's edge?

With the shotgun unsheathed, I lope through widely spaced willows, my heart thumping, whether still or again, I couldn't say.

I find them exactly where I last saw them and assess their physical state, as I just did my own. They look fine, a bit bored and shivery and then wide-eyed when they see me running toward them with a drawn weapon. The one who flipped his packraft would later tell me he'd worried I'd shoot him because he had messed up his run.

"Where did she go?" I snap, still in overdrive.

"Who?"

"Who? Who?! The bear that almost killed me!"

They never saw her. She must have circled wide, crossing the river farther upstream. When I search the beach near my raft after filling them in on the details, I find, as I thought I would, paw prints and fresh dung trailing upstream.

Back at our base, my boss put the empty bear-spray can up on our warehouse "wall of shame," with my name and the date penned next to it, where it now hangs together with melted forks, broken paddles, bent tent poles, and a shotgun barrel plugged with dirt that had exploded when the guide pulled the trigger. But I felt no shame in my surviving and was not yet ready to chuckle at it.

I've been mulling "fate" much since that day. Is it mere chance? What were the odds that my carelessness would coincide with the presence of a foraging mother bear? Of all the riverbanks in the refuge, why this one? Does your number come up in some perverse lottery with cumulative probability, with too many days spent exposed to the wilds? Being at the wrong place at the wrong time is part of bad luck. Mistakes in volatile situations then can be the timber that breaks your back, your avoidable contribution to disaster. If fate flows from character, as my line of work and enthusiasms do, then my run-in on the Hulahula was inevitable.

I can't fully attribute this bear's restraint to her sense of self-preservation, to wanting to avoid injury, or to her concern for her cubs. I prefer to believe, no doubt naively, that on some level I mattered to her, that she spared me out of compassion. I admire, perhaps love her for not removing this perceived threat violently, especially given the harshness of her existence. Yes, "love," the big scary, overused, underused, clichéd word. But I have no other label for what washed through me then as it does now. Empathy mixed with gratitude approximates the emotion. Call it Stockholm Syndrome or anthropocentric projection, if you must. Unarguably, she left intact my violable self, at least its physical aspect. I would have been an easy kill, but she kindly passed when she could have battered, a force majeure in a pelt.

In this context, I cannot stop thinking about stuff that daily percolates through the news, about police brutality, our war on countries, on terror, on drugs, about imprisonment, rioting, eco-sabotage or other forms of civil disobedience, or even about our daily apolitical dealings with each other. When words or threats fail, pepper spray could do the job of bullets. Embargos could replace bombs. Like myself, the victims will be grateful, the cost to society less.

Perhaps we can learn from wild animals, or in some other way, to apply the least force necessary, responses appropriate to each transgression, each conflict. And perhaps the practice of killing "trouble bears," those that keep raiding garbage cans or have sampled human flesh, is not sound management but rather futile retribution. Killing the perp doesn't bring back the dead or ease the survivors' pain. But they wrongly say preying bears acquire a taste for it and sometimes seek more.

To pack or not to pack heat in the backcountry—I struggle with that also. I have fired a shotgun in the air as a warning once, and when I did was glad to have brought one, though my shooting scared the clients. It drove home the point how quickly wildlife watching can degrade into something else, how quickly thrill shades into terror.

I think of her sometimes, or rather, quite often, the one that spared me on the Hulahula: out there, under the midnight sun, drifting through crimson fall-heather, hiding in coastal fog, weary, horny, grouchy, content, pot-bellied or bony, digging her den, grubbing for roots, defying boars, or birthing more twins—hoping that she has not met an untimely end. I think of "her" not of "that bear," as if I really knew her. I'm not alone in this. Others who've been less lucky but survived feel the same way. I am bound to her not by friendship or blood or compassion, but by black blazing terror. Only death can sever our bond, hers or mine.

CHAPTER 25

ESKIMO SUMMER ON THE MATHEWS

A Dall sheep cape being cleaned drapes from the ceiling. In the log home's dim living room, it gathers this fall day's wan light. The rich, nutty meat sits in a wardrobe-size freezer nearby. As the year wanes, putting up stores becomes an urge only those who inhabit lean land far from grocery aisles truly appreciate.

Seated around a rustic table, we're visiting with Berni and Uta Hicker, Bavarian immigrants and homesteaders on the Brooks Range's south side for almost four decades. Neatly corded spruce and birch, solar panels, a windmill, and a generator, cozy their Wiseman operation Arctic Getaway, a cluster of rental cabins and outbuildings. Pioneer relics authenticate the grounds: a whipsaw, a Winchester repeater, rusty leg-hold traps, huge blacksmith bellows... Kitty-corner in the groomed, grassy yard, a penned gobbler dreading Thanksgiving eyes a white chicken companion laying prized eggs. Breakfasts are served in the main house, a 1910 dance hall in which Inupiat and Anglo miners and the Depression-era conservationist Robert Marshall jigged here during a flash-in-the-pan gold rush on the Koyukuk River's Middle Fork. So had Arctic Refuge advocates Olaus and Mardy Murie, wilderness honeymooning during the 1924 presidential election. "Territorials" couldn't vote, but Wiseman folk held a mock election, supped at the roadhouse, danced in the Hickers' hall until 5 a.m., and raffled a sheep off—an Inupiaq hunter had smartly copied the Anglos' profit scheme. Due to a surfeit of 45 men, called "tag dances" unleashed a "mad rush by all the stags, and a raucous melee" in which five women changed partners about every five steps. The hall's antique piano is a prized possession of the Hickers.

This morning, Berni fixes coffee with their good old German Melitta filter, lately fashionable among hipster baristas, pour-over coffee that could float horseshoes. He flips sourdough pancakes for two couples in the breakfast room. Our hosts enjoy the brief annual lull before vans disgorge scads of aurora tourists in this enclave of 14.

I admire Uta's raised bed outside, lush with five kinds of salad greens. "Don't you have problems with moose raiding?" I ask. Berni chuckles. "I wish. Let 'em walk right into our kitchen," he says in his Old-Country Alpine lilt. Federal fiat exempts Wiseman residents from rifle restrictions that safeguard the pipeline's silver thread three miles away, fetish of a hastier, noisier world.

We, its emissaries, rumbled in unannounced yesterday on the gravel two-lane linking Fairbanks and Prudhoe Bay. With each hour of leadfooting to beat sunset—dodging semis and shrapnel they flung at our already spider-webbed windshield—autumn's flare had intensified, except on the shoulders, which traffic, always sparse, had blighted with dust. It's my favorite road, a spring-board for bargain Arctic ventures, with belly-flopping potential. The Hickers let the three of us crash in their sauna, and in a cabin under construction, which I preferred despite its rough concrete floor, since its windows admitted rays weakened and in shorter supply in late August, 60 miles north of the Arctic Circle. We'd given a lift to their son, Leo, who was taking aircraft mechanic classes in Fairbanks and whom they homeschooled, as they did Julia, the sister with bird-of-paradise hair streaked electric-green. The siblings, fluent in German, as acquainted with lynxes as with calculus, had both won scholarships.

We unload from two vehicles at a wooded cut farther north on the Dalton Highway. Leo shuttles our truck back to the Middle Fork Bridge, where we'll beach our packrafts at trip's end. Geared up, we follow the creek bed upstream, rock hopping, avoiding wet feet as long as possible. A golden eagle gyres in the gently bluing sky bowl. At one point, cliffs of slanted limestone lamellae along the ditch narrow into goblin gates.

From near the ravine's head, leaning into my traces, wheezing like a chain-smoking dragon, I zigzag 4,000 feet up the ramp of a steep, sustained ridge, first on tundra, then on flaked bedrock, to a plateau birthing a Mathews River tributary. Tom Moran, a lanky, six-foot-five playwright and science writer, mountain biker, and marathon runner, steps uphill pretty much in a straight line, as deliberately as a heron. His longtime buddy, Jay Cable—clean-shaven, lantern-jawed, looking as if dirt wouldn't stick to him, though a few extra pounds do, to his six-foot frame—has to pause in the ascent as often as I. He grew up in Skagway and as a ten-year-old joined his chief park ranger dad on patrols. Now, he maps forest fires remotely for the University of Alaska's Geophysical Institute. Jay placed first in the Iditarod Trail Invitational, a thousand-mile winter bike race to Nome, during which Tom suffered frostbitten toes after pushing his ride through an overflow but "finished the damn thing anyway." Teamed up again, both won the 2018 Alaska Wilderness Classic, an ankle-twisting, multiday challenge of routefinding, river fording or travel, and staying awake jazzed on caffeine gum while lugging every ultra-light gadget needed. That year's racers crossed the Brooks Range from Galbraith Lake on the North Slope to Wiseman, a distance of 85 miles.

"We hike pretty fast, do very long days (when necessary), and don't stop to rest very much," Tom had warned me in an email. Should the Mathews run low because the snowpack was gone and it hadn't rained a lot lately, "there could be a lot of walking." This, I know from my research, is typical male behavior that athletic competition heightens: men running as a pack take fewer breaks.

At 60, I've seen 17 summers more than these guys, so I had shouldered my pack with some concern. To my relief, I manage to keep up, if at the expense of nourishment. My lunch is buried in my backpack, and breaks just long enough for leaks force me to subsist on one energy bar for the initial nine-and-a-half-hour leg. Fine dining doesn't rank among my companions' priorities. Nearing Wiseman, they inhaled Yukon River Camp pizza slices stacked on the center console, by then cold and rubbery. I quickly learn to snack on the go.

On the saddle, wind panpipes a monotone dirge on paddle shafts strapped to my pack. The world opens, a book of sagas, an arena of giants, with prospects far west into Gates of the Arctic. To the north, close to Atigun Pass on the Continental Divide, a summit, freshly powdered, blinks from shrouds. Range upon range marches toward every horizon, paling as they recede. The view encircles more scenery than you could explore over the most fruitful hiking career. I realize I'll only ever dip my toe in it. Unlike the glut of choices that normally stuns us, this wealth leaves me primed, not dissatisfied.

Refreshingly, after the shale-y mud at the pass, the season enflames the tundra farther down-valley in the Arctic version of Indian summer. A rash of ruby bearberry leaves glistens as if freshly painted. Willows burnish the air with the glow of cognac commercials while we thread stands hemming the feeder stream single file. Fall has been less showy in Fairbanks recently due to leafminer infestations. The larvae's hunger imprints emerald birch leaves with silky-white labyrinths before turning them a sickly yellowish-brown. Still, enough splendors remain to savor what Wallace Stegner called "that old September feeling."

Dead matter drops even in evergreen forest during winter's rude disrobing: dwarf birch and willow, balsam poplar and blueberry leaves—rustling shallows of orange, burnt sienna, scarlet, canary yellow, burgundy; and night, sooner and sooner each gilded day. Robert Frost thought nature's fleeting palette is the "hardest hue to hold," the flight of seasons, "Nothing gold can stay." Inevitably, "leaf subsides to leaf." Best not to cling but to embrace the grand letting-go. I say this also because too much foliage blocking sight lines rattles me, as it did old-time Inupiaq hunters born on the coast.

Between drizzles, light spokes of a heavenly wheel march across smooth, open slopes until afternoon clouds meld into a foreboding pewter backdrop.

Our camp, on a bluff amid black spruce, the tree line, overlooks the Mathews's too-shallow braids. Lichen so deep it preserves footprints makes sleeping mats optional. It's 14 more miles to the Bettles River, from where, with greater depth likely, we can paddle to the highway. As the temperature dips, Jay and Tom build a driftwood fire befitting the racers' minimal-impact philosophy, on an outcrop below the high-water mark.

By morning, frost has stiffened socks and boots and crystallized dew on the tent fly, but my water stayed liquid. When I treat the bottle topped off in the current, a snowflake shows next to the smiley face of my ultraviolet-light SteriPen that signals successful filtering. No kidding. Each draft of the delicious elixir provokes pain of the palate and a grimace closer to one during dental surgery.

We meander downstream beneath clouds cruising pelagic skies, fording the Mathews repeatedly, tracking open forest brittle or spongy underfoot, and skirt the lip of two canyons in search of water to buoy our miniature rafts. The blueberries are past their prime, rendered mushy by meat-locker cold. Pale, blushing lowbush cranberries, conversely, have changed into globules of tartness, a windfall people and bears await. Despite the brilliance, underneath it, much of the vegetation looks tired—anemic, droopy, nearly spent. Within two weeks, poplars and birches will have shed all their glory. Plunging into chilly spruce shade, I cannot help but recall the Northumbrian monk who compared the human lifespan to a sparrow flitting through a lit mead hall: a beacon flash, quick luminescence that winter's void bookends. That sparrow could have another go, unless the hall has been barred. *We* get only one turn on this earth. The Welsh long-distance hiker Colin Fletcher quoted an "otherwise unsuccinct" paper, which puts a secular, ecological spin on his compatriot's observation: "Organisms are relatively transient entities through which materials and energy flow and eventually return to the environment." The same can be said about rivers, and yet in their essence, like animist souls, they endure.

As the sun's arc flattens daily until, three weeks hence, darkness and light briefly hang in equinoctial harmony, nature, holding its breath, braces for partial shutdown. Streams will skim over and sap will congeal under bark. Ground squirrels will go narcoleptic for months. Grizzlies will fit themselves into dens to dream of fawn kills on greener pastures. Wood frogs will clot into olive hailstones, yet months later revive thanks to antifreeze sugars that soak vital cells. The geese and cranes will have fled, and with them fellowship's clamor.

Berni said to expect sheep hunters here. Sure enough, we spot smoke wisps, a meat rack, and humongous mule tracks, sooty campfire rings. Ravens accenting some bushes like notes in a musical score draw us to a skinned, headless trophy black bear. We stand and stare, loath to approach flesh scraps melting off ribs, viscera, sausage links among scarlet ruin, feet suggesting an arthritic or a captive's, broken on a different kind of rack. The birds, before taking wing, scattered digestive claims-stakes. This carcass, this mess, complementing the Hickers' hide, sharpens our own mortality. It's not pretty. Death and scavenging seldom are. But from it, life will spring, next year's fox kits and raven chicks.

At the end of a mercifully mellow day, we pitch our second camp in a meadow near the river's edge. Tom scales a bluff, scouting the down-valley stretch, while Jay and I laze by the tents. The few big, lethargic mosquitos in mine must have forgone procreating this late, hanging around for lack of alternatives.

In the morning we launch at a gravel bar here and, without too much scraping or bumping, soon reach the confluence. The Bettles River easily doubles the volume, maintaining the Mathews's gin clarity, which causes bottom cobbles to pop like gems that a hand lens magnifies. For the ecologist David George Haskell, "To experience the passage of time in an animal body is to experience sensory diminishment." But I, despite cellular decay, feel sensory overload currently, with colors as sharp and vibrant as those of a toddler's toy searing my retinas. Perhaps, this is an optic rallying, terminal lucidity in a landscape-loving species.

With the ceiling tearing and a barely risen sun on our backs, digging hard to catch the plaited flow's deepest, sapphire channels, I already sweat inside multiple layers.

Until the advent of hot air balloons, humans knew no smoother travel, rapids and rocks notwithstanding. A shoreline observer sees rafts zipping past as bright satellites; for a boatman midstream, landmarks rotate as earthbound constellations. A glimpse of eternity lies in this swirling. You *can* step into the same river twice. Rushing constantly seaward while also arriving, it maintains itself. Despite often quickly changing scenery, each river also reveals a unique character—dare I say "personality"? Presently, a fog front pours over an upland fall, dappled, a mist avalanche at slowed speed that never advances beyond. Tatters ghost above the opposite bank, baring Wiehl Mountain's craggy mien randomly. Civilization has shrunk to the rare buzzing plane, with its cargo of hunters and oilfield commuters. When quiet reigns, I hear twin paddle-blades drip as the shaft rests on the drum-taut tube. Breezes carry the rich rot of compost to us. The sun worshipper's madeleine, scent equivalent of the post-party blues, it spurs memories of days lost, youth vanished, opportunities squandered. Fall's flavor, rivaling that of the best kind of chocolate or romance, is bittersweet.

Final narrows sluice us to Sukakpak Mountain's foot and into the Koyukuk's Middle Fork, sweeping, milky, jade-green. "The last 380 million years of geologic activity could not have produced a more perfect peak," in the opinion of one guidebook author. White quartz veins the horned peak's marble bulk. Its ancient seafloor, pressure-cooked and uplifted, resembles a deadfall marten trap, apparently, for which it was named. The local Nunamuit ("Land People," an inland branch of Inupiat) saw objects familiar to them in the topography. Even from the varied angles the river's wheeling affords us, I cannot solve this optical riddle. I instead savor diamond moments free of thought, being present in what might be this year's last hurrah in the sun.

"The seasons and all their changes are in me," Thoreau journaled on October 26, 1857, five years before his death at the age of 44. My knees and toe joints, achy since the headwaters saddle, concur. So will my knuckles and shoulders tomorrow. When Ibuprofen is a staple, "Vitamin I," ingested twice daily, your heydays are done. Yet, as for the ecstatic John Muir, still, "There is at least a punky spark in my heart and it may blaze in this autumn gold…"

CHAPTER 26

THE MANY COMFORTS OF SNOW

It is over two weeks past the equinox, the fulcrum at which day and night at the Arctic Circle poise in balance. Lately, I've been avoiding backcountry overrun by going where nobody goes or when nobody goes. So, I've thoroughly monitored snow conditions in the Brooks Range for weeks, to optimize daylight and temperatures and darkness for star extravaganzas and auroras on a trip, but also fretted about yet another early spring breakup—"corn snow" and slush ruin adventures, just as too many people will. The day before we left Fairbanks, the mercury at Anaktuvuk Pass plunged to minus 40 assisted by wind chill. (That was when I stupidly blistered my heels tromping to the store in rubber boots.)

The window for bliss is a peephole. A mere 15 degrees Fahrenheit make the difference between zero gravity and sand in the gears. I once missed that sweet bracket on the Grand Canyon's North Rim, where it is even narrower. In the days' climbing temperatures, snow glommed onto my skis, mixed with pine duff and possibly topsoil. Skiing resembled walking after stepping into fresh, quickly setting concrete. A companion who had forgotten his wax applied a butter stick—in vain. It was that kind of trip.

This time, I need not have worried. We disembark from the single-prop plane into a calm, sunny minus 30 degrees, welcomed by diamond dust sparkling at eye level. Sunlight glancing off the horizontal planes of tiny crystals causes this effect. Sundogs, and rainbow auras edging cirrus clouds, both reflections from the prismatic dust, often forecast heavier snowfall. On the wind-scoured tundra tableland across from the airstrip, two dozens antlerless caribou graze by cratering shallow snow. Those that do not end up in village freezers will get a head start on the spring trek to coastal calving grounds.

Inupiaq women and men mill about, unloading cargo: store provisions and special orders from Fairbanks. We three skiers stick out like white-bellied Alaskans on a Hawaiian beach. While we assemble our sled loads, inquisitive villagers ask us our destination, what kind of tent and stove we have, and "How many days you guys gonna be out for?"

"About nine," I say, "to Coldfoot," a truck stop with an airstrip off the Haul Road to Prudhoe Bay. I in turn ask if Skiku recently has been to town. The Anchorage nonprofit whose name combines an Inupiaq word for ice—*siku*—with "ski" brings Nordic fun to Anaktuvuk. Volunteers coach young Nunamiut ("People of the Land," inland Inupiat) as they do those at the other ten village schools in the Northwest Arctic Borough. At sessions with the air of spring carnivals, you may see tots schussing atop instructors' skis, clinging in pairs to an adult, front and back.

Skiing is a young tradition in the home of sleds, snowshoes, and snowmachines. The Norwegian explorer, novelist, and playwright Helge Ingstad, who lived at Anaktuvuk for nine months from 1949 to 1950, introduced this pastime of Norse gods and goddesses here. "The Eskimos watch my manœuvres with wonder," he wrote, "the small boys are particularly interested. Now and then they borrow the skis, and it is astonishing how quickly they copy me." Having returned home, the discoverer of the Viking settlement L'Anse aux Meadows sent back twelve pairs of skis and poles as thanks.

When I mention him to a woman, she points across the valley: "That's Ingstad Mountain."

When I comment on the caribou, and that the people must be happy to have meat in their freezers this spring, she points to another valley and says, "They have been seeing wolves up there." When we're rigged up, she offers to take our picture. "The famous before and after shots," I joke, not knowing yet what awaits us.

While many Nunamiut still see skiing as a novelty, the sliding boards gripped Alaskans early on. They founded their first ski club in Nome, in 1901. The Norwegian-American Leonhard Seppala, known for his 1925 feat during the "Serum Run" precursor of today's Iditarod race, stuck a 103-foot ski-jump landing on the southern toe of Anvil Mountain, the 1,200-foot peak that inspired the original name of that mining metropolis: Anvil City. Skiing Sámi reindeer herders hired to teach the Inupiat husbandry played a large part in the early twentieth century, on the Seward Peninsula and at reindeer stations encircling the Brooks Range from Shungnak to Barrow. Another Norwegian skijored on sea ice behind a husky and directed ski-jump construction at a pressure ridge while pack ice pressed Vilhjalmur Stefansson's doomed *Karluk* in its vise near present-day Prudhoe Bay.

We ski past the town dump and climb our first slope up to the bench, where the caribou interrupt their meal to gawp at us before prancing off. We then flush a large flock of ptarmigans still in winter attire, disappearing until they launch.

I'm towing more than 70 pounds, a fully loaded plastic sled. An ergonomically shaped split pole with ends carabinered to a hip belt on the downhill keeps the beast from nipping at my heels. Uphill, I lean in, a draft horse in its traces. A blue tarp secured with bungee cords keeps the load dry and prevents getting it scattered along the trail. The stately pleasure dome riding in this *pulk*—our "Home Away from Home"—is a tipi tent with an ultralight titanium woodstove that can be disassembled. A thin metal sheet rolls up into a tube kept together with slip-on rings for a six-foot stovepipe. Its length is half a foot less than the national snowfall record for a 24-hour period, which Alaska holds. Enough alder and willow branches for firewood poke from the snow, and I'll cut them with a folding saw. I brought spare slip-on ski bindings and enough down to dress an entire polar patrol, sealed in waterproof bags in case of overflow mishaps. There is roughly 20 pounds of food. Snowshoes bungeed to the top of the load could come in handy if the terrain gets too steep for my wax-less skis or during camp chores in deep powder. Roughly one hundred miles separate us from Coldfoot, a destination that sounds intimidating.

The sled is a loaner from Sven, who climbs ahead of me, a slick molded number advertised as being "Unaffected by Temperatures below −60° F." I'm not sure *I* would be. The manufacturer demonstrated its sturdiness to Sven by driving a truck over it.

Sven "I can't grow a beard" Grage, a clean-cut native of Hamburg in his late fifties, taught German, outdoors skills, and soccer at a Fairbanks high school for 20 years. Now retired, he works part-time in an outdoors-gear store, as does Jacob Buller, the last but not least in our triumvirate. Like me, Sven fell under the spell of the North as a young adult. Jacob, half my age, pilots airplanes on ambulance flights in the Interior. Last year, he worked at a blue-ice runway on Antarctica's Union Glacier near Mount Vinson for an outfit specializing in expedition logistics. He got to ski a "10k loop groomed and flagged" and ran a marathon there. Born in Anchorage, Jacob is another wilderness racer, a weight minimalist. I, at this point, cherish creature comforts and am willing to pay the price in extra weight (and the airline's price *for* extra weight). He's whittled his winter racing gear down to 30 pounds, which entails alfresco bivouacs. "Makes you feel like a badass when you just stretch your sleeping bag out on a sleeping mat in the snow," one email said. Ah, the enthusiasms of youth—I remember them well. I have not engaged in serious snow camping since my Denali ascent 28 years ago. My credo for traveling—*heavy and steady, not light and fast*— always has served me well. It's the old hare-and-tortoise contest.

The snow on the bench is "slab," wind-packed, hard and dense. My skis' steel edges barely dent it, and it rings cavernously, like a roof someone putters on. Now and then it collapses in light floes under my weight. I'm surprised how little there is. Rocks and tundra plants surface intermittently, so we pick our way with care. Slab is a pavement often stepped with lamellae, finely etched by weathering. Igloos are built with slab sawed into blocks. But, hitched to the 50 or a hundred Inupiaq words for snow, that image is a misleading Alaska cliché. The Inupiat *do* build windbreaks and hunting blinds from slab with antler or bone machetes, with which they also excavate traps drifted over. But the Inupiaq *iglu* or "house" names a structure girded with spruce, or driftwood or whalebones on the coast, and roofed with sod.

As to the discernment of snow types: Inupiaq is a polysynthetic language, that is, words can be tapeworms, accruing suffixes to a stem that add specifics, comparable to English whole phrases. Thus there is *piqsiq*, "low, blowing snow," and *pukak* or "depth hoar," large, ornate, hollow crystals from ground vapors frozen or from other temperature gradients or rain or surface melt water percolating downward. Concealed by a drier overburden, this stratum is the best to melt for drinking water. Its weak bond with layers above it triggers avalanches, sometimes signaled by the *whoomp* skiers hear while slab sags under their weight. *Siqoqtoaq*, the "sun *crust*," can glaze it, which melts by day and re-freezes by night and handicaps moose that lighter-weight wolves chase. Some plants in spaces thus sealed manage jumpstarts in the spring, while this greenhouse also saves them from desiccation by wind. *Qamaniq* is the bowl in the branches' snow shadow at the base of coniferous trees; it shelters spruce grouse and snowshoe hares and hides ambushing lynxes. *Qali* collects on the boughs.

In an amalgamation of traditional and modern knowledge, many winter ecologists now use this lexicon as convenient shorthand.

My favorite Indigenous snow term by far is *qurriniq*, an Inuit one: "snow delicately tinted yellow by the urination of dogs." I've seen crossbills peck at it for salt. But do not melt this, or similar stuff near your tent, for tea. The late Mike Mallon, among Canada's leading linguists for the Inuktitut language, also listed *ivvuuaqtuut*, "snow that falls down your neck when you wrench open your Arctic entryway's door after a blizzard"; and *singirniijarnaq*, "snow that flows into your boots, soaking your socks while you wallow in drifts." A person could study snow her whole life and never run out of new insights or surprises. Some people do become hooked. Among the substance's many pleasures for me are the honed observations and playfulness it engenders. Vocabularies of snow-and cold-loving chionophiles the world over bear witness to varied ephemerals and how these aggregate. Their semantic precision highlights what cultures other than ours deem important. The language of snow is a language of survival. Recreational skiers—mostly Alpine—coined beauties like "crud," "corduroy," "cold smoke," "death cookies," "champagne powder," "boilerplate," and "Sierra cement." Scots creations embody sheer poetry by their sound alone: *feefle* ("snow swirling around a corner"); *flindrikin* ("a light snow shower"); *skelf* ("a large flake"); *glush* ("melting snow"); and *snow-smoor* ("suffocation by snow"). One wonders how common that last kind is. In mid-April, when our Fairbanks cabin roof wetly calves with a rumble, the side overhanging the path to the outhouse, you're more likely to have your neck broken.

We descend the plateau to the Anaktuvuk River. Lenses of antifreeze-colored ice shield it. The ribbed snowmachine tracks of Nunamiut hunters and trappers, like the one we're now on, web parts of the park. A snowshoe hare browses, a "low-bush moose" standing on its hind legs in the stream's willow fringe. He's another camouflaged creature. Snowshoe hares, ptarmigans, and snowy owls, which roost often on tussocks, evolved wide, weight-distributing feet; so did lynxes in the boreal forest to the south. Even caribou did. Their concave hooves splay, distributing their weight, printing sets of big apostrophes with each step. Oversize feet drew attention, finding other uses as well. The hare's inedible hind feet functioned as washcloth, pot scrubber, or children's toy dog. A feathered ptarmigan amulet foot made a boy a fast, tireless runner.

A rock ptarmigan (formerly "snow chicken") can weather minus 40 degrees. The genus name *Lagopus*, "hare-footed," to which it belongs, points to its culottes legs. The birds molt into more feathers in the fall, especially on their toes. This helps them keep warm but also contributes to their nivean nimbleness. Their claws grow almost twice as long in time for that season, for traction and as digging tools. They float atop the immaculate surface, probing for buried catkins and willow twigs, and later, spring buds. Quick-change artists, all ptarmigans switch from solid umber, chestnut, and black-barred gold to mottled to all-white plumage and back again within the year. The sun's shifting arc—length of daylight or "photoperiod"—not snow cover starts these makeovers. With the earth unrobed earlier in the spring now through global heating, ptarmigans sometimes no longer blend in.

Their daisy chain tracks get snarled between bushes; it's a regular chicken dance plaza in here. The birds gather in large winter flocks. Fifty or sixty could be hazed into a seine net in one coup. They follow caribou and feed where those paw snow to reach lichen and frozen berries.

The phrase "in the dead of winter" never made sense to me. Snow keeps a perfect record of creatures that passed through, narratives that the season and survival script. New snow is a white page awaiting a story. Wind, sun, trees, and wildlife will fill it while revising each other's lines. To decipher them is to regain land literacy. The root *text*-, "woven," from the Latin verb *texere*, binds textural details to textual ones and evokes snow crystals interlocking.

On a steep downhill pitch I remove my skis, but the sled pushes until I gallop across the hard pack to avoid braking and wiping out. I end up doing a face plant in softer snow. Elsewhere, we herringbone uphill with splayed skis. Sidestepping up with a sled? Not so much. Having lost the snowmachine track, we traverse off a bluff with the sleds swinging perpendicular, threatening to yank us off balance. A bottom thicket entangles me, and I unclip my harness and bindings to crash on through. Less than an hour later, shortcutting across a river bend, we flounder in powder that willows gathered, which mantles them against frost. Each of us seeks a better course, but all sleds hang up on stumps and in narrow gaps. "I'm not going there," I think, watching Jacob struggle.

And promptly get stuck in a different spot while from the bushes, the ptarmigan gallery cackles crazily, hidden.

Snow cover, a layer cake of differing moisture, density, and weathering processes, has its own geology, reminiscent of Grand Canyon strata, but deposited super-fast. The most important environmental feature of arctic and subarctic zones, it spreads unevenly across them, like wealth in a nation. "The sparse snow is driven by fierce winds which bare large areas and compact the snow firmly where it lodges," remarked Laurence Irving, who studied physiological cold adaptations among the hardy Inupiat and birdlife at Anaktuvuk. "Many exposed areas are blown free from snow, thus clearing the vegetation for the caribou." Conversely, in forested valleys, with trees as windbreaks, snow mires linger. Facing eight months of snow each year, caribou spend more than two thirds of their lives in it and therefore choose winter ranges smartly. In mountainous, boreal forest, also called "taiga" or "snow forest," they skirt bottomless pockets that slow them down and make finding lichens harder. Shallow autumn snows entice the majority of the Central Arctic Herd, which feeds the Nunamiut, to winter on tundra north of the Brooks Range. Their coats of tubular hair provide great insulation. Ingstad spoke of fur clothing so warm that hunters sometimes lay down in a sudden snowstorm and went to sleep.

We decide to lie down and to go to sleep a scant nine miles from the village, in the lee of clumped head-high willows. We planned to camp early to practice a good setup and smooth out any kinks. Soon steam plumes from Sven's Kelly Kettle, a double-walled can for melting snow by feeding little sticks to a fire on its baseplate. Hot drinks reanimate us, and I'm glad to exchange ski boots for mukluks, and Jacob and Sven do so for down camp booties, which they'll wear inside their sleeping bags. Staying hydrated means getting up at night to relieve yourself, in Sven's case repeatedly, and you don't want to fumble with frozen footwear when seconds count.

Shivering badly, Jacob eats "in bed." The tent's skin cannot hold the wood heat, which grants short relief nonetheless before we fall asleep and again before breakfast. After pouch-meal dinners of freeze-dried food, Sven and I also turn in, slipping into our mummy bags fully dressed as our chugging stove weather-vanes smoke into the powder-blue dusk.

This morning, the key-ring thermometer on my fly-fishing vest with a pocket for every occasion reads minus 20. The vest keeps batteries, camera, snacks, and vital Ibuprofen near my body's warmth, within easy reach. I carry a notebook in it too but already decided not to scribble during the day, since I'd risk losing digits. It's bad enough to slip out of my mitts for an occasional snapshot.

We breakfast on oatmeal and instant coffee as warmth from another fire briefly suffuses the tent. Planning to skip hot cereal, I brought oatmeal–chocolate chip cubes. They're hard as marble dice, inedible jawbreakers. Hot water bottles prepared last night, kept in the bags' foot ends, remained unfrozen. Mine are light-weight dirtbag thermoses: Nalgene bottles with duct-taped foam quivers. Even lukewarm sips during the day make a difference.

The hardest part every morning is wrestling your dogs into boots stuffed into insulated over boots. Sven and Jacob keep theirs in the sleeping bag, but in mine, there's no room. Regardless of preparations, three figures sprint in place, swing legs, or hop, trying to aid circulation. We put on boots last, after packing, just before leaving, inserting toe heating-pads as we do hand warmers into our mittens.

I am not on the twelve-foot "Norwegian skates" on which Sierra Nevada miners raced each other, double-poling down the slope; or on "boards seven or eight ells long" that a 13th-century Norse text exalts. The sweet spot in length for straight downhill did not change in 600 years: Viking skis were the same size as most of the Forty-niners'. That's twice as long as mine. Still, I dream, like the skald, that I could "pass the bird on the wing, or the fleetest greyhound that runs in the race, or the reindeer which leaps twice as fast as the hart."

Alas, there'll be none of that.

I've hiked faster with heavy packs. We average a mile and a half an hour, even with little trail breaking. The route to Ernie Pass rises 1,200 feet, but worse is the river ice, which we trace for long stretches, detouring around hillocks and side hilling on the banks. The guys have attached sticky synthetic skins to the undersides of their skis, while I, cheapskate that I am, flail nude on this rink. Even with steel edges and a fish-scale pattern roughing the kick zone, each ski veers in a different direction, and I find no purchase for tugging the sled. The poles, which I jam down ice-axe style, help very little. This isn't skiing, it's ski walking. I quickly fall behind.

Crystals sprout from my fleeced shoulders and chest: frozen condensation. Old-timers took frequent tea breaks on the trail not just to hydrate in the dry air; they also brushed off moisture that frosted parkas hung inside out on a tree, with a beater of antler or rib, restoring fur's insulation. One secret of efficient winter travel is not to sweat, to shed just enough clothes to dodge hypothermia.

The scenery compensates for the drudgery, when I get a chance to absorb it. I move through a duotone musical piece, if only at a lento pace. For the poet Nancy Campbell, "music and snow are not natural bedfellows, because "one of the markers of fresh snowfall is quietness," the absorption of sound at the ground level and among laden trees through its trapped, tiny air pockets. My mind, weaned on movies, however, demands a soundtrack, a rhythm to lumber by. Tchaikovsky's "Waltz of the Snowflakes"—an airy confection spun around harp, triangle, and piccolo—would seem twinkly twee in this setting. Grieg's "In the Hall of the Mountain King" peaks too abruptly and forcefully and is too on the nose. This high country does not rush or pound. It calls for something built on Gregorian pacing and moods, the Estonian Arvo Pärt's "Cantus" perhaps. Among classical composers, only a northerner could match the soul of this vastness.

Winter here plays variations on white and azure. Some south-facing mountain slopes glower slate-gray. The tundra and range beam bridally under the cloudless sky. A haze hangs on the odd summit like exhalations. "The skis glide exquisitely through a mountain world bathed in sunshine," Ingstad wrote about one such Brooks Range day—he must not have hauled a dead steer— and "The farthest white-clad tops stand out sharp against the blue." Our shadows stretch gauntly in the morning light. Oblique rays heighten the snow granules. The mountain world slumbers muffled, except for my clattering and the occasional crunch as I scrape over an ice lump, outcrop, or pressure ridge. For miles, a few puny willows half encased in the overflows are the only visible vegetation, none reaching above our knees. Stone clefts in the valley's flanks, their throats filled with mystery, beckon to be explored. (I know that waterfalls terminate some.) But there's nei- ther time nor strength for detours. Though I've traveled this valley repeatedly, it now appears foreign, a different land altogether. I recall days when smoke from a North Slope tundra burn turned this skyline into a phantom.

In any expanse that snow blankets, droughty plants, fire scars, and retreating permafrost can be briefly forgotten. It is easier to pretend there that the Arctic—and we—will be okay.

Predictions about the future of snow in the Brooks Range are difficult. Science better knows snow in the Alps than is does the Arctic's. Field data are spotty, and conditions vary much from one year to the next, even in periods of supposedly stable climate. "To date, we really don't know what long-term changes are underway," admits UAF geophysics professor Matthew Sturm, author of a field guide to snow, also a veteran skier.

Researchers like him believe that there will be, and maybe already are, more rain-on-snow events. His work in the Arctic Refuge this March revealed significant rain icing near the pack's bottom caused by a 40-plus-degree thaw. He feels more confident stating that winter in most years starts later and ends sooner than it used to.

Why does this matter beyond the realm of skiing?

Always close to the melting point and containing up to 90 percent air by volume, depending on type, snow is an excellent insulator, a benign habitat. Lacy flakes in low-density new layers are the best. Bears depend on it keeping their dens cozy, as do ground squirrels, true subterranean hibernators. Grizzlies don't really hibernate but lie in torpor. Some wake up sporadically and go for a walk. And even the comatose ones are about to reappear here in mid-April. I've watched Kodiak brown bears roughhouse on slopes of steep uplands at this time of year. Cubs chased each other, up as fast as down, on crampon claws, chest-deep in snow, like puppies chasing a ball, while the ragged mom reclined in the sun.

Grizzlies in forest settings choose den locations at the base of trees on north faces. This orientation ensures that plenty of snow pillows their chamber during cold snaps. They bring bedding inside that includes spruce and pine boughs and duff. An entrance through which a bear narrowly fits minimizes heat loss; snow covers it quicker than it does larger ones. At air temperatures of minus 60 degrees, the snow layer directly above the soil can be a balmy 30. *Pukak*, this temperate zone, is the winter abode of voles, lemmings, shrews, and weasels. Spring uncovers paths and seed caches that the voles memorized, miniature haystack mattresses, and the trunks snowshoe hares girdled. The underground dwellers modify *pukak*, burrowing three-dimensional trail mazes that let them live and feed screened from foxes, snowy owls, and great grays, which all hunt by ear. Imagine for a moment a vole's terror as its dim existence implodes in a flurry of daylight and chandelier dust before talons squeeze the life from it, too fast for it to even glimpse a dished, ringed face with an amber stare.

Streamlined least weasels, with their keen sense of hearing and smell, patrol some of the same tunnels. They tackle prey ten times their own weight, such as hares. Their sleekness does not conserve heat well, and to keep their hyper engine stoked, they feed up to ten times a day on meat they stash. At full speed in powder, the white-phase ermines bodysurf rather than dash. Vilhjalmur

Stefansson saw ermine skins sewn to the back of Eskimo parkas for agile power and grace.

I could use some of both.

With Jacob and Sven out of sight, I leave the groove their sleds scored into inches of snow. There's a quiet thrill in marring an untracked expanse. It sparks a sense of discovery, as a fresh snow duvet gives tranquil novelty even to places busy and familiar in the main season. For a few seconds, I can believe I'm the first here, the only person for miles around. (And except for my trail mates, I am.) "Snow provokes responses that reach right back to child-hood," the land artist Andrew Goldsworthy said; he sculpts the stuff into abstract delights. For me, it has always borne romantic notions, a wish to live in and know northern climes, the frisson of "To Build a Fire" and of *Two Old Women*, a Gwich'in tale of persistence and derring-do. "Every boy," the father of boreal ecology, William O. Pruitt Jr., said, perhaps overstating his case, "has dreams of a life in the Great North Woods."

Another 20 caribou flow up Greylime Creek. Hoar feathers the ice that plugs one of the river's bottlenecks with sequins that flash here and there as I approach. My poles' rhythmic croaking accents each kick and push with crane calls and a squeak of Styrofoam. I crest *sastrugi*, hardened, sharply eroded remnants of snow dunes. The term is Siberian. So is the mood. A headwind drives nails into the afternoon, and one thumb quickly goes numb inside my shells. Snow grains saltate on the ground. They're debris of flakes, fine sugar drifting. My face, mildly sunburned already, is raw. The cold paints my skin with a metal varnish while my torso cooks inside sundry layers. Headwinds can make a landscape oppressive, as if nature itself wanted to hinder your progress. When I don a neck gaiter, my sunglasses fog up. When I take them off to wipe them, my eyes instantly water. Before this is over, frost will have nipped my muzzle. No skin off my nose, at least not until after I've returned home. I'll lose seven pounds over the course of five days. Someone should market Arctic skiing as a weight-loss regimen.

We make camp a few miles before Ernie Pass, above Greylime, by a scant break of willows. Open water, amazingly gurgling nearby, spares us having to melt snow. But even after stomping the site on skis, it is too soft to walk on. When I try, I break in up to my crotch. We therefore set up the tipi on skis; gather wood and heat water on skis; eat dinner on skis; and piss on skis. (In the V-stance, of course.) I misjudge how much water my Kathmandu Curry needs, and the meal—leftovers from a forty-day canyon hike years ago—is a bit al dente. We step off skis only before we crawl into our bags. When Jacob's white-gas stove briefly turns the tent into a tepid Turkish bath, we decide to melt all snow outside in the future.

We've covered almost twelve miles today.

It snowed overnight, I can tell from fluff shushing down the tipi sides. It covered a huge pile of wolf scat mixed with bone splinters on a ridge above camp, the wolf's urine mark, and his palm-size tracks. A pink Frisbee in which I planted the tent pole to prevent it from spearing into the snow and thus keep our living space from shrinking shattered today.

Icy brume dims the day. The forecast promising milder weather has let us down. I bought an arborist tree-climbing belt to harness my sled, trying to save money on gear, as usual. Its metal buckle saps warmth from my bare fingers, and I struggle to close it. I pull a muscle on my ribs in the process. Unlike a backpack's hip belt, it can't be tightened once it is on. By the time I'm geared up, Sven and Jacob have vanished over a rise half a mile ahead. Having worked as a guide for decades, I am not used to lagging. Snow flies, flightless alpine relatives of daddy longlegs, as a last-ditch measure self-amputate up to five legs to survive mounting cold by preserving their core temperature. What reasons have I to complain? And what is life like for a one-legged insect?

An old shoulder injury is acting up, so I pop Ibuprofen like candy. My fleece mittens are so bulky that I have to crank down the Velcro straps on the ski-pole loops to secure my grip. This is causing tendonitis on the back of my hands, which within days swell into catcher's mitts. (Back home, after the trip, I won't be able to turn our cabin's doorknob.)

A small herd shadows us on the way to the pass named for a hiking companion of conservation icon Robert "Bob" Marshall, who'd come north as a forester but under the spell of these mountains quickly forsook his original mission. Ernie Pass straddles the Continental Divide. In June, snowmelt from where I rest for a minute will trickle, then tumble, then roll toward the Yukon River and into the Bering Strait. That from a hundred yards behind my back will join the Beaufort Sea and Arctic Ocean by way of the Anaktuvuk River.

We pick up the faint trail of skiers that preceded us by a day or so. They're participants in a race from Galbraith Lake on the Brooks Range north side to Wiseman. Going light, they pull no sleds. Luckily, they hit just the right gully downhill from the pass. We heard that steep ravines and stairs of frozen cascades could make the descent sketchy here. Instead, it stays gradual, easy for a change, with the occasional ice patch where in the summer Ernie Creek frolics.

Marshall, the first white man to poke around in these parts, named the fold that the creek beyond several headwaters junctions splayed Valley of the Precipices. A skim of snow on the river ice makes for good traction, keeping me from doing the splits mounted on skis today. Clouds, sun, and mists alternate on this stretch, singling out cornices, summits, and ridgelines cold-sintered in nature's porcelain factory, smooth and blindingly white.

At a terraced section, a special treat waits. A caribou herd drawn toward the pass condensed the snow where they stepped. Wind then chiseled away the softer surrounding matrix, sculpting tracks that stand out in relief, not as the usual imprints. Thus inverted, they look rather substantial, as if the animals left pieces of themselves in their hurry. As a bonus feature, the lone spoor of a wolf parallels the caribou's, also raised. I bet the lone hunter followed her prey, though I can't say for sure whose tracks are older.

We enter the tree line near a ghost grove of balsam poplars crowning a knoll, a camp with a great crust that keeps us from postholing. And there are views—except that the world has reverted to gray-on-gray. A dark apron farther south, this trip's first black spruces, traps what little light there is left. From my Crazy Creek chair I take in the "Gates" of Gates of the Arctic National Park down the valley. In the time-honored tradition of explorers of a so-called "terra incognita," Marshall christened these doorjambs with the entitlement of a demiurge, "two gigantic white posts...rugged and bristling with unscalable crags," centerpieces of the North Fork of the Koyukuk whose tributaries he mapped: Boreal Mountain and Frigid Crag.

I've put twelve more miles under my crappy belt.

This afternoon's laidback pace and accommodations encourage the swapping of tales. We mostly spin skiing and other outdoor yarns, as people on such a trip as ours are wont to. Sven tells of a common acquaintance, a state employee, no less, whom the Fairbanks REI store banned for unseemly complaining about gear he had bought. He also was blacklisted at an annual race. He'd hidden in the woods, waiting for a contestant who had wooed away his wife and, cursing, jumped his rival, stripped the guy of his skis, and javelined those into the selfsame woods.

Jacob shovels a low snow berm around the tipi to block drafts.

Snow laves the tent again, and it continues falling all morning. Yesterday, I frostbit the tip of my thumb; today, I burned it on the stove, which also marshmallowed a fist-size hole into the synthetic filling of my sleeping bag. I notice pinholes in the tent walls from cinders the stovepipe ejected. (That's what the sieve-looking thingamajig in the stove kit is for, then.) The dynamics of fire and ice are a theme of this trip.

You know it is cold when you're so layered that you can barely reach your behind when you go to the bathroom. I, Michelin Man, have dreaded this moment for three full days.

Alaska's Inupiat and Athabaskans excelled at improvised winter camping. To *siwash*, a corruption of the French voyageurs' racist *sauvage*—"savage" or "wildling"—meant bedding down atop campfire embers buried in the ground. Or else, a fire whose heat the back of a spruce-bough lean-to returned warmed a sleeper's front and back. Both methods depended on boreal forest for wood and snow accumulation. Where deep drifts were rare, hunters built a *quinzhee* near trap lines or kill sites. They'd piled a circular mound of loose snow, ten feet in diameter and six to eight feet high, using a snowshoe as shovel. This was left to settle and fuse for a couple of hours and then scooped out from a two-foot-wide entrance they then sealed with a caribou hide. A snow bench for sitting and a candle or lantern would turn any such place into a frost-palace haven. Sven has dug *quinzhees* with students, even twin ones connected by a tunnel, mimicking lemming apartments. A snow bench seat and a candle or lantern turn any such hole into a frost-palace emergency shelter.

Marshall, less savvy or underprepared like myself, described one *siwashing* stint without blankets or a reflective cutbank as "alternately roasting and chilling, with little sleep" though "fairly comfortable as such nights go." Jacob would have loved the then 30-year-old Marshall.

Shuffling down lower Ernie Creek, farther into the tree line's embrace, we earn another moment of beauty. One hundred ptarmigans roosting in spruces sail away like a streamer of gulls, spooked by us.

A bully headwind again pipes up, and my fingers never get warm. Frozen breaths armor my beard with mini-icicles, which offer partial protection and crunchy refreshment. My camera battery died; I could be next. There's about a foot of snow here, and Sven and Jacob's combined weight poorly compresses it. With every third or fourth step, one of my skis sinks inches, requiring wearying lifting. Two sleds and skiers ahead of me not only should plow a nice trail but also, glazing it, make it slippery! "Ski" comes from an Old Norse word for a split piece of firewood. I might as well strap two half-logs to *my* feet. It pains me to think that once I canoed 90 miles on this stream in three rip-roaring, fluid days.

We come upon a camp of our predecessors: three dismal slit trenches in spindrift near the trees. Jacob says racers pack up and start again as soon as one gets too cold.

At a break past the confluence with the North Fork, catching up to the guys, I tell them I'm done for. Perhaps, somewhere between the Mathews and here, old age at last did catch up with me, within merely four years.

I'm bummed. Broken down, out of shape, out of luck, out of sorts.

This is not a malady that a hot meal and a night in the bag will cure.

I will try to get out. Abort. Surrender. Cancel the rest.

Another camp where we waltz around on our skis doing chores and settling in, this one, tucked against the evergreen fringe. At least it is sheltered from wind. Tucked into the evergreen fringe, it sits on the threshold of the Gates, with Boreal Mountain on one side and aptly named Frigid Crag vis-à-vis.

Four wing nuts for the stove have frozen into a cluster, and I breathe on them to separate them. The many ways in which clothing and gear can malfunction symbolize human existence for me.

It's too late in the day to contact any charter companies; none operate in the winter from Coldfoot. But I ask Sven to text Melissa in Fairbanks with an update. She will try to book me a flight in the morning.

Last night was the lousiest yet. When I went out to water the front yard, glared at by Pruitt's "heat sink of celestial space," I thought I would die if the sleeping-bag zipper were to fail upon reentry. My air mattress had deflated to the point where my hips touched the ground, and I shivered inside a sarcophagus rated for minus 34. I know it was not quite that cold, though.

As my piss plashed the snow, making more *qurriniq*, northern lights flared above Frigid Crag. Even their neon shine could not brighten the pit that had swallowed my soul. Still, they were a proper parting gift, a bookend to the Anaktuvuk diamond dust eons ago. "You take them as much for granted as you would starlight outside and only become especially thrilled when there is unusual coloration to them," Marshall wrote about the auroras.

I beg to differ.

"I can hear it getting warmer outside already," Jacob quips as the sun peeks over the mountains and he from *his* mummy sheath and the stove crackles and pops. I've named the stove Moloch, and this morning, sacrificed more fabric to its omnivorous skin.

We receive word per InReach that a plane will be on its way later today. The pilot suggests that we move down the river to a suitable landing spot on the ice. He will find us there. The bill will be close to four thousand dollars.

Three miles beyond, before a chain of turquoise overflows, we park the sleds and mark a runway with willow branches to assist Max, the pilot, with his depth perception. We've checked for bumps, boulders, driftwood, and pressure ridges that might foul him up. I've given the group gear I carried to Jacob and Sven and consolidated mine. They'll have two more ten- to twelve-hour days with cold nights to Delay Pass, where they'll turn east, climbing from the North Fork toward a second divide, sublime Glacier Creek Pass, and another day's slog to the obsolete Nolan mine and then on to Wiseman, Marshall's "Arctic Village," where, overwintering in a 16-by-18-foot cabin, he eagerly timed the first color blushing the southern sky. The two will arrive there a couple of hours before their scheduled return flight, and catch a ride to Coldfoot.

Sven and Jacob wax their skis in anticipation of the overflows downstream.

A hum that is not Brooks Range silence swells. Soon, we spot Max, skimming up-valley, perfectly punctual. The landing lights of his Helio Courier herald the end for me.

Like stories, not all journeys have happy endings. "What is defeat?" one of Hemingway's character asks and, trying to take the sting out of it, answers himself: "You go home." His contemporary, the poet and critic George Edward Woodberry, believed that "Defeat is not the worst of failures. Not to have tried is the true failure."

Thus I console myself, with literature, humankind's tracks on a single page of the ages. And snow is a great reminder that nothing will last.

CHAPTER 27

ANCESTORS, ENDLINGS, AND A REVENANT

Eyes watering in a breeze that snatched its sting from the pack ice, I scan the coastal plain for signs of life. My binoculars frame horizon segments the sun blurs, a mindbender like Prudhoe Bay's gas flares, which snap and yaw above industrial installations 150 miles to the west. A liquid glare melds earth and sky. Distant "lakes" separate, then coalesce, dissolving firm ground into quicksilver, a landscape of uncertainties. When polar fronts straddle warm ground, light flexes into mirages like this, supple and transient as tundra denizens. More than other shores, and not without irony, the continent's farthest-north suggests limits; its luminous emptiness unmoors assumptions, urging us to reconsider the scale of things, their importance, and beyond that, the scope of our ambitions.

My eyes catch on a pair of boulders swimming amongst tussocks on this inland sea. Changing position ever so slightly, the mounds look too bulky to be grizzlies, as well as the wrong shade of brown. A "Forward, hard!" activating four paddle blades propels our blue rubber raft, which scrapes across gravel, its blunt snout nuzzling shore. Ravines and willow clusters downwind from two grazing muskoxen allow us to sneak up on them in a line and hunched over, in an effort to reduce our silhouettes, to appear small and non-threatening. Screened by topography as much as by the animals' poor eyesight, we pause frequently, considering how far we should push our luck. The clicking or whirring of cameras alone could invite an attack. We also don't want to harass the roaming haystacks.

One hundred yards. Fifty. The bulls raise their prizefighter heads, sampling the wind. Each skull alone weighs as much as two heavy-duty sledgehammers and, with the backing of 850 pounds of muscle and attitude, can hit with comparable force.

The dark masses seem to absorb sunlight, to gather gravity like black holes on the hoof. We freeze. Catching sight of us, they neither charge nor turn tails but step away, nimble as dancers despite their weight, the hemlines on their wool skirts trim and swaying in sync with feet in prim white stockings.

When muskoxen feel threatened, they circle or line up in front of their calves like armored cars on a parade ground, a reaction honed through millennia of skirmishes with bears and wolves. An alpha bull may break rank without giving advance notice. Taut as a spring, he will launch from a wall of fur, horns, and bossed foreheads, ready to gore or throw any intruder. (Incredibly, one rutting bull lunged at a low-flying airplane in an attempt to hook the landing gear.) While a circling-the-wagons instinct served muskoxen well before the advent of humans, it contributed to their decline throughout Alaska before the mid-1800s. For centuries, Inuit hunters had dogs pursue fleeing herds, forcing *oominqmak*—the Bearded Ones—to align within range of arrows or spears. Yankee whalers wintering in the western Canadian Arctic and traders who provisioned them with meat and skins shot muskoxen with rifles instead, felling one at a time at a long distance, for coveted carriage robes, too. Entire kin groups faced the bullets standing their ground like statues. Expeditions wanting live specimens for eastern zoos and museum exhibits wiped out whole parental defense lines before they could capture the calves sheltered behind them. One college man who risked his own skin in the Far North for that of an ox called it "cruel butchery." It was as much sport as "hiring a pack of hungry curs for an afternoon, and turning them into your neighbor's sheep pasture" for an execution by firing squad. "You do not feel the triumphant exhilaration which results from successfully pursuing the noble moose or elk," he admitted.

Tied closer to sparse rangelands, with large bodies harder to sustain, muskoxen have always been less numerous than caribou. During the Pleistocene, herds flowed back and forth across much of the ice-free interior, western, and all of northern Alaska, contemporary with mammoths and mastodons; but climate changes during the Holocene probably hastened the erstwhile decline of a species that glaciers and wind had lathed.

Trying to restore the region's biodiversity, the federal government imported 34 Greenlandic muskoxen in 1930. By ship and by train, the transplants arrived in Fairbanks. The university still keeps some of their offspring at its Large Animal Research Station in our cabin's neighborhood, where, skiing the trails, I sometimes see them in their enclosure with the reindeer as they plow through the clearing like dark ships through icy wastes. Five years after the seed herd had arrived in the Interior's forests, 31 muskoxen were crated and then barged to Nunivak Island in the Bering Sea, where they prospered. In 1969 and 1970, Nunivak muskoxen were shipped to northern Alaska, including 63 that formed the core of a herd in the Arctic National Wildlife Refuge, the state's contested northeastern corner. Those must have been the world's most-cosmopolitan muskoxen. Upon their release, several, confused or headed home to Greenland, wandered onto the sea ice, but Inupiaq herders straddling snowmachines pushed them back to shore. The new herd grew and dispersed for the next 15 years, expanding their range as far west as Prudhoe Bay. In 1986 the refuge population peaked, numbering close to 400 animals. "Cycles of one year, five years, a thousand years: all these different cycles spinning around. The cycles of the wildlife, the different species and how they come and go. This sort of gets into your head and keeps going on and on," the travel and science writer John McPhee said in an interview; he structured much of his nonfiction accordingly.

To everybody's surprise, a 2006 survey of traditional muskox habitat north of the Continental Divide came up short. Although muskoxen can be difficult to spot from the air and some may have been overlooked, their numbers were down everywhere. Pilots counted only one muskox within the refuge boundaries. It is easy to imagine this loner as one of the two shag piles our paddling crew approached on the Aichilik River, which, unbeknownst to us then, could have been the whole herd.

Pressure from subsistence hunters could easily have played a role in the slump, at least until 2006, when muskox hunting in the refuge was suspended. Biologists believed that, despite its legendary fleece, the refuge's last muskox would not see another spring.

What triggered this downward slide of a species that had survived rampant glaciation? Poaching? A mysterious disease? Toxins in the water or soil?

We'd been looking at creatures the future might only know as museum exhibits, an animal now seen as "a marker species for climate change." Residents of Kaktovik, nestled against the Arctic Ocean's blue sweep, increasingly comment on erratic weather, which may afflict the muskoxen. Wetter springs deliver snow dumps deep enough to stop even the dozer bulls. Untimely thaw-and-freeze episodes encase grasses and sedges under three-inch solid ice, thicker than hooves can crack. Population crashes have also been linked to a lungworm explosion and a bacterium normally found in domestic sheep and goats. Freezes no longer tamp down parasites sufficiently. Malnourished cows may give birth to weak calves, or leave in search of greener pastures in the Brooks Range or Canada. Not too long ago, 13 muskies drowned in a flood on the Colville River west of the refuge; others got stranded on raw barrier islands, where they pawed sand for sustenance and starved to death after the sea ice melted, mingling their bones with bleached driftwood from the Mackenzie delta.

Perhaps more disturbing to people who view wilderness as simply another theme park, some North Slope grizzlies figured out how to breach muskox formations and kill several animals in a herd, sometimes without feeding on the carcasses. Decidedly rare, multiple or "surplus killings" have been recorded for species ranging from spiders to orcas. Most cases occur when the scales of risk and effort tip to favor the predator, while environmental or genetic disadvantages—weather, starvation, disease, or deformity—weigh in against prey. The proverbial blood lust of the fox in the henhouse may be nothing but a projection of human proclivities, an assignment of irrationality to creatures that cannot object. Evolutionary progress, the fine-tuning of survival, seems to drive animal surplus killing. In a land of feast and famine, it makes sense for bears, as it does for people, to stockpile whenever they can. Though they may take the occasional caribou calf, barrenlands grizzlies scrape the barrel's bottom while their southern cousins fatten up on salmon. (Muskoxen do thrive in places like downtown Nome, where bears are absent or find diverse, abundant, less combative food.) More importantly, nature goads all beings into realizing their full potential. Surplus killing polishes instincts, reflexes. It calibrates skills. Much pleasure springs from physical mastery, from the deft pitting of bodies against each other and of wits against world—any athlete, hunter, wild child, or animal intuits this.

Evolution never tires of new designs. Congruent with science, many Inupiaq elders believe that wolves shaped the caribou and vice versa. The same selective pressure keeps working on muskoxen and bears: in the keen presence of each other, both become faster, stronger, smarter, more alert, more enduring—or else drop from the race. Species are not fixed, yet rarely do we get to witness their changing. At times, gene flows stagnate before drying up; at other times, they merge, gain momentum, and animate bastard organisms. A recent Arctic example comes in the form of hybrid bears.

In the spring of 2006, a trophy hunter led by a guide killed an animal on Banks Island, Canada, that resembled a polar bear with cinnamon legs and dark circles around the eyes. Closer inspection also revealed a dished snout, humped back, and long brown claws for raking berry bushes and backhoeing tubers and ground squirrels from rocky soil—all typical grizzly features. At seven and a half feet, this bear was much shorter than the average polar bear but had the small head suited to pulling seals from their breathing holes in the ice. DNA tests confirmed the unique animal to be the result of a polar bear female and a grizzly male mating. In 2010, a Canadian Inuk killed the most recent confirmed hybrid, which was pillaging vacant cabins. DNA samples showed it to be a second-generation mix. While both species have produced fertile cubs in zoos, crossbreeding had never before been documented in wild populations.

What should we call such crossovers? Grolar bears? Pizzlies? How will we pigeonhole a rapidly shifting world? The dilemma runs deeper than mere problems with taxonomy.

To some biologists, these liaisons spell trouble. As the Arctic sea-ice disintegrates and straits like the Northwest Passage open, closely related, formerly separated species—belugas and narwhals, bowheads and right whales, among others—will pair off more frequently. In this scenario, more common or far-ranging species could "absorb" endangered ones or smaller regional populations. Think humans and Neanderthals. Genetic blending can lead to animals with successively less vigor and talent for survival. Still, compared to a Shih Tzu, White Fang was one hardcore mutt. So was Buck. And look at us. Our DNA carries traces of Neanderthals and Denisovans, both extinct. Hybridization is much more common in nature than previously thought. And it can bestow adaptive advantages. In general, Darwin theorized, "It is not the strongest or the most intelligent who will survive but those who can best manage change." Arctic hybrids in theory could develop into species well adapted; natural selection, however, takes time—millennia, not just decades. Evolution is on speed now, and we're pushing it.

Geneticists say that polar bears branched off from grizzlies, and rather recently. About 125,000 years ago, growing ice sheets isolated a group of brown bears in the far north of their range from its ancestral stock. Initially, these holdouts scavenged seal carcasses washed up on beaches; later, they began to hunt seals that surfaced near shore or that hauled out to rest on the ice. Fur of a lighter shade and other traits that benefited them in their new habitat cropped up and, selected for, became permanent until the sleek, white hunter *Ursus maritimus*, the "sea bear," had taken shape.

Like hybrid whales or northern bears, the last muskox topples notions of ecosystem stability, the linchpin in theories that satisfy our cravings for harmony, permanence, and smooth functionality. It compels us to accept extinction, to refrain from fixing what is not broken but also to ask ourselves if our hands truly are clean. It raises questions that cut close to the bone. Can we embrace nature unruly, nature in flux? Is human-caused local extinction, the muting of voices in a landscape's register, less lamentable than its global counterpart? And ultimately: do we dare reassess our responses to environmental threats, or are we bull-headed enough to repeat destructive behavior, hastening our own end?

You must come face to face with extinction to fully digest it, and I'm not speaking of dinosaur bones, mammoth tusks, or bird skins in cabinet drawers here. Those are mere body parts, bereft of individuality's flame. On UAF's West Ridge, in the Museum of the North, reposes a mystery bull from the ice. Blue Babe, mottled with vivianite, a mineral rust glowing like midnight from the peat overburden, is a mature steppe bison (*Bison priscus*)—a species better endowed in the headgear department than its Great Plains kin—that breathed his last 36,000 years ago. Animated by torchlight, his likeness belted across mankind's oldest wildlife art galleries, cave walls at Altamira and Lascaux. In 1979, a placer miner's hydraulic-jet water cannons on a creek outside Fairbanks sluiced Blue Babe's remains from the muck. Called to the cold hollow, Dale Guthrie, a slim, bearded University of Alaska paleobiologist with a ponytail, ID'd the animal, a common one once in Alaska's interior. *Bison priscus* thrived between twin peaks of the last ice age that dropped sea levels by converting water into glacial caps. A gateway and natural larder, Beringia's "Mammoth Steppe" welcomed Eurasian megafauna into our continent's younger margins. Camels, ground sloths, Beetle-size armadillos, and an assorted herbivorous menagerie relocated, trailed by people and dire wolves. Forest-loving descendants of Beringian bovid populations survived climate change and predation until about 400 years ago near present-day Whitehorse, a Yukon steppe-bison graveyard atop goldfields. Puncture marks showed that American lions had killed this bull before first snow, and then silt from a nearby slope preserved it. The type and placement of scratches, and clotted blood under the nose's skin—a sign of strangulation—also hinted at lions as the killers. Further dismantling the bison, ravens had pecked flesh around the eyes; other scavengers gnawed on the bones. The horns' growth patterns revealed his age (eight or nine years), its underfur the season of his demise (early winter).

With the name, Guthrie also honored Paul Bunyan's famed helper, which a blizzard had buried up to the muzzle, tingeing the ox as it does frostbitten toes. Guthrie cached his Blue Babe piecemeal in a university freezer as the mummy emerged, keeping the hide in ethanol. A talented artist as well as a hunter, he later researched and designed a plaster mold and mounted the skin, aided by a Finnish zoologist and Russian mammoth experts, one of which had allegedly learned from the man who'd embalmed Lenin. Thus saved, the bull was carried in solemn procession from the workshop to his new resting place at the museum. In celebration, Guthrie carved a portion off Blue Babe's neck and stewed it and then dined on it with his wife and friends. The uncooked chuck resembled beef jerky. The prepared dish, served with burgundy, unsurprisingly tasted like mud.

Freed from the Subarctic's meat locker, the state's most famous fossil still lies entombed, behind glass in the entrance hall of the museum. Visitors at the display case murmur in awe as they behold this member of paleontological royalty. Skin patches missing from the restored rump and hump betray feline and scientific appetites. Beneath the lethal horns' lyre-shaped sweep, with his legs folded under, chin resting on a snow-white catafalque, Blue Babe seems merely asleep. Meanwhile, on the African Serengeti, lions and wildebeests enact the same timeless ritual, that all-or-nothing roll of the dice, a dance joining life to death, hunters to the hunted. But the question butts in, for how much longer?

A cautionary tale lies in the bones of the last mammoths. In 1999, hunters on St. Paul Island—with 70 square miles the biggest of the Pribilof cluster's spent volcanoes—stumbled upon a sensation: a 40-foot-deep lava tube beneath tundra, housing a charnel hoard. During a 2003 expedition to Qagnax Cave, named after the Aleut word for "bone," University of Alaska Anchorage scientists sorted its faunal debris. Among more than 1,750 fragments, most from foxes the pit had devoured, lay five woolly-mammoth shards plus two teeth. Mammoths made up one-third of Alaska's paleo-mammal biomass, so that alone hardly warranted much excitement. But dates obtained by various methods at different labs did. Radiocarbon decay measures showed that this animal bulldozed through the island roughly 5,700 years ago, 4,000 *after* its last known relative roamed our continent.

Bugling trunks still shattered the silence on Siberia's Wrangel Island about 4,300 years ago, centuries after the completion of Giza's Great Pyramid. Wrangel Island was another high-ground refugium, one thousand miles north of today's Pribilofs, on Beringia's northern periphery. Insular woollies could be ten percent smaller—fairly common in deprived, confined populations—but they were no dwarf race like California's Channel Islands mammoth; they rivaled African elephants in height. The mainland's mammoths forged on until circa 10,000 BCE. Each of the reddish-orange, strawberry-blond, or chestnut-brown jumbos Hoovered the equivalent of four alfalfa bales daily. Wetter, warmer years turned steppe into tundra and forest, with the behemoths' decline reinforcing the trend. Saplings no longer trampled became woods less reflective than prairies. Snow no longer compacted, like a down blanket, screened warmer soil from cooling winds.

Nineteenth-century rumors of the mammoth's survival in an Arthur Conan Doyle-style lost-world scenario were owed to a zoologist aboard the US Revenue Cutter *Corwin,* to whom the Cape Prince of Wales Inupiat offered fossilized bones and tusks in trade. Bering Strait dwellers long familiar with half-buried pachyderm parts they carved into adze blades, harpoon tips, knife handles, and amulets took them as proof of mythical creatures tunneling underground that died when they surfaced, upon inhaling. It was a good explanation for why they'd never found a live one. The hulking shape the collector sketched onto the ship's deck during his inquiries fleshed out the chimera whose continued existence his visitors might then have affirmed. Who knew what wonders these vast spaces hid, even this late in the race? Given the absence of complete skeletons, the related Greenlanders over 2,000 miles farther east conceived of the *kiligivak* (the Inupiaq *kiligvak*) whose carcasses baffled them as a creature with six or ten legs. In their folktales it was a trophy of distinguished hunters, together with the polar bear.

Outlier species, from dodos to giant tortoises, often lingered—or arose—on predator-free islands until sailors, settlers, or ecological shifts doomed them. The question of what finished St. Paul's holdouts has intrigued paleontologists. They considered "overkill," the idea that early human arrivals hunted wildlife to extinction—70 percent of North America's megafauna simply disappeared. However, except for stray Aleut kayakers, Russian sealers in the 1780s were the first people to land on St. Paul.

UAF researchers tackling the mystery in 2013 cored lake sediments on St. Paul Island. The layers revealed poor water quality during the tuskers' twilight days; algae and aquatic insects sealed up in the muck profiled the region's dwindling ice-age lakes. Nitrogen isotopes of an organism's diet leave unique, local signatures in its skeleton, which underscored creeping aridity before the St. Paul bruisers' end. Lack of freshwater, for Matthew Wooller of UAF's Water and Environmental Research Center, was "the smoking gun" of causes that jelled into a dire situation. When melting ice caps shrank the island to its present dimensions, its shaggy tanks ran out of fuel.

This, among the most compelling studies ever to pinpoint prehistoric extinction, is yet another reminder of the balancing act required of small populations in changed circumstances. Compared to the St. Paul scenario, droughts and sea level rises we trigger will seemingly strike overnight. *Mammuthus primigenius*, one of the last in a line of at least six mammoth species, through millennia failed to adapt to the threat. *Homo* not-quite-so *sapiens* and fellow creatures now at best have decades to do so. Our kind evolved to fear the sabertooth cat or the short-faced bear on the steppe, not seas that inched upward and signaled the Pleistocene's end, or those that do currently, at the end of the Holocene climate break. Still, this diagnosis of a far-future blind spot collides with the novelist David Mitchell's truth that "Anticipating the end of the world is humanity's oldest pastime." Depending on our political leanings, we just predict the apocalypse to ride in from varying quarters.

Unsurprisingly, Alaska's state fossil keeps making the news beyond grinding rivers and coastal storms baring the dome-headed grazers' remains. Bioengineers want to replicate the woolly mammoth as a niche-filler in rewilded experimental settings or "Pleistocene parks." This in part seeks to remedy the melting of permafrost by beating back encroaching boreal forest. It is also a sort of apology to species we've sent to their doom.

Biological extinction has its counterpart in the cultural. And the same economic-political system drives both. In a breakdown exacerbated by the climate crisis in particular, through displacement, every 40 days, somewhere on this globe a language flickers out. The year 2008 saw the death of the last person fluent in Eyak (a language related to Athabaskan ones), formerly spoken around my one-time hometown Cordova and the Copper River delta and on Qe'yiłteh, Kayak Island, in the eastern Prince William Sound, where Russia made its initial landfall in Alaska. The deceased, Marie Smith Jones, then 89, was what is known in both humans and other animals as an "endling"—the last of her kind. While her people endure, not all nuances encoded in Eyak do. Much ethno-botanical lore, for instance, is lost, including species taxonomies, another casting of culture onto biology. Michael Krauss, the head of UAF's Alaska Native Language Center, whom I knew, worked closely with Mrs. Jones to salvage as much of her knowledge as possible and to develop teaching materials, analogous to captive-breeding efforts. The linguist with white hair and the gleam of bonhomie and impassioned scholarship in his bespectacled eyes became conversant in Eyak. But there was no one left to converse with. "Should we mourn the loss of Eyak or Ubykh any less than the loss of the panda or California condor?" he asked, quite sure of the answer.

It has been said that the loss of each Indigenous tradition-bearer equals a library burned to the ground, the loss of a language, a bomb dropped on the Louvre. And that Hebrew is the only language ever fully revived from the written to spoken state. "Old knowledge that we need to learn anew is leaving us," the Chickasaw writer Linda Hogan observes. The extermination of cultural and biological treasures sometimes coincides in a literal conflagration. The Rio de Janeiro fire of 2018, which razed 122 rooms of Brazil's Museu Nacional, consumed all recordings of chants in extinct Amazonian languages, thousands of pre-Columbian artifacts, a part of the zoological collection, striking feather art by the imperiled Karajá tribe, and a fresco from Pompeii that had weathered Vesuvius's eruption.

So much gets lost in translation alone. Each language uniquely parses the world at a most basic level through the kinds of things it differentiates, from car brands, stock options, and breakfast cereals to healing herbs, constellations, the life-cycle stages of whales, and types of forest spirits or ice. Globalization drives both forms of extinction, the cultural and biological. We know that the first abets the second, as hunter-gatherer vocabularies anchor modes of respect for the other-than-human. "In a state of emergency, a democracy is not the best form of government to have," Barry Lopez said about our grim present. "*Elders* is the best form of government to have [emphasis and subject-verb disagreement his]." And he was not referring to the Washington gerontocracy. He was thinking of seniors in touch with the nonhuman world, who over decades of paying attention learned what works and what doesn't: "The fact that these people are still on the face of the earth with a coherent culture tells you that they've consistently made the right decisions through drought and starvation and disease." Our hurried, youth-obsessed culture has sidelined this expertise.

Outlining a philosophy of sound land management, another such elder in our midst, Aldo Leopold, cautioned that we must preserve every cog and wheel—and by implication complete workshops—when tinkering. The realization that we don't even hold all the blueprints or fully grasp the interlocking of parts can be as humbling as a face-off with ice-age beasts, or mastery of a non-European language, its foreign sounds, grammar, hidden meanings and relationships.

CHAPTER 28

SWEET SCENTS, SWEET HOMES

A sprig from a creosote bush enriches the steam in our shower stall with notes of the western Grand Canyon: tarry, resinous, bitter. I carried it carefully wrapped in my luggage the last time I returned to the Subarctic from my former tramping grounds, the high desert Southwest. The sprig's scent conjures a dear place and time more suddenly than fossil or feather or driftwood burl on a desk, jump-starting memory, as would satiny wildflowers between a book's pages. Call it schnoztalgia, aromatherapy for the homesick, or, like Helen Keller, "a potent wizard that transports us a thousand miles and all the years we have lived."

It's been January for five leaden months outside the two-story Fairbanks cabin. Winter swaggers with the dearth of smells symptomatic of that season's deprivations. A sachet of lavender blossoms in my pillow guarantees sweet vernal dreams at least. The bouquet of snow has been described as "tingling and fresh." It is not, at least not at 50 below, when nostrils freeze shut. When you're able to siphon through your snore-hook, the monotone of old snow reigns supreme. Vapors carry more scent molecules and move more freely in warm, humid than in cold, dry air. Also, wet, "hydrated" particles stick more easily to the nose's olfactory membranes. Beyond 55 below, as the molecules living bodies emit cease to move, even wolves, which can pick up scents of one part per billion, turn anosmic. (That's a dandy word for "smell-blind," and it contains "nos.")

But knowledge of the facts does not make such absences easier to bear.

We are predominantly visual beings, underestimating or taking for granted what the nose knows until a head cold or exotic virus leaves us not blind, not deaf, not mute, but—what? We have "anosmia," which sounds like a snob's sneeze, but no common word (or solace) for the impairment of smell. Moreover, our scent cliff notes lack refinement, suggesting disinterest, an emphasis elsewhere, or inadequate training. Place names derived from smell, such as Stink Creek (a Yukon River tributary), are even more rare than those we get from hearing (Gates of the Arctic's Rumbling Mountain; the Kenai Peninsula's Whisper Lake), which visual coinages vastly outnumber.

Not every culture prioritizes the senses thus. A dearth of smelltalk characterizes some cultures more than others. Linguists speculate that, unlike the low-key Arctic and our odor-poor sanitized cityscapes, tropical rainforests foster olfactory fluency. A now extinct shrub inspired Native Hawaiians to coin the term "Octopus Fragrance" for the delicious orange-like scent of its flowers. This was an appropriate metaphor, as their morning and evening exhalations slipped from the dense groves like that contortionist from its reef lair. The Suyá, a hunter-gatherer tribe of 150 native to Brazil's Mato Grosso rainforest, classify animals by their odor, rather than, say, by their gestalt, behavior, or habitat. They use these same categories for people, and to a lesser degree, plants. "The Suyá think in smell, whereas we only react to smells," the authors of an anthropological study sum up a more visceral take on existence. The Jahai of the Malay Peninsula have a dozen terms for types of smell. One puts fresh blood, raw meat, mud, stagnant water, and even some species of toad into the same class. Most English speakers cannot differentiate toads by sight, or detail cinnamon scent beyond calling it "spicy." Mind you, English also has spot-on words for odor nuances, all of which though refer to other things: "earthy," "fishy," "citrusy," "gamey," and so on. But this concerns the average person's vocabulary, not Faulkner's or Thoreau's.

Soupçons of change, however, aerate the industrialized world. The Japanese, attuned to the aesthetics of daily-life practices and sensations, compiled a list of their nation's hundred best aromas tied to specific districts. The winners, chosen from a write-in contest, included cultural as well as natural scents: grilled eel, sulfurous hot springs, the mustiness of used-book stores, and the punch that marinates herbal-medicine shops. The responsible ministry hoped the initiative would raise awareness and spur efforts to protect an olfactory heritage.

Unlike the rest of sensory input, scent impulses bypass the thalamus, hominid seat of language and logic, zapping straight to the amygdala and hippocampus, the brain's reptilian regions for fight-or-flight responses, emotion, memorization, and navigation, where they're archived. This lumping together of functions makes sense. Memories, after all, are mental journeys frequently tinged by feelings. Some scents teleport us across space or time. When I travel south from wintry Alaska in a jet's stale interior—a pressurized climate bubble, like those cored from glacier ice—Phoenix welcomes me as soon as the cabin door opens with a cocktail of heady particulates, as if to a different season.

"Smells linger in a way that light does not, revealing history," the science journalist Ed Yong writes. This is metaphorical truth, not just physics. I have no early-childhood olfactory souvenirs, but Inupiat people comment on the smell of wolf being their earliest remembered scent, one they associate with their mothers and with feeling sheltered. Generations of women carried babes on their backs snugly inside parka hoods lined with wolf fur. Developing brains etched those discrete sensations into shared neural pathways. Adults may blow on a pelt's long hair to release its scent, a distant wild whiff unlike a dog's. Inhaling deeply, they revisit their infancy.

After 25 years in the North, I can tap into a file of odors complementing locales, the ecologist Christopher Norment's "catalog of experience and desire." Strengthened by slivers of the past wed to volatile parts, I am absorbing Earth's essences, trying to safeguard each one in my recollection: Freshly split spruce, a fuel that warms you twice. A dwarf lupine field in the Arctic Refuge—like wading knee-deep in ambrosia, bumblebee heaven. Brisk nose tickles from Labrador tea crushed underfoot on the tundra. Wormwood or "stinkweed's" menthol soothing flesh in a steambath. This sage is the northern herbalist's cure-all, the Athabaskan and Inupiaq chicken soup or Tylenol. Nine essential oils have been distilled from it. One of these, the mild narcotic absinthin, mellows the neural regions that process pain and anxiety. I've joined Dena'ina men self-flagellating with stink-weed switches and can verify rumors that you taste the whip after you've stopped flogging. It's a sign of the herb's potency, of the active ingredients' quick diffusion through the bloodstream. In order to be tasted, a substance has to dissolve in a liquid. Smell and taste, both forms of chemical perception, overlap, although smelling is more nuanced and expansive. To fulltime foragers, the first locavores, their diet must have felt cartographic or mythical, with each scent-flavor hitched to a place of origin.

At the opposite end of spring's floral awakening, we find the poignancy of deciduous fall, the putrescence of stranded, spent salmon, the rankness of walrus or whale melting into Nome's driftwood beaches, which stops you almost like a wall. Incense from newly lit woodstoves in Fairbanks proclaims the begin-ning of autumn, though it carbonizes the air. I close my eyes bent over smoked-salmon strips and see a fishcamp with tiered A-frame drying racks, the meat conserved like my August days on the Kobuk. A pair of beaver-fur mitts I once owned honored a moose's sacrifice when I warmed my numb nose tip by blowing into the buckskin palms—the Koyukon seamstress had smoked the hide after tanning it, for durability.

Scents ground us in nature's cycles, in death and rejuvenation.

Scents cling to us even bodily: fetid river muck or mud brined tides. And have you ever boarded a plane outbound from rural Alaska, smiling at the cured-bacon haze coming off hunters who've spent nights sitting at campfires?

Each treasured scent evokes an embrace, a friendly pat on the shoulder at least. Even outhouse interiors braided with cigarette smoke connote rusticity, quiet cabin stints in the city's hinter-lands. The stench weakened during cold snaps, when frost furred the walls with sparkling sequins. I've stored surprisingly few stinkers in my mind's vault. The fumes from the crappy coated Special Forces raingear that I wore only once—just about daily for a month of my Arctic traverse. The seepage of unwashed socks infusing Cordova's old library and the reek of its cannery, which taints the whole town with a seal's breath of fish guts and blood. (In all fairness, I must mention the real puffs we heard through our open bedroom windows when harbor seals hungry for spawning salmon patrolled Eccles Creek during high tides, which at new moons and full moons flooded the path to our walk-in rental.) DEET, which I once licked off a girl on an alfresco date and which masked her skin's latte creaminess, brings back that affair's acrimony. The pall of charred wood with ashtray overtones that chokes Fairbanks bronchia and moods too frequently now is another scent I could do without. It heralds our flammable summers—and upwind Canada's—as unambiguously as does the claustrophobic non-view from atop College Hill. In my once-again hometown, I sense conflagrations before the air visibly thickens.

You can smell the climate emergency not just in the grown presence of wildfires but also near permafrost slumping at North Slope cutbanks and gutted bluffs. Scientists at UAF's Toolik Field Station in the Brooks Range foothills compared the rot of decaying plant matter mixed with mud to that of a tent stored wet for months, or to a damp, moldy room—in other words, the inside of my first Fairbanks residence, a shack leaning on muskeg. For me, that melting soil summons freshly turned earth, turf trenches cut into Irish moors I visited as a youth. A "metallic ping" the Toolik researchers noticed stems from the extremely high concentrations of carbon dioxide being discharged. While the gas is odorless, its taste is sharp and faintly acidic, like soda water. The peaty burps contain methane, too, an organic compound over 80 times more damaging to the atmosphere than carbon dioxide. Methane also is odorless but often mixed with hydrogen sulfide, a result of animal digestion and the decomposition that contributes the rotten-egg smell. Here, in the winter, you can make methane from decaying organic matter in lake bottoms visible. It builds up under the ice, and when you puncture the lid and light the escaping gas, it leaps up into a man-size flame. (Don't lean over the borehole while doing it.) A legacy of the last ice age, permafrost encapsulates one sixth of our planet's soil and traps these gases in much older, deeper sediments—as long as those stay frozen. Bodies of water, warmer than the ground, speed up that release and act as valves. One lake in the Arctic that scientists studied, and from which they heard gurgling, vented flatulence equaling that of 6,000 dairy cows daily. Even vaster reservoirs slumber in Arctic continental shelves, which, awakened by warming, plume toward the oceans' surfaces.

Through Alaska's thawing soils we sample extinction with our bodies. Emanating from it are sins of the past and present, the fug of the future.

Biologists have long researched how fragrances impact creatures' wayfinding. Ants putting down pheromone trails lead others to a food source. Pigeons, petrels, bees, and possibly bears and mice use odor maps of their neighborhoods to return to dens or nests. On the flipside, regional scent dialects that the anal glands of river otters secrete help those to distinguish strangers from kin. Lynxes run ID checks and can tell if a conspecific is in heat from urine sprayed onto tree stumps. A delicious citrusy tang wafts around crested auklet rookeries; both males and females emit octanal, a liquid also found in tangerines, which serves as a mate attractant and possibly, mosquito repellant. Puffins, with nostrils at the base of their beaks, zero in on their colony from a distance of almost 500 miles. Similarly, certain campsites of Inuit, inhabited over centuries and "surrounded by the smell of their things," in Knud Rasmussen's words, developed distinctive auras, which hunters could latch on to on their approach.

Wolves signal territorial boundaries in conspicuous places, as dogs do on lampposts, if they can, on top of a rival's leavings. It's a literal pissing match, not for volume and for a different kind of range. In addition to cooking away from any tents, I too water rocks around mine before turning in, generating a force field in lieu of an electric fence that, I hope, will deflect bears. Pack members also flag den sites and dominance in that way, and food caches they have depleted. Reinforcing the messages, glands between their toes perfume the ground when they're digging.

On the subject of body excretions, I simply cannot avoid the sex lives of porcupines. It comes as no surprise that males joust by weaponizing quilled tails, and orange incisors that grow throughout their lifetime, replacing denture worn down. The prize of combat is the chance to mate with an ovulating female, whose vaginal mucus lured these suitors. A bout's winner, as a rule the heftier opponent, splashes the damsel with urine, often while both perch in a tree. A female not yet ready shakes the droplets off and skedaddles. I don't want to deprive you of the happy ending, although scent has no part in it. Consummation takes place on the ground. To spare him the pain, she curls her tail over her back, underside up, covering most of her quills.

Equally indelicate weasels, scared witless, anoint careless trappers with "stink bombs" justly famous and taunt scientists with scat on top of undisturbed traps. Such property markers, normally left on trails—oh, the irony—make excellent bait for catching other weasels. The slender droppings attract conspecifics, as does "anal drag," the weasel version of grizzly butt dragging for laying a scent track.

Conveying facts less glaring to us than to bears, glands in their plate-size paws hook pheromone junkies as adept as the ants and with noses that make bloodhounds envious. Foot fetishists of the carnivore world, non-territorial polar bear males, widely dispersed, latch onto receptive females in sea-ice tracts. The olfactory bulb in the brain of their bruin cousins, five times larger than ours, translates scents 2,000 times better than ours. It detects food, danger, or mates up to two miles away. Especially during the breeding months, grizzlies whizz purposely and by "stomp-walking" grind that fluid into the earth as if squashing bugs or foes. Such "mark trails" show clearly near prominent trees against which bears rub, not to scratch an itch, but to impart skin odors and rectal lubricant. (Field biology does get messy, and its practitioners call a stick what it is, except that they do it in Latin.) Boulders or, in Denali, Park Service signs, make handy posts too. Grizzlies and black bears have favorite trees, ursine chat rooms, where ranges adjoin. Olfactory fingerprints spreading more than 20 distinct compounds curb bear brawling by establishing hierarchies. The where, when, how much, and how often of chemical Sticky Notes, far from subtle, vary between the young and the old and between females and males.

Hair that researchers gather from wire snares and the rough bark of trees through genetic analysis discloses the sex, numbers, and relatedness of bears in a given area. I have stopped for inebriating Nootka roses in our woods, but never for these hair strands. The biologist Anthony Cupri, who preps rub trees with gauze, says it turns almost black from oils and dirt in the fur and "really smells like bear." A few people can smell grizzlies in nearby brush, but I have to watch the body language of caribou for reassurance. They can sniff out lichen under five feet of snow, and when they are grazing, heads down, I am at ease.

The scent postings different species leave in a busy square mile, if they were visible and if lines connected them, would look like a colorful vintage subway map or that of a village's trap lines or a snarl of spaghetti, if you're not familiar with either.

As on land so in water. An olfactory prompt from a beloved location—a cascade in Utah's Wasatch Mountains fragrant with mosses and columbines—led a University of Wisconsin biologist to discover how salmon smell home. A stream's unmistakable chemistry, the scent of natal waters, reels in mature salmon, imprinted in their youth. Greater carbon loads now burdening oceans impair the fishes' wayfinding.

"For many animals, scent is the primary window to the world," Bernd Heinrich writes in *The Homing Instinct*. It orients us as well. Our ancestors heeded the dinner bell of ripe or fermenting fruit. A dash of decay warned of meat spoilt. Scent still bestows survival benefits, as it did in our species' past. Incidentally, the now-cliché, exoticizing "Eskimo kissing" that Anglo explorers first mentioned is an affectionate greeting among family members and friends in which the nose and upper lip nuzzle the greeted person's forehead or cheeks while breathing in. Mongolian nomads, Native Hawaiians, Arabian tribesmen, Southeast Asians, and the Māori follow a similar custom. The Arctic *kunik* was practical, since furs covered most of the body outdoors. But it may have deeper roots. Many diseases have scents that give them away. Ammonia hints at kidney failure, stale beer at tuberculosis, and freshly plucked fowl at measles. (Dogs, which can tell identical twins apart by their smell, have been trained to recognize "biomarkers" of Parkinson's, COVID, and diabetes.) Besides, clinical trials have proven that joy, fear, and disgust can be smelled. So, *kunik* yields clues to the emotional states and physical health of others. Last though not least, human odors, like those of many mammals, influence mate selection. Germans, approaching this from the dour end, express antipathy toward a person with the phrase "I can't stand the smell of her (or him)" instead of "the sight of her (or him)." By extension, each household has a unique smell, a composite of the family members' microbiological "odor prints" preset by genes and augmented by their cooking, other habits, and the house's microclimate and furnishings. Germans have a word for this: *Familienmuff*—"family funk." As evidence, I submit some homemade granola a Nome acquaintance once gave me, which was virtually inedible. A miasma of cat piss and room freshener clung to it. The recall alone makes me queasy.

Thus, scents unveil the hidden as much as they resurrect the nearly forgotten. Gaminess betrays distant caribou, trekking upwind, or sometimes hangs in their wake; musk spells a weasel in the bushes or marmot under rocks. Once, at the end of a ten-day trip on the Noatak River, the sea announced itself through a breeze redolent of sex long before the first gull had winged in overhead. Plankton releasing dimethyl sulfide gas creates this scent, which others describe as "seaweed-y" or "like oysters." It rises in varying concentrations from marine fertile hotspots. Aerial gradients above surface slicks of this byproduct limn fishing charts for the tubenoses: petrels, albatrosses, and shearwaters.

Unlike signature sounds currently studied, scentscapes remain a sadly neglected aspect in the concept of place. We take pictures, record noisy seashores or forests, measure the density of their species, but depend on a spoken or written archive for scents. Scents, which we cannot arrest otherwise, need the storyteller, the writer, to blossom, to have their praises sung.

CHAPTER 29

THE BOUNTY OF THE BONE PILE

66**I**f it gets any closer, I'll have to turn around."

Poking its nose in our direction to sample the sharp October breeze, a juvenile polar bear 30 yards across from us—one of the two dozen foraging on the pile of bowhead whale bones on the sand spit—gingerly steps into the sea. It's slowly heading our way. So, Robert Thompson, a local hunter, a friend who guided the celebrity photographer Sebastião *Salgado and with whom I have* worked on the Hulahula, puts his all-terrain vehicle (ATV) in reverse, pulls back and, ready for a quick get-away if we need it, parks facing away from the bear. The Utah writer and environmentalist Brooke Williams calls ATVs "those annoying modified golf carts that can go anywhere," but just this once, I appreciate them. A stone's throw is as close as I ever want to be to polar bears, knowing they could run down a horse at a short distance and do brain half-ton walruses. With one hand clamping the ATV's rear rack, I aim my point-and-shoot camera with the other, trying to keep steady. I'm so excited I'm shaking. When I last saw a white bear, on a rafting trip in the adjacent refuge, it snoozed four football fields away, but a shotgun lay next to me, unsheathed and ready. For Robert, a portly Vietnam vet of the 101st Airborne, the legendary "Screaming Eagles," a former paratrooper like myself, with frost hair and eyebrows like bits of black felt, this encounter is routine; the only thing ruffled is the wolf trim of his drab army parka. On the Hulahula, he'd let leftover pork chops sit overnight in a pot in our kitchen area, in case he became hungry later, or "for breakfast," which concerned me, since he kept the Remington inside his tent and slept as if hibernating.

His placid demeanor hides fiery convictions. There's not a national magazine or international film crew that comes into town that does not interview him. An activist, he has traveled to Washington D.C. to testify and overseas to attend conferences. Unlike most of his fellow villagers, who would benefit from oil revenues and who depend more on marine animals than on caribou, he is staunchly against drilling in the refuge. He founded REDOIL—Resisting Environmental Destruction on Indigenous Lands. In a village whose residents stand to make money from oil jobs and leases, he is part of a vocal minority. At the house, he was talking about building a wind turbine to meet his Kaktovik family's electricity needs. "I guess I'm an elder now," he said to me in his sixties, surprised how time had snuck up upon him. As if ecological wisdom came with age.

The polar bear on the sand spit, contemplating whale chops and deciding we are not worth its while, returns to rummaging through the bowhead ruins.

Akin to wildlife in other Alaskan towns—moose roaming the outskirts of Fairbanks and muskoxen prowling the runway in Nome—polar bears cruise the streets of Kaktovik, an Inupiaq village of about 300 on Barter Island, set against the stark shores of the Beaufort Sea. My first night, having visited Robert at home, he pushed his .45 Colt upon me; bear spray would have offered only scant protection. On my way down the street, to Robert's B&B, my eyes drilled into Stygian shadows below the houses on stilts, raised above the permafrost, like the one we lived in in Nome's lovely-named Icy View subdivision. It was a comfort to know that here in Kaktovik the front doors stay unlocked, allowing escape into an Arctic entryway, the "mud room," if you are chased. My second night in town, when barking dogs alerted me, I looked out the bedroom window at a plump shape galloping down the main street under jerking pale smears of northern lights, chased by the truck of the community's polar bear patrol, which, starting at sunset, orbits Kaktovik all night long. The men and women of this guard carry twelve-gauge shotguns with beanbag rounds and cracker slugs for deterrence, and, in extreme cases when non-lethal means prove ineffective, they won't hesitate to shoot an aggressive bear, as Robert once did in self-defense, right on his doorstep. You may legally kill a black bear or brown bear in Alaska in defense of life or property if you did not provoke it or attract it with pet food or garbage. Owing to their protected status, you can only shoot to kill polar bears if they attack someone, unless you're Inupiaq.

In laidback Kaktovik, gunfire signals trespassing polar bears, not crime. But these interlopers also mean tourist dollars: as word spreads about the layover of mammal rock stars otherwise rather evasive, polar bear viewing has fast become a cottage industry. Robert earns the largest share of his income in just twelve weeks. He's a popular guide; his 2017 season already was fully booked the fall before. I've seen him so busy that he rushes out of the house chewing a handful of coffee beans instead of a decent breakfast.

In Kaktovik, as in far better known Churchill, Manitoba, and elsewhere along the Arctic coast, polar bears get stranded on shore after the pack ice—their launch pad for assaulting seals—breaks up in the summer. This year, it went out a month early, in July, the earliest ever, because of global heating, Robert said. That, however, was only a portent for 2017, when global sea ice reached a record low. The bears linger on shore in a "walking hibernation," scrounging for food scraps and napping to conserve energy, waiting for freeze-up, when the cold once again puts a lid on the vast Arctic Ocean. Depressing for some people, the area around Kaktovik hosts growing numbers of bears each summer, and, as the Arctic remains ice-free longer and even the winter ice thins, these guests lengthen their stay.

It's not surprising, then, that their shortened hunting season has affected whole polar bear populations. Numbers of the southern Beaufort subgroup—one of 19 that inhabit the Arctic—which include the Kaktovik bears, have dropped substantially, to 900 animals, in the past three decades. (The exact peak number is hard to determine, but is thought to have been as high as 1,200.)

According to the USFWS, among these, the most-studied polar bears besides Churchill's, fewer cubs now survive. Over the years, the agency's biologists also have noted that the bears' size has diminished.

Polar bears are used to at least a partial fast during their summer months on land, but for the bears near Kaktovik, survival rations can be found close to town, at the bone pile near the airport hangar—the remains of bowhead whales that locals butcher on shore for subsistence. Three whales have been taken this fall—the community's yearly, allotted quota—keeping families fed. The remains mark the spit like carcasses of some extinct race of giants. Scraps of spoiled blubber and muktuk (black, rubbery whale skin eaten raw) from people's freezers on occasion augment this cetacean buffet. An ATV puttering out to the bone pile loaded with such bounty is like a dinner bell ringing. From miles away, bears resting on the sliver barrier islands catch a whiff of the rank deposit and swim or walk to the smorgasbord, where dozens might gather at once. There they'll feast, peaceably as a rule, now increasingly landlubbers, sometimes mingling or mating with grizzlies as the climate spirals wildly. Up to 80 furry gourmands commute near or through town during ursine rush hour. Their pigeon-toed tracks stitch muddy roads, clues of bear intentions, bear hungers.

Even when they don't ghost through people's backyards or curl up under living room floors or steal fish heads from chained dogs, white-bear proxies dominate in Kaktovik: spray-painted on a rusting, storm-blasted dumpster; on a Welcome to Beautiful Barter Island sign; and as logos on van doors and sleds and the defunct B&B Dance With Polar Bear—its name, riffing on a Hollywood movie, a spelling error rather than invitation.

Before I can knock on Robert's door, I have to navigate a porch that's a still life of body parts and implements: a pot with chunks of unidentifiable meat chilling in the cold air (his fridge is probably full); a caribou leg for his dogs; snowmachine parts (time to prepare for winter); a gas tank; and, like a cluster of fallen angels, a brace of white-phase ptarmigans that still need plucking. On a driftwood stump near the shed, a mossy polar bear skull grins; it's not a scene for tender romantics.

The juncture of loitering bears waiting for freeze-up, the windfall of a bone and blubber cache, and a nearby community eager for economic opportunities, has resulted in a burgeoning bear industry in Kaktovik. Robert, one of seven Coast Guard–certified tour boat captains, makes a good living from the castaways at the whale skeletons between September and November. His boat *Seanachaí*, Irish for storyteller, is aptly named—the man who can watch bears making beelines to the bone pile from his living room armchair regales visitors with tidbits about life in America's Far North. After serving me wildfowl and caribou in his kitchen nook, he shares a favorite one, a technique for how to clean a polar bear skin. "You stuff it through a hole in the ice and let shrimp pick it clean," he says, adding that he's also seen bears steal from set fishing nets and one pull a net to shore.

He then talks about local tourism. Overall, this Arctic community has learned remarkably well how to coexist with stranded megafauna and benefit from them. In the past six years, small ecotourism outfits like Robert's have sprung up like summer's glacier avens, cashing in on the trend. Lay and prominent wildlife photographers fly into Kaktovik on twin-prop planes, armed with lenses as long as my forearm, lured by the package of a whaling culture, auroras, and views of the Brooks Range blue with distance—but foremost by the thrill of meeting Earth's largest land predator in its home environment.

And therein lies a dilemma. Many visitors crave that calendar shot, a keepsake the years won't distort, unlike a memory, to validate the experience and justify the expense—even without the round trip to Fairbanks, a three-day polar bear viewing excursion can set you back thousands of dollars.

In the bid for satisfied clients, rules and ethics the USFWS has been trying to implement are easily compromised. Robert worries about accidents and tighter regulations as a consequence. Some guides have fed bears from the back of tour boats to attract them. The prescribed distance of 30 yards that keeps bears from getting stressed and tourists from getting killed has been breached repeatedly. Tourists push to approach ever closer, and a few have forsaken boat captains who refuse to do this, traveling instead with those who will. Any interaction with the bears, such as harassment or attempting to draw their attention, is discouraged to keep them from getting habituated. Still, some people, hoping for that prize-winning photo, ask their guide to make a bear stand up on its hind legs. The guides, if caught in any violations, risk losing their license and cabin boats with powerful motors, an investment of at least $60,000.

Locals fear that outsiders will launch boats of their own in an attempt to muscle in on the state's latest boom. Already, tour operators from urban Alaska and even the Lower 48 siphon off a good deal of the profits. They arrange transportation and chaperoning by natural history or photography guides, at best purchasing boat rides or accommodations at one of Kaktovik's two lodges or its only bed and breakfast. Bruce Inglangasak, a lanky, mustachioed boat captain in a camouflage suit and a watch cap embroidered *Get Wild About Nature*, earlier expressed his frustration to me about guides from the south trying to muscle into the business, a sentiment widespread among his peers. He politely removed his wool glove before shaking my hand and quickly made his point: "It's our God-given right. We live here, and nobody knows these animals and waters like we do."

I'd love to hear more about this from Robert, but he has to fetch his granddaughter from school. His daughter's boyfriend swamped the Toyota truck driving on the spit, so Robert roars off on his ATV.

To get a better picture of the polar bear tourists, I visit one of the two hotels in town. On the way there, I notice a white bear napping in the sun near the lagoon. I'm surprised how the people here always know where bears are. While I stand in the dirt road glassing the sleeping bear, my eyes tearing up from the wind, everyone else is doing their errands, unfazed. Could you live with bears as you would with dumpster ravens?

When I open the door to the ramshackle Waldo Arms, some French tourists are fueling up on greasy burgers, while others, bent over laptops, edit their polar bear images. Fringed bowhead baleen with scrimshaw designs lies on the pool table, enticing souvenir hunters to leave a few more dollars in the community. A bucket near the TV catches drips from a leaky ceiling. *DO NOT FEAR THE WIND* message board graffiti pontificates beneath the felt-tip pen cartoon of a bear. I'm not welcome here. Once, when I brought my lunch sandwich in because it was raining sideways outside, the proprietor sniped at me, "We run a business here." Never mind that I'd led dozens of clients into their over-prized trap through the years.

After their lunch, an old school bus conveys visitors to the boat launch for an afternoon tour. Others pile into the back of a pickup truck, dressed like the upscale cast of an Arctic survival show. In their fancy goggles, balaclavas, Gore-Tex pants, and red Canada Goose Arctic Program parkas or cold-water immersion survival suits, these polar bear pilgrims stick out like tuxedoed penguins where the dress code is decidedly working class.

Tourists here expect a more personal experience than in Churchill, where crowds are trucked in on Polar Rovers (deluxe Humvees on steroids that can hold 50 passengers) and the mobile Great White Bear Tundra Lodge, a Ritz-Carlton–Trans-Siberian Express on fat tires, parked right on the fasting bears' turf. Dinner smells wafting from the lodge windows magnetize the bears, which, tourists complain, come begging for food rather than exhibit wild behavior. From elevated viewing platforms, the bears are also never encountered at ground level, a drawback for many photographers; boat decks in Kaktovik, on the other hand, bring them face to face with *nanuk*.

Among photographers who visit Kaktovik, an unofficial ranking as arcane as the Boone and Crockett Club trophy hunting register (which scores animal attributes such as fur color and antler or horn size) rules the clicking, blazing camera competition. Bears grimy from foraging in the bone pile or rolling in the dirt are undesirable, but smeared with blood, they become interesting, living up to their "killer" image. Cubs playing, males fighting, bears swimming, or mother-and-cub motifs are also highly coveted, as are photos with a bear mirrored in the still waters of the lagoon or gazing directly into the camera. "I got my $7,000 worth right there," one telephoto junkie tells me at Robert's B&B, recalling her capture of a blond mother and cub in the shotgun scatter of late sun. Return visitors crave a particular image or get hooked on the adrenaline rush. A few, such as Shayne "Churchill-is-so-passé" McGuire from California, then become tour guides who finance their passion by bringing other seekers to Kaktovik. "I don't like to see animals harassed," McGuire says in a voice thick with emotion about flight-seeing helicopters pestering Churchill bears. But out on the lagoon, even here in Kaktovik, three or four tour boats often corral bears.

McGuire's reservations match my own: we do debase much that we claim to love. Some force darker that compassion might be at work here, though, some mechanism of repression. In *The Uninhabitable Earth*, David Wallace-Wells writes that "It can be curiously easier to emphasize with them"—"them" being animals stranded or otherwise stressed—"perhaps because we would rather not reckon with our own responsibility, but instead simply feel their pain, at least briefly."

Waiting for my flight from Fairbanks to Kaktovik, I spoke with a couple in the airport lobby. I asked about their expectations for the trip there. He said he was looking for an American paradise, the sort of place Lewis and Clark had encountered. Many who step from an airplane into this northern outpost share his romantic passion. The more perceptive soon realize that this paradise comes with pitfalls, bear-size shadows, and thorns. Robert Thompson and Bruce Inglangasak regard Barter Island not as a Garden of Eden but rather as their backyard, an image that even in the context of the whole country seems appropriate.

Not all residents welcome the opportunities ecotourism brings. There is concern that pictures of butchered whales, bearskins, or skulls—a normal part of the landscape here—could provoke animal rights groups and environmentalists. Occasionally, locals who need to go to Fairbanks or Anchorage for medical treatment have not been able to get seats on fully booked planes. Tired of the recreational takeover, one old-timer angrily tried to chase off bears while tourists were watching, and almost got killed when his ATV did not start up again right away. Envy of those few who are lucky or savvy enough to tap this newfound wealth can also sour the atmosphere in a community where members have depended on each other for millennia, surviving through sharing and cooperation.

To counter the negative effects of tourism on the locals—bears and people—the USFWS, in concert with the school, mentors Kaktovik youth ambassadors, who greet incoming visitors and try to educate them about Inupiaq culture and bear viewing etiquette.

Perhaps this community will balance the presence of tourists and bears in the future, but it currently faces a different tightrope act: the environment that has supported both Indigenous people and polar bears for millennia is shifting below their feet. As pack-ice changes curb the polar bears' hunting, rotten shore-fast ice inhibits Inupiaq hunters' ability to intercept migrating whales. Sea level rises and coastal erosion worsened by surf that storms agitate put Arctic coastal communities at risk of flooding, and bears will lose den sites.

Humans stand out as one of the most successful species on Earth, in part because of our adaptability—the Inupiat are a testament to that. But the highly specialized bears are not so blessed. Locked into fairly fixed behaviors and bound to evolution's slow clock, the chances that they'll handle the threats to their place of origin are slim. Their loss will be ours as well.

Uncommon since mammoths last grazed these parts, more intense and frequent wildfires on the North Slope spew additional carbon; the largest tundra blaze on record, above permafrost by the Anaktuvuk River, in 2007 released the same amount of carbon as that biome absorbs *globally* in a year. Watercourses and lakes freeze later in the fall, while the spring melt sets in earlier. These patterns have made Arctic lands hospitable to red foxes that are pushing northward, cannibalizing and replacing smaller, native Arctic foxes.

Since my last visit in 2017, COVID has shut down tourism in Kaktovik. More bears spend more time on shore and the pack ice much less. Relations between villagers and the USFWS have chilled with the current administration's suspension of oil leases that the previous one auctioned off. Kaktovik's runway has been relocated inland from the spit near the bone pile, with a price tag of $38 million. A storm in 1986 had completely flooded it, and another in 2000 half of it, and annual, partial flooding at the hangar continued throughout the 2000s. As the land becomes mired deeper in the Anthropocene, like an aging, ailing person, it has more and more bad days. By the time this book is printed, who knows what else North Slope villagers will have seen?

Unlike that Vegas deal, what happens in the Arctic does not stay in the Arctic. Each barrel of crude that stays buried buys precious time for the planet's other-than-human inhabitants, and for us.

POSTSCRIPT

This collection opened with an essay about the highest point in the state and finishes with one about one of its lowest, at the continent's northern edge. The writings in between span 33 years, the most formative decades of my life. Rivers have been a constant in them, the sinews connecting highpoints and low points, outlier and main events, as they do Alaska's elevation extremes. Radiating from the boreal heartland, snowmelt carried from the slopes of Denali and my beloved Brooks Range feeds the marine bodies that cradle this state: the Beaufort and Chukchi and Bering seas and the Gulf of Alaska. It recirculates to the peaks by evaporation. In a boat, you merge with this loop, if only for a short while. Every one of these rivers meets the Pacific, a word that also describes an ideal state of mind. They have taught me much more than what shines through in the preceding pages, though I cannot commit all their lessons to paper quite yet. There always are stories behind the stories, without enough room or time to tell but a tiny fraction. One could call these untold tales "energetic loose ends," though the essayist Edward Hoagland may have meant to convey a writer's conflicts and idiosyncrasies with that image.

I no longer believe essays—a purling, fluid, highly excursive form—became my passion and strength by coincidence or from lack of staying power for longer projects. Their paragraphs digress like coils or may even switch channels, to always return to the overall course of an argument or a theme. Their source isn't always obvious; their destination, a sea of rest and tranquility or mingling with other currents, sometimes surprises even myself. Like rivers, trails and routes smoothen linear travel as they do trains of thought. And, as the literary scholar Jeffrey C. Robinson noted, walkers, "almost always bona fide essayists, are urged from somewhere to ambulate on paper about ambulation." Thus are the nature of things and things in nature revealed. (Take *that*, Jacques D.!)

I am certain streams will continue to give if I give them my efforts. Perhaps what's needed is a walk and float from headwater origins to an ocean. I have never done this—few people have. It requires more patience and a yen for quiet obscurity, for snowfields and springs, continuity and completion, not just floatable middles and ends. Perhaps, someday I will embark on such an endeavor, or at least my ashes will. In the metaphorical river of human existence so often invoked, rapids represent danger, excitement, highlights, turmoil, and crises, each hiding slicks of reprieve, places to pause and reassess. But any focus on wave crests is like loving a mountain's while ignoring its roots. The much-maligned stretches of flatwater in between, which sometimes account for the bulk of miles paddled or rowed, dole out opportunity in equal measures.

Discussing vocations and aspirations, a former outfitter boss once asked me what else he would do. "All I know is camping," he'd said, downplaying his carpentry skills. My life's great blessing has been that I got to learn, foremost, what rivers know. Career-wise, that also has been the main handicap, since cash grows more abundantly elsewhere. For richer or poorer, far from ever exhausting their wealth, I too am haunted by waters. That is, flowing waters. "Our nature consists in movement," Blaise Pascal realized, and "complete rest is death." So it is for the rivers.

ACKNOWLEDGMENTS

Even the longest journey begins with the first step, and after that, you take one day at a time. Putting together a book is a journey too, one fraught with setbacks and moments of joy. Along the way of putting together this one, many people have offered support. And as any wilderness traveler knows, logistics, planning, route-finding, and morale are crucial. I would like to thank Thomas Guy for some early mock-ups. With two beautiful covers for the manuscript, it was easier to envision my destination, the book it could become. Fellow author Tanyo Ravicz, who introduced me to Hancock House Publishers, was there when the going got tough, talking shop with me when dusk threatened to settle in and batting subtitles back and forth. Chuck LaRue, flintknapper extraordinaire: I liked yours best—*Two and a Half Decades of Not Ending Up as Bear Scat*—but unless you're Tim Cahill or Bill Bryson, no editor would condone it. Elisabeth Dabney, literary agent and longtime Alaskan, assessed the terrain for me and ages ago assisted with materials for that book tour from hell.

This has been my first venture into Canadian book publishing, and I quickly learned that there are professionals on both sides of the border that care greatly about wildlife, visual flair, and polished manuscripts. Doreen Martens spared me some embarrassment (e.g. "Louis and Clark") and helped make the prose flow, like all rivers should. Emily Morton wrapped it all up in an attractive package.

Thanks go to all the Alaska Native elders who imparted their knowledge, and opened their homes to me, and fed me. In what I have learned from them and many others, I've been an eternal student, a hunter and gatherer of knowledge, never the expert.

In the realm of guiding, I can't thank any former bosses except Cliff Ghiglieri at OARS, John Crowley, then manager at Canyoneers, and Tour West's Terry Brian, who died tragically, snorkeling in the Fijis. Terry would sometimes light a stogy above Lava Falls and considered it a good run if at the bottom it was still smoldering. Gordon Janow, of Alpine Ascents in Talkeetna, generously let me tag along with their yaks, a trip on which Maren Jostad, Dylan Cembalski, and Fura Kancha Sherpa expertly cooked and led this headstrong guide and kept full wine boxes on the camp table, and good coffee, not keto-diet yak-butter tea. Matt Thoft of Silvertip Aviation arranged air support on the Ivishak, Canning, and elsewhere beyond the mere call of duty. My favorite colleagues have been Kielan Partlow, who increased our tips on an all-nurses trip by wearing nothing but a sarong and who wrote a fine review of my river anthology—we lived it daily, bro'; and Michael "Mac" Dukart of Jackson Hole—sorry, Mac for deserting you, mid-wave, while surfing the double kayak near San Francisco and again on that hike above the Yampa confluence. (I fondly remember us on Sixmile Creek and the Dolores, though, and playing cross-country bocce beside that river.) Fairbanks falconers Randall Compton and Bennett Wong never tired of my inane questions, while Toots let me carry her without taking a chunk out of me. Matthew Sturm kindly shared his snow expertise. I learned much about Project Chariot from Dan O'Neill who did the original research and resurrected the nickname "Firecracker Boys" from historical obscurity.

Versions of some of these essays first appeared in the following publications: *Hakai Magazine, Alaska, Sierra, San Francisco Chronicle, Canoe & Kayak, Cirque, High Country News, Adventure Journal, Zoomorphic, Backcountry Hunting, Earth Island Journal*, and *Snowy Egret*. I appreciate these magazines being early testing grounds for the breaking-in of my boots, so to speak. I'd like to single out Susan Sommer, editor at *Alaska*, for indulging my whims, obsessions, and silliness over the years.

Above all, I am grateful to Melissa Guy, my backcountry companion of lo, these many years and my guide through the tangled muskeg of matrimony. (She asked that I don't call it a "swamp.")

Written words, to borrow a line from the Anthropocene critic John Green, are signs and gifts, "like trail markers in the wilderness." To me, they are the wilderness proper, a teeming, untamed abundance in which to lose myself.

ABOUT THE AUTHOR

Michael Engelhard worked for 25 years as an outdoor instructor and wilderness guide in Alaska and the Canyon Country. He received a Master's degree in cultural anthropology from the University of Alaska, Fairbanks, where he also taught very briefly—indoor classrooms just weren't his thing.

He is the recipient of a Rasmuson Individual Artist Award, a *Foreword* INDIES and Independent Publisher Book Award, and of three Alaska Press Club Awards. His books include *Ice Bear: The Cultural History of an Arctic Icon*; his account of a solo trip from the Canada border to the Bering Sea, *Arctic Traverse: A Thousand-Mile Summer of Trekking the Brooks Range*; and *No Walk in the Park: Seeking Thrills, Eco-Wisdom, and Legacies in the Grand Canyon*.

A Luddite fence sitter and migrant by training and inclination, he moves wherever his needs are met best, just like the peoples and critters he so admires.

RELATED TITLES

Wolves, Grizzlies & Greenhorns
WERNER, MAXIMILIAN

Death & Coexistence in the American West

Werner recounts the two-and-a-half years he spent tracking down and looking after a wolf pack that was rumored to have settled in the Centennial Valley of southwest Montana. Along the way he encounters and reflects on the lives of other animals, including deer, elk, fox, coyote, skunks, and grizzly bears. But he also encounters other humans too—ranchers, hunters, land and wildlife managers, cowboys—who offer their own, often conflicting perspectives about the natural world, other animals, and how both ought to be treated.

978-0-88839-537-5 [paperback] 978-0-88839-578-8 [epub]	5½ x 8½, sc, 352pp	$26.95

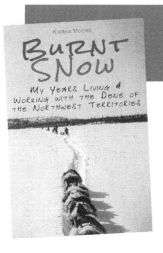

Burnt Snow
MOORE, KIERAN

My years living & working with the Dene of the Northwest Territories

The reflections of the authors encounters with some of the leading figures of the North are quite humorous and consequential in the later development of the North. He describes the Indigenous Elders who would influence him in countless ways, and how their teachings are later, the source of northern survival in otherwise seemingly impossible situations. This book reflects the people of that time, and their lifestyle of living off the land in total independence and their incredible life-skills of survival.

978-0-88839-100-1 [paperback] 978-0-88839-356-2 [hardcover] 978-0-88839-265-7 [epub]	6 x 9 272pp	$24.95

The Power of Dreams
NEADS, DAVE & ROSEMARY

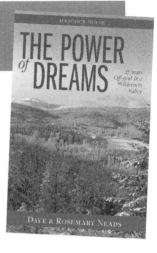

27 Years Off-grid in a Wilderness Valley

The Power of Dreams tells the story of a couple, already in their 40's, who uprooted themselves from urban life to follow their dream of living in the wilderness. They settled in a remote mountain valley called Precipice Valley, part of the ancient trade route linking B.C.'s Chilcotin plateau to the Pacific Coast.

Surrounded by mountain vastness they lived there for nearly three decades, much of it in near-total isolation. Their dreams sustained them while they carved out a lifestyle that was both rewarding and challenging.

978-0-88839-718-8 [paperback] 978-0-88839-742-3 [epub]	5½ x 8½, sc, 246pp	$24.95

Land of Bear & Eagle
RAVICZ, TANYO

A Home in the Kodiak Wilderness

A celebration of nature and of the peculiarities of the Alaskan bush, Land of Bear and Eagle: A Home in the Kodiak Wilderness builds from personal experience to a rounded, loving portrait of a place, Cottonwood Homestead, and a way of life. In these essays and sketches, by turns humorous, meditative and lyrical, the author goes beyond the challenges and triumphs of wilderness living to explore his environment and to examine the relationships among the plants and animals and the people he meets. Along the way, he wrestles with his doubts and reconsiders his assumptions about life.

978-0-88839-722-5 [paperback] 978-088839-703-4 [epub]	5½ x 8½, sc, 278pp	$24.95

Hancock House Publishers

19313 Zero Ave, Surrey, BC V3Z 9R9
info@hancockhouse.com | 1-800-938-1114
www.hancockhouse.com

hancock
house